Praise for Marilyn Paul's
It's Hard to Make a Difference When
You Can't Find Your Keys

"A book to help you organize and clarify your mind as well as your desk. A unique, rich, and unusually practical book—dare to read it."
—William Isaacs, author of *Dialogue* and *The Art of Thinking Together*

"In the midst of the hecticness and anxieties that define living for so many today, we all need a quiet place to stand. Marilyn Paul's book shows how that place can be our office, our home or even the way we go about our everyday affairs. Who would have thought that the mess that is my desk could be a vehicle for deep personal learning—about myself as well as about how to be more effective in the world?"
—Peter Senge, Founding Chair, Society for Organizational Learning and
    author of *The Fifth Discipline*

"The thinking person's solution to chronic disorganization. Paul grounds her seven-step path to becoming truly organized in a thoughtful examination of the complex reasons why disorganization is costly and yet why it can be so difficult to change."
—*The New Leaf Newsletter*

"Disorder can seriously damage self-confidence, relationships, and your reputation. It results from the conscious and unconscious choices we make, and willpower alone will not get us out of it. We need to look at the physical, mental, emotional, and spiritual issues related to how we organize our lives. . . .
It's Hard to Make a Difference When You Can't Find Your Keys is a superb resource packed with sound advice and a holistic sense of organization."
—*Spirituality & Health* magazine

"Too many advice books drop us at the doorstep of change and leave us stranded. Marilyn Paul walks us through the door and helps us make sense of what's on the other side."
—Douglas Stone, coauthor of *Difficult Conversations: How to Discuss What Matters Most*

"Marilyn Paul's approach to healing disorganization is a wonderful balance between the practical and the spiritual. If clutter and disorganization are suffocating your spirit, you must read this book!"
—Cheryl Richardson, author of *Stand Up for Your Life* and *Take Time for Your Life*

"A brilliant, provocative, and profound book. Marilyn Paul delves deeply into human nature as she discusses organization, and she offers remedies for the disorganized that respect one's intelligence as well as uniqueness. Her approach is innovative and totally convincing. This book goes far beyond all that has previously been written on this subject. A wonderful book that I am using in my own life and recommending to my friends as well as patients."
—Edward Hallowell, M.D., author of *Driven to Distraction* and *The Childhood Roots of Adult Happiness*

"Marilyn Paul has managed not only to uncover the secrets to becoming organized, but perhaps even more miraculously she has been able to convey this information in a way that anyone can follow in her new book, *It's Hard to Make a Difference When You Can't Find Your Keys*. Knowing where everything is, or 'your stuff' is will help you save time, reduce stress, and stop beating yourself up."
—Cherie Carter Scott, Ph.D., author of *If Life Is a Game, These Are the Rules* and *Negaholics*

"Marilyn Paul has transformed 'organizing' into a path of growth for the adventurous soul. Her empathic and creative work shows how the messes of everyday life are an intrinsic part of deepening one's spiritual path. *It's Hard to Make a Difference* is a must-read for people seeking to bring more of their true selves to light."
—Marc Gafni, author of *Soul Prints: Your Path to Fulfillment*

"For teams and workgroups, disorganization disrupts communication and undermines morale—and makes it just plain difficult to get things done the right way and on schedule. Marilyn Paul's unique (and totally engaging!) insights into how to create great team performance will be of value to any organization. No more chasing our tails fixing things in ways that cause more chaos!"
—Ginny Wiley, President, Pegasus Communications, Inc.

"*It's Hard to Make a Difference* is a well-honed and practical tool for organizing all aspects of life. This book serves as a benchmark for, even while it transcends, the category of 'self help.' Paul shows us how our approaches to organization serve as a window into our bedrock values and identities, reflecting the most fundamental aspects of how we choose to engage the world. She proves an expert guide through the territory of change, allowing us to move past the exhortations and the guilt to personal choice and productive action."
—Russell Eisenstat, coauthor of *The Critical Path to Corporate Renewal*

"Based on her work with a broad spectrum of managers and professionals, Marilyn Paul helps readers confront two hard and often denied facts about our own disorder: the chaos we create is more stressful than creative; and it wreaks havoc on the lives of our family, friends, and coworkers. By showing us the way back into a world of calmness and order, she gives readers a great gift—the freedom to be truly creative and effective."
—Robin J. Ely, Associate Professor of Organizational Behavior, Harvard Business School

"Working parents need to be organized in order to balance all the demands of their busy lives. The approach in *It's Hard to Make a Difference When You Can't Find Your Keys* can help busy parents transform their chaos into purposeful effectiveness. I highly recommend this valuable resource."
—Linda Mason, Chair and Co-founder of Bright Horizons Family Solutions and author of *The Working Mother's Guide to Life*

PENGUIN
COMPASS

IT'S HARD TO MAKE A DIFFERENCE WHEN
YOU CAN'T FIND YOUR KEYS

Marilyn Paul has a Ph.D. from Yale University and an M.B.A. from
The Johnson School at Cornell. She has been a consultant, workshop leader, and coach for twenty-five years. She and her husband,
David Peter Stroh, co-founded Bridgeway Partners to help clients
improve their ability to work together to accomplish meaningful results. Their approach combines individual development and organizational change with a strong emphasis on the four levels of human
experience: physical, mental, emotional, and spiritual. Their many
clients include New Balance, Pfizer, the National Urban League, the
Home for Little Wanderers, Dana Farber Cancer Institute, Johnson &
Johnson, Shell, and Jobs for the Future.

Marilyn began creating her seven-step method for personal and organizational change over twelve years ago and speaks frequently on
the topics of personal growth, leadership development, managing
workload, and improving work and home life. She can be reached
by e-mail at marilyn@bridgewaypartners.com, or visit her Web site
at www.marilynpaul.com. You can also visit the Bridgeway Partners
Web site at www.bridgewaypartners.com.

It's Hard to Make a Difference When You Can't Find Your Keys

The Seven-Step Path to Becoming Truly Organized

Marilyn Paul, Ph.D.

Penguin Compass

PENGUIN COMPASS
Published by the Penguin Group
Penguin Group (USA) Inc., 375 Hudson Street, New York, New York 10014, U.S.A.
Penguin Books Ltd, 80 Strand, London WC2R 0RL, England
Penguin Books Australia Ltd, 250 Camberwell Road,
    Camberwell, Victoria 3124, Australia
Penguin Books Canada Ltd, 10 Alcorn Avenue, Toronto, Ontario, Canada M4V 3B2
Penguin Books India (P) Ltd, 11 Community Centre,
    Panchsheel Park, New Delhi – 110 017, India
Penguin Books (N.Z.) Ltd, Cnr Rosedale and Airborne Roads,
    Albany, Auckland, New Zealand
Penguin Books (South Africa) (Pty) Ltd, 24 Sturdee Avenue,
    Rosebank, Johannesburg 2196, South Africa

Penguin Books Ltd, Registered Offices:
80 Strand, London WC2R 0RL, England

First published in the United States of America by Viking Compass,
a member of Penguin Putnam Inc. 2003
Published in Penguin Compass 2004

10 9 8 7 6 5 4 3 2 1

Illustrations and diagrams by Mark Stein Studios

ISBN 0-670-03194-1 (hc.)
ISBN 0 14 21.9617 7 (pbk.)
CIP data available

Printed in the United States of America
Set in Garamond Light with Diotima display
Designed by Carla Bolte

This book is dedicated to my mother, Betty Byfield Paul, of blessed memory, who taught me that digging out, clearing things up, and letting go are some of the most worthwhile work one can do.

Contents

Introduction: Organizing as a Path to Growth

Would you like to find things easily or stop running late? Do you wish it would take less effort to manage day-to-day tasks? Would you like to reduce your stress and experience your home or office as a pleasant haven? Ten years ago, as I fruitlessly tried to clean up my office yet one more time, I would have answered yes, to all of the above questions. I was looking for genuine relief from my chaos, mess, frenzy, and lateness. Now, my life is much easier because I applied some known principles of self-transformation to my chronic disorganization and I now live an easier, more creative, more connected life.

Living as a disorganized person is tough. We often pile up belongings that we don't use, spend hours looking for lost papers or other objects, pay our credit card bills late and lose our credit ratings. We make our homes and workplaces uncomfortable and unattractive. We take on too much, overbook ourselves, can't keep appointments or get to them on time, and miss important events. Disorder can be a nightmare, and those who suffer from it often feel locked in, unable to escape.

We suffer because we betray deeply held values such as integrity, dignity, and responsibility. Disorganization damages reputations, self-confidence, and relationships. Even though we can get a lot done and are often very successful, we are often haunted by the sense that we could do or be more if we weren't looking for things so often, or experiencing so much pressure. We get in our own way. Those of us who are disorganized often feel tremendous shame about the way we are living. So, in addition to everything else, we have to hide the disorganization (as much as we can).

Most disorganized people truly want to live without the chaos. They want to arrive at appointments on time. They want a sense of calm that is difficult to find in a swamp of disorder. There are plenty of books and classes about how to create order in one's life, but the advice doesn't take into account the depth and meaning of being disorganized. Transforming chaos into order—getting organized—is often described as a series of action steps fueled by will. The message is: Don't do *X*; just do *Y*. This book is different. I help you understand *why* you are disorganized, and I'll give you a clear method to follow to help you change your ways over time. Not only will you learn how to get organized, but you also will acquire new skills, work through emotional wounds, develop more powerful ways of thinking, and deepen your connection to life energy. Clearing up your external messes can lead you to a path to deeper self-knowledge and a sense of inner peace and order.

By profession, I am an organizational development consultant. My job is to help people in organizations work together better. I enable people to build stronger teams, communicate well, and develop effective organizational strategies. I am interested in change at all levels. I use a multiplicity of theories, approaches, and tools to support people to live more fulfilling lives.

It took me years to apply my professional knowledge about change to my own crushing habits of disorganization. I had an aversion to organizing. I thought I would become rigid and compulsive, that I would have to give up my creativity and self-expression. Yet, as I took on more responsibility, raised my sights and saw more possibilities for myself, I kept stumbling. I ran late, missed appointments, forgot to return important phone calls, couldn't find vital documents, misplaced airline tickets, lost receipts, and became overwhelmed by my long to-do list. It was an impossible way to live.

I read many organizing books and tried to "fix" my problem. But I couldn't do it. Much as I tried, I couldn't make the changes in my life that I wanted to. I discovered that I was up against something that was harder and more complex than I realized. I was going to have to draw on all of my expertise to accomplish my goals.

The first step was to take my disorganization much more seriously. I needed to stop thinking that I could "solve" my problem. I abandoned quick fixes and became much more interested in the complexity of my challenge. I brought respect and compassion to my messy ways instead of disdain and impatience. I studied how I was creating my mess. As I became more responsible about the unwanted consequences I was creating, I changed the behaviors that led to those consequences.

As I became more organized, I faced a number of paradoxes. Contrary to my previous belief, I became more, not less, creative. That was a big surprise. I freed up time and attention to be even more expressive and more creative. I experienced an emotional aliveness that wasn't possible for me when I was in a frenzy so much of the time. I discovered that busyness and frenzy are different from emotional fullness. And I discovered that I was often well repaid for the "wasted" time I invested in getting organized. I got time and energy back in spades.

In some ways, the path of organizing is an inquiry into how to live well and fulfill your potential. Perhaps the most surprising benefit is that by getting organized, you can learn valuable lessons that foster growth and character development. You'll start to see that organizing is a way to express self-love and self-care. Organizing is also a way to take on responsibility. You will discover that beliefs such as "I have too much to do to get organized" or "Organizing is a waste of time" don't support you anymore. You will learn that you can manage your own tendencies to be distracted easily or forget what you meant to be doing. You'll balance the time you spend in a "flow" state, in which you are deeply engaged with what you truly love, with creating the conditions for this flow state to take place. Living well is ultimately about loving yourself and others, connecting with what really matters to you, and taking actions based on what you truly care about. Being organized actually can improve your chances of doing so.

This approach is founded on the premise that it is the whole person who creates disorder, and therefore it is the whole person who must create a new, meaningful way of living. It shows you a path for change, identifies many crossroads along the way, and points out where and how you can choose to modify your behavior. It enables you to reframe organizing from an unpleasant *should* into a vital and exciting part of your quest for growth and learning.

This book is for you if you want to experience more clarity and freedom in daily life. It's for you if you can no longer bear the stress of running late or losing things; if you have been longing for sanity and simplicity, but have been unable to make it happen; if you have realized that you can't move forward in your work because you are hampered by your clutter and lateness; or if you have been meditating for years, and still live surrounded by clutter. It's for those of you who have attention deficit disorder and who want a sympathetic guidebook on how to manage distractibility.

This book is for those of us who are suffering and know it. We are painfully aware that disorganization:

- Blocks our true self-expression because we are mired in details, can't find things, or can't get comfortable.
- Reinforces our distractibility, which in turn reduces our creativity or effectiveness.
- Fosters an ugly, unpleasant environment that impacts our sense of well-being.
- Causes stress and worry, which is exhausting and drains our vitality over time.
- Causes us to feel stuck, depressed, or ineffective, which can lead to a deep depletion of spirit.
- Leads us to break agreements, offer more than we can give, and then let others and ourselves down.

Being disorganized often feels like a permanent state—and yet it does not have to be. Healing is possible. Deep personal change can come from addressing disorganization in your life. Join me and others who have pursued this path of learning and reaped great benefit from changing their thoughts, feelings, and behaviors. It takes courage and receptivity to move from self-blame and impatience to inquiry and learning, but it is worth the effort. You'll start feeling more self-confidence, more energy, and more joy in just living. Welcome!

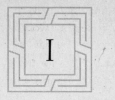

I

Laying the Foundation

1

There Must Be a
Desk in Here Somewhere

My desk was piled high with papers, empty coffee cups, and unopened mail. Perhaps there was even an outdated check lurking in there somewhere. I couldn't tell. The floor served as my filing cabinet. I didn't put papers into files because I was afraid I wouldn't find them again. I still couldn't find them easily, but at least I thought I knew their general whereabouts.

I was a management consultant at a demanding firm. My clients and colleagues counted on me to deliver excellent, timely work. I did deliver, most of the time, but at great cost—recurring late-night work sessions; anguished preparation time; and frequent, frantic searches for missing information, my hair standing on end because I couldn't find the folder with the *critical* data. Some of the intensity stemmed from the very nature of my work, but much of the pressure came from me.

Even though I tried to focus and to feel balanced and self-confident—I had practiced meditation for years—my life and work grew ever more stressful because I was usually running late. Rushing to the airport for business trips, I'd skid into the jetway, my heart pounding, just before the crew closed the door. Sometimes it was a high, sometimes I hated it.

Running late for meetings, forgetting something yet again, submitting invoices way past deadline, I was creating havoc around me. I valued integrity, but I often broke agreements because I double-booked myself. In addition, I had several years of unfiled taxes. I would lie there, sleepless, worrying about the size of the debt ($1,000? $50,000?), but I still couldn't get my tax returns in the mail. And despite my M.B.A., I had no clue what I owed on my credit cards, because I couldn't find the last set of bills (or any set of bills, for that matter).

My personal space was also very messy. When I invited people over, I would swoop through my apartment and throw the clutter into a closet or stash extra belongings under the bed or in the tub, and hope that people didn't peek behind the shower curtain. Things would stay in the closet, only to be buried by the next sweep through. I rarely hung up my clothes. My sink was piled with dirty dishes. I would often lose phone messages. I longed to live in a peaceful, beautiful space. I wanted a sanctuary, but I created chaos.

Embarrassing? Very. Could I tell anyone what my life was like? No. I wanted to change, but I got little help from the many books on organizing. To organized people, and in most of the organizing books, the obvious answer is: Pull yourself together, create a plan, and "just do it" or "do it now." Put the keys in one place. File or throw out the mess on the desk and the clutter on the floor. Get rid of the excess stuff in the closets. Put everything in its place. Decide to be on time. That made sense to me, too, so I would try to "do it now." I'd sort the papers on my desk, finally get the dishes done, and then frustratingly I'd be disorganized all over again. What was my problem? How could I fix it? I had accomplished a lot in life. How come I couldn't master the ordinary tasks of every day?

What is challenging is that chronic disorganization—like a chronic weight problem—feels as if it has a life of its own. I truly wanted to be different; I wanted to live without chaos and lateness. I just couldn't seem to do it. I would get completely fed up with the mess, the frenzy, and the panic. I would say, "Okay. This is it. This weekend I am throwing everything away. I'm clearing off the desk and the floor, hanging up all the clothes and doing all the dishes. I am creating some peace in this place. And, from now on, I'm arriving on time."

But that declaration never worked. After many, many wasted weekends of failing to clean up and failing to have any fun or relaxation, I hired a professional organizer—I'll call her Jane. We sat at my desk in my home office and after several painstaking hours, we had cleared it off. She even gave me a system to stay on top of things. I put everything in a logical place. What a relief! Success! I was organized!

Or was I? By the end of the next day, there was a fine spray of clutter on the desk. By the end of the week, the desk looked as if we hadn't touched it. With dismay, I called Jane back. She arrived with a little scowl (such a mess? so soon?) and we cleared the desk again. After another week, not surprisingly, the mess was back once again. How did the desk and papers do that? I wondered. Where was the clutter coming from?

I was too mortified to call her back once again, and realized that I was on my own with a mountain of papers. These papers were not just on my desk, though—they littered my office floor, filled my closets, and spilled across the kitchen counters. I had a chaotic office, a disorganized kitchen, a messy car, an unlivable home. Since I had been meditating for a long time, I had developed a small capacity to observe myself with compassion. As I mulled over this discouraging situation, I came to a key realization: *I (me?, not me!) was the one creating the mess.*

I began to see that I created my own mess through the choices I made and my unconscious habits. Becoming aware of this was hard for me, but the more I looked, the more I could see that I was taking actions that led to chaos. A simple example was my very messy car. At the end of the day, I could bring everything in, or leave things in the car. If I left things in the car, it became an ugly, unpleasant mobile storage unit.

I was the agent of this mess. I was the source of this chaos. I was very effective at creating it. I was taking actions every day that amplified my inner and outer disorder. *It followed that if I created it, I could uncreate it.*

It was not so easy, though. It took a while to find a way out. Step by step, I discovered a new approach. I decided to apply my extensive experience in change management to this profound challenge and *change myself*. I established my purpose for organizing, created my vision for where I wanted to go, took stock of my current situation, got good support, and put into practice a few simple strategies. I worked through frightening feelings. Incredibly, I began to experience changes in myself and my life. The frantic, chaotic messy life I was living became less frantic, less chaotic, and much more satisfying. I discovered that order was possible and valuable and didn't ruin my creativity. Oddly enough, some order helped me be more creative.

It was clear to me that simply deciding to change doesn't produce change by itself. Deep personal change requires fundamentally shifting how we think about things. It asks us for the courage to face our difficult feelings. It demands a more profound understanding of what motivates us. We then must use every tool available to help us shift our typical ways of behaving. Habits are strong, but they can be altered. The method described in this book takes the focus off the external chaos and gives us a chance to look at our contribution to it. The principle is that when we change our thinking, process our feelings, and build new habits, our environment will change.

In the end, and you may not believe this now, you may come to see your disorganization as a great gift, because it has launched you on a path to deeper personal discovery. This is a very human, practical path. Your healing will be very tangible. You'll not only discover a deeper love for yourself, but you'll also be able to find your keys in the morning. The nightmare will start receding. The terror of lost checks or lost jobs will decrease. The panic attacks will be less frequent. And why? Because your healing is holistic. Your inner healing will be matched by your outer healing. Your inner fragmentation will lessen and so will your outer fragmentation. Your greater inner coherence will be matched by your outer coherence.

Using the approach described in this book, I have changed the way I live my life. Today my taxes are paid, my closets are free of clutter, and my kitchen sink is free of the accumulation of dishes. I can get to meetings on time, and the general level of havoc has died down. I deepened my relationships (and finally found my husband). Along with that, I have moved farther toward the goals that I had been trying to accomplish through meditation. I have more peace of mind, less frenzy, and a much deeper awareness of the power of spirituality in my life.

Other people who have undertaken this journey also have altered their lives dramatically. Mary is a highly successful training director at a large pharmaceutical company. Her success derives from her enthusiasm, her command of her work, and her creative approach to problem-solving. She wanted composure, yet often came into meetings with "folders flying." When she came to see me, she was working late at the office most nights—catching up from the day's work, sorting through the piles of paper on her desk and trying to get some of the reading material off her office floor. She genuinely wanted to create some order, yet she felt exhausted, and ineffective. She couldn't think straight. She was fed up with being disorganized because it was eating up precious time with her family. She could barely stand the rush in the mornings, looking for socks and boots, making lunch at the last minute, getting the kids out the door late again. She also knew that her stress was taking a profound toll on her body, soul, and marriage.

As a training director, she had taken several courses on professional effectiveness and stress management. They hadn't helped her much, however, because she couldn't implement the many tips: "I get lots of good ideas from these courses, and I do try them out, but I often slip right back into my old ways of doing things." She had reached a point where she was open to deeper change.

As she followed the seven steps on this path, she observed, "This method helped me change a few key habits. I feel like I found a path out of what looked like a trackless jungle. I no longer have to sit in my office late, spinning my wheels. I can get home much earlier, without guilt. I've learned how to get ready the night before so that we can all leave the house in good shape the next morning. I feel much more connected with myself and my family. I am much clearer about what is important to me—both my priorities and my sense of deeper purpose. I feel like I am back on track in my life."

Charles, a lawyer in solo practice, has an impressive office downtown. He didn't meet with clients there because, in his words, "it was a zoo." There were books open on the desk and the floor, and piles of folders in disarray. All surfaces were covered with clutter, even the chairs. Yet, he was reluctant to try to clear it up because it would ruin the delicate order that he had created. At any given time, he knew—sort of—where everything was.

Often, he felt completely unproductive. He sat, numb, panicking, but unable to take action. His behavior reminded him of a quote he once heard: "Hell is when things freeze." He lived that hell often until a deadline was close, and he would be galvanized to act. But the pain he felt was enormous.

For him, his lateness was what finally brought things to a head. He was a single dad, and his teenagers were also always late to activities. At work, he, his colleagues, and his clients all knew that he couldn't be counted on to meet deadlines. He tried to arrive at appointments on time, but something always got in the way. He was tired of breaking agreements and being unreliable, and he sensed that his chronic tardiness was damaging his business. He was good at what he did, but other people didn't want to hang around waiting for him. He had difficulty building the deep trust he wanted with his clients. Trust was an important part of his spiritual growth and his deep desire was to be fully present for others and to bring a sense of presence to his work.

As he worked through the steps of this approach he said, "The first few occasions I arrived on time, no one else was there, because they expected me to be at least a half an hour late. I now realize that I can be on time to every appointment. It does take some planning and awareness of my thought patterns. However, I like knowing that I can keep my agreements. I can be present. I am developing real integrity. My clients are learning to trust me in much more profound ways. I feel the presence of a much deeper trust in my life."

Helen, a counselor in a city youth agency, also has some administrative responsibilities and counsels at least fifteen kids a week. She had so much paper piled on her desk, floor, and chairs that she could not use her office for counseling. She and the kids were always looking for a spare room or office where they could meet. She is single and has no children, yet her home did not feel welcoming—even to her. There was no place to eat, since the kitchen table was piled with newspapers, magazines, and mail. She ate most of her meals standing up. It was time to create some space for herself.

Now she says, "It was a nightmare. There was no place for me, neither at home nor at work. I was always running. Now, I feel much more confident about handling it all. I'm more calm and deliberate in my approach. I've gotten my house back under control. There is a place for me to sit. Stuff is no longer scattered on the floor and piled on the kitchen table. Now I know how to keep it that way. It's much easier to think clearly! My home is a sanctuary for me, not just an extension of the nightmare. I feel so much more centered, joyful, and powerful."

What helped these people change is that they saw what you probably see, that being disorganized depletes your energy and that making change is worth the effort. You expend far too much energy hunting for lost objects, making unrealistic plans, scrambling to meet deadlines, and apologizing for being late. You end up running on empty because you exhaust your reserves as you deal with the impact of your own chaos. This is one of the many paradoxes of organizing: you don't organize because it feels as if it's a waste of time, yet you then waste a lot of time contending with the mess. Clearing up your messes gives you a chance to encounter the physical world and recraft your sense of mastery in it, to redirect your energy toward what has the most personal meaning for you. You begin to see the importance of personal growth in this area. As an ancient teacher once said, "Who is master of the world? He who masters himself."

Organizing is deeper and more powerful than I once thought. It's not only about freeing ourselves from clutter or putting "everything in its place." It's about expanding our sense of personal efficacy. It's also about discovering courage and dignity, and living our true life purpose. Organizing allows you to listen much more carefully to your inner voice, because you are quiet enough to hear. Being organized means:

- You can **find what you want** when you need it.
- You can **keep track of important information** and lay your hands on it when you want to.
- You can **complete your tasks** in a timely way.
- You can **arrive at your destination when you choose**.
- You can **keep agreements** and make agreements that you can keep.
- You can **take action when you want** and seize new opportunities as they arise.
- You can **focus** on what is important to you.
- You can do all of this with a great degree of **presence of mind**. You are able to pay attention to what you decide is important. This presence of mind also allows you to live with more awareness of a greater Presence, if that is what you are seeking.

As you can see, this is an action-oriented definition. It is not about achieving surface neatness or compulsive timeliness. Being organized means you can live your life fully and move full steam ahead. This is the deep order that is possible when you connect with your true intent and your sense of dignity and self-worth.

How Do I Get Off This Merry-Go-Round?

Freeing up energy involves seven steps. These steps build on each other. For clarity's sake, I list them in order, and this order is a useful way to begin. Over time, you will find yourself working a few steps at a time, in your own way, in your own order. Don't be overwhelmed by these steps—I'm just giving you the overview here. This is the map for the rest of the book. In the seven steps, you:

1. **Establish Your Purpose.** In the first step, you have an opportunity to explore your deeper purpose for getting organized. You look at how disorganization is a stumbling block for you. You identify what being organized can do for you and you make a deep commitment to change.

2. **Envision What You Want.** Now you create your vision for how you want to live your life. You visualize the details of how being organized can contribute to your life vision. You imagine how much better your life will be and you find some role models to help you see that you can change.

3. **Take Stock.** You take a very realistic look at what you are doing to create chaos and frenzy in your life. And you examine the thinking, beliefs, emotional attachments, and spiritual orientation that lead you to disorganization.

4. **Choose Support.** Support, lots of it, is crucial to make this kind of change. You identify all kinds of support for yourself in this process.

5. **Identify Strategies for Change.** You learn what it takes to become organized—how to clear up the backlog successfully, how to build new systems and new habits. Then you incorporate the basics of time management, handling purchases and possessions well, learning to focus, and making sure that your word is good.

6. **Take Action.** You use implementation tools to put the approach into action. You set reasonable goals, you allocate time, you energize yourself when you get stuck, and you get good help.

7. **Go Deeper to Keep Going.** You learn to take care of yourself better and you do the deep emotional work that can free you from destructive habits and emotional pain. You deepen your understanding about how you want to live and what it takes to live that way.

As you can see in the Seven-Step Change Cycle diagram (page 12), purpose is central. You start with purpose and you return to purpose. You focus on your purpose for getting organized, but, ultimately, you are getting organized so that you can do more of what you really want to do in life.

I call this a cycle because in getting organized, you go through many rounds, and you work through many layers. The blast-through-the-mess approach or the this-weekend-I-am-going-to-get-totally-organized method doesn't work for most people. Rather, you go through a cycle of working through the mess on your desk, learning to keep your desk ready for action, and then moving on to clearing the clothes off the floor. And that deepens your commitment to getting organized because you see the good results, which in turn allows you to go after what you really want in life because you are not getting in your own way so much. You get clearer about who you are. This is a cycle for life.

As you go through these steps, you'll see what really works for you. You'll get to know yourself better and you'll take more effective action. You will change. You'll find it easier to get things done. And on the nightmarish days, you'll still find ways to keep your energy moving. You'll also see that this path is a powerful way to improve the quality of your life.

What It Feels Like Along the Way

Using this method you will become aware of your current thoughts and choices about possessions, time, agreements, and focus. You'll begin to see trade-offs that you hadn't seen before. You'll see small changes that you can make. You'll work differently with your fear and anxiety. You will cultivate new habits slowly, one at a time, so that you can adjust to a new way of living. You will delve more deeply into the meaning of your mess, and you'll start to understand your own brain—how you think and what distracts you.

Step by step you create some order, then a little more . . . until you establish a substantially clearer space. This learning process takes time and repetition. For example, I had to tackle my desk as if it were Mount Everest. I made thirty or forty attempts. I know this sounds exaggerated, but I had to get my figurative hiking boots, pack, and ice ax, and go after

The Seven-Step Change Cycle

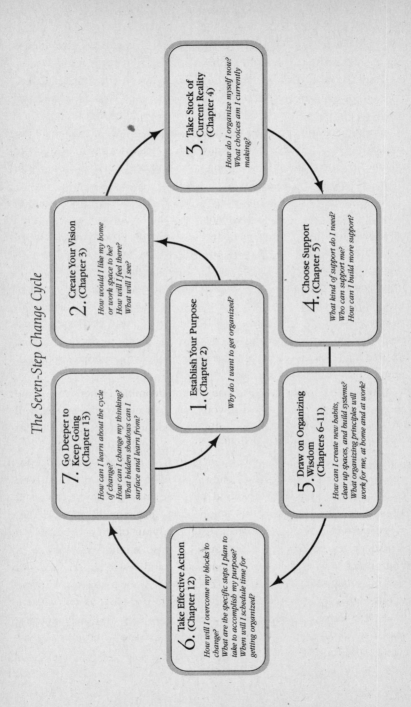

1. Establish Your Purpose (Chapter 2)

Why do I want to get organized?

2. Create Your Vision (Chapter 3)

*How would I like my home or work space to be?
How will I feel there?
What will I see?*

3. Take Stock of Current Reality (Chapter 4)

*How do I organize myself now?
What choices am I currently making?*

4. Choose Support (Chapter 5)

*What kind of support do I need?
Who can support me?
How can I build more support?*

5. Draw on Organizing Wisdom (Chapters 6–11)

*How can I create new habits, clear up spaces, and build systems?
What organizing principles will work for me, at home and at work?*

6. Take Effective Action (Chapter 12)

*How will I overcome my blocks to change?
What are the specific steps I plan to take to accomplish my purpose?
When will I schedule time for getting organized?*

7. Go Deeper to Keep Going (Chapter 13)

*How can I learn about the cycle of change?
How can I change my thinking?
What hidden shadows can I surface and learn from?*

my desk with determination. The "mountain" defeated me many times, but eventually I did conquer it. (I have a little flag waving at the top.)

Determination to change must be mixed with a healthy dose of compassion. You weave will and kindness together as you undertake this transformational journey. You develop self-acceptance and let go of the shaming inner voice. You see that you can't force yourself to change just by bossing yourself around. You develop a much deeper motivation to change and grow and, in so doing, you find the strength to go after more of what you want in life.

As you begin to get organized, you feel more and more confident in your ability to incorporate order into your life. You also experience a stronger sense of professional effectiveness and "presence," because you aren't wrestling with time and objects as much. This sense of presence—sometimes called "mindfulness"—signals the ability to be fully available for life and its challenges, and is a guiding principle in this method. It's hard to be "present" when you can't find your keys or when you're running half an hour late. It's also hard to be present—and connected to others—when you're spending another Sunday cleaning up the office or you're too embarrassed to welcome people into your home.

You will begin to have a sense of homecoming. When you come "home," whether to your house, your office, or even your car, you will become energized and engaged rather than depressed. Home enhances your sense of belonging. You might begin to feel that there is actually a place for you. You may experience a sense of grace and peacefulness because you are not struggling so hard to get to a place on time or to meet deadlines. Your blood pressure may go down. You will wrestle less with bills, receipts, phone calls, and e-mails. You can find a deeper sense of the sacred. For example, your office can become a sanctuary for meaningful work, and you also might find a space in your home that allows for contemplation and reverence. You might start to sense that life is short and you don't want to scatter it to the winds, doing everything and seeing everyone. Finally, as you clear a place for yourself by becoming organized, you may well begin sensing your true aspiration. It's easier to hear your calling when there is less pandemonium.

An Integrated Approach to Change

Using this approach, you will work the seven steps in cycles, alternating between focusing on objects or time and working with your emotions, thoughts, and life energy. You'll engage four levels of self in order to enter a new way of living:

- The physical level—what you do day-to-day, the actions you take that produce the chaos
- The emotional level—your feelings about disorder, order, timeliness, and possessions
- The intellectual level—what you think, how you think, and what you believe
- The spiritual level—your deeper sense of meaning and purpose; your values and your sense of the sacred in time, space, and material things; your connectedness with your source of strength and courage

Most personal change efforts fail because they are limited to one or two levels. Using this process, you will draw on knowledge from all four realms so you can truly transform your life. Think of this work as clearing your path of inner and outer obstacles. Everything has energy, and freeing up energy occurs on several levels at once. As you make changes, your well-being increases, and this frees you up to live your true purpose. You experience more composure. You connect more deeply with a greater energy and vitality. Every action that you take matters. Every time you flex your inner muscles to do something different, you are building the strength for more. Athletes lift weights. You do the dishes, throw things away, file the papers, and put things back. This is your discipline. Building discipline builds your strength and power. Each action that you take towards change helps you take the next action. I will remind you often that this is a journey of small changes. Over time, small changes add up to great transformation.

You'll become more aware of how your disorganization causes anxiety and your anxiety causes disorganization. Running late often leads to panic. Losing the car keys leads to rage. Missing an important deadline can lead to despair or self-hatred. The life of a disorganized person can be a roller coaster ride of feelings. Fear, anxiety, despair, resentment, are among the many feelings that are intensified by disorganization. Moreover, emotional upsets are disorganizing. When you are too mad to sit down and pay the bills, when you are so resentful that you can't focus on your work, when you are too depressed to remember to stop at the grocery store on the way home, your life tends to be more chaotic. If your feelings often knock you off your feet, if you are so overwhelmed by floods of emotion that you cannot take care of your daily needs, then it is time to make steadying yourself a serious practice.

In the end, much of this is about micro-changes in how we think about taking action. We see how our deepest beliefs and feelings affect our everyday actions, which in turn affect our results. We can see clearly how if we do what we have always done, we will get what we have always gotten. We will be in the same situation over and over again, unless we fundamentally change. Each time you put your keys back in their place, each evening that you clear off your desk, each time you make a promise that you can and do keep, you are growing toward more satisfaction and well-being.

Every step of the way, there are exercises so that you can put this approach into practice. These exercises won't take you a lot of time, but when used, they can be very powerful. Try these out. Try thinking of these exercises as explorations into a new way of living.

Create a habit of noting what you are learning. Keep a journal in a book or on your computer and pick a time every day to write a few sentences. For example, go directly to your journal when you open the computer and set a timer for five minutes and write. Or keep your journal by your bed and make a habit of reflecting on your day and noting what it was like for you. One pointer: Do not take notes on random pieces of paper thinking that you will copy them down someday. If you like jotting down occasional notes, make it a practice to carry a small notebook with you.

Part of the reward of this approach is that not only will you begin to uncover your floor and desk, but you will also start to create a nurturing space in which you can know and love yourself more fully. The beauty and power of this path is that you can work both outside in—clearing clutter can help you feel more serene—and inside out—as you heal your inner chaos, it may become easier to clear off your desk. You can uncover your core purpose and have the space to do something new, meet a new person, or take a risk. It's paradoxical perhaps, but as you clear up your surface messiness, you become able to enter the genuine, alive messiness of life more freely.

2

What Is Your Compelling Purpose for Organizing?

Recently, Melissa, one of my clients, told me, "I don't like being disorganized. I waste a lot of time looking for things. I hate the way my apartment looks. I miss appointments because I forget to write things down. I'm looking for an exciting, responsible job, and I know I need to change. But when I have free time, I don't like to spend any of it cleaning, or putting things away. I want to visit friends, go to the movies, have some fun."

Melissa has summed up a core dilemma around getting organized. She wants to get organized, but she doesn't want to spend any time doing it. She wants the results, but isn't ready to change herself to get them. So far, she has managed to escape most of the pain of her disorganization. Melissa is known by her colleagues to be a little scattered, but she is delightful, and her forgetfulness is easily forgiven. She hasn't lost a promotion or a life partner because of her disorganization. Without a good, strong reason to change, Melissa won't. She doesn't think that it is worth the effort, and, right now, she doesn't pay a high-enough price. What Melissa has not yet recognized is that a few well-chosen organizing habits can actually save her time and energy, reduce her stress, and help her find and flourish in the job of her dreams.

By contrast, Ruth, a single mother and a high school teacher, is well aware of the price that she pays for being disorganized, both at home with her children and at work with her colleagues. Ruth's life has become painful to her. Her habit of overbooking herself and running late has led to a chronic feeling of being squeezed. Her indecisiveness has led to taking on more than she can handle. She feels pressure almost all of the time. She can see clearly that organizing would bring her more of what she wants in life. She is ready to change so that she can do more of what is really important to her with less of that frenzied feeling.

Most disorganized people have no interest in being organized for its own sake. Why get organized if you don't enjoy the process or value the result? You probably don't want to get organized just to be tidy or punctual (even the words might evoke distaste). When you create order not for the sake of order alone, but to manifest something that is deeply important to you, you get the fuel for change.

A strong, meaningful purpose for organizing will be the motivation and pivot point around which your organizing will take place. When you forget why you ever started getting organized, when you want to give up, you'll draw on your purpose and that will give you direction and energy. Organizing is hard work—it entails a change of mind, heart, and action. Like other worthy endeavors that demand a lot from you, it requires determination, commitment, and grit. If you set out to build a business, be a good athlete, or learn another language, you would prepare yourself with a clear intent. You have to do the same thing for getting organized.

Finding things when you want them, feeling less stress, living in a pleasant place, keeping agreements, experiencing fewer family fights, keeping your desk clear: as good as these reasons are, they won't sustain you when the going gets rough. You can probe your good reasons for getting organized to reveal your purpose. For each good reason, you ask a question: Why do I want that? Why do I want to find things more easily? So that I can have a greater sense of readiness for action, for example. Why do I want to feel less stress? So that I can experience greater health, energy, and well-being, so that I can enjoy my life. Why do I want to keep agreements? So that people see me as reliable and trustworthy.

As you build on your reasons to develop a strong purpose, you start to see that organizing can help you bring more desirable *qualities* into your life:

- The *confidence* of finding things when you need them
- The *reliability* of showing up when you say you will
- The *beauty* of living in a place that is aesthetically pleasing
- The *creativity* of working in a supportive atmosphere
- The *responsibility* of meeting deadlines
- The *integrity* of knowing that your word is good
- The *calm* of knowing that you can count on yourself

■ ■ ■ EXERCISE ■ ■ ■

Take a moment to write down a few qualities that describe what you are longing for. Ask yourself what qualities you want to express in your life. Would you like to be serene under pressure? Would you like more self-confidence? Would you like more open-heartedness? Your list might include: self-esteem, security, relaxation, peace of mind, more energy, freedom, creativity, access to knowledge, reliability, serenity, clarity, focus, beauty, perspective, or spaciousness.

■ ■ ■

Another way to discover your purpose for organizing is to think of something that you would really like to do or to be in life and you can't do it because you are disorganized. For instance, if you truly want to take leadership in your community, develop a strong, intimate relationship, create a loving family, or be known as a trustworthy healer—but you can't do those things because you are unreliable, chaotic, chronically late, messy, or break your promises—then you have a strong purpose for getting organized. Purpose is about who and how you want to be. Your purpose for organizing will support your life purpose. Your life purpose is often about something beyond yourself, or bigger than yourself; it is about your contribution. While you don't need to know your life purpose to get value from this book, you may discover it in the process of clearing up your mess.

■ ■ ■ EXERCISE ■ ■ ■

Ask yourself why you want to get organized. What is your disorganization preventing you from having or experiencing in your life? Think for a moment about why you picked up this book: what do you hope to gain from getting organized?

■ ■ ■

At first, Ruth answered the question about her purpose with her good reasons: "I want to get organized so that I can find things. My mess is my stumbling block, I just spend too much time looking for my keys." And, later, she began to realize: "As I get organized, I can start to be more of the person that I want to be, loving, strong, a good teacher and very present for my family. I can do more of what I care about doing."

It took Melissa a little longer to find a compelling purpose. After considering her lack of professional focus, she said, "I want to get organized so that I can stop feeling so confused. I don't really know what is most important to me." And as she explored this question more fully, she said, "I am ready to experience more dignity and listen to my inner guidance for my purpose in life. I think I am ready to take on more leadership in my community, but when I am running around so much, I don't trust myself to follow through on things."

■ ■ ■ EXERCISE ■ ■ ■

The following sentence-completion exercise will give you more ideas about your purpose for organizing. You can say these out loud or write them down. Try completing each sentence in five different ways.

When I am more organized, I will experience more . . .
I will have more . . .
My disorganization keeps me from . . .

Now complete the following sentences and see what information you glean about what you might gain from organizing. Some of these sentence stems will resonate with you, others won't be important.

If I could find things easily, I would . . .
If I stopped rushing, I would feel . . .
If I worked through my backlog, I could . . .
If I lived in a beautiful space, it would mean . . .
If I really felt at home, I would . . .
If I really cleared my desk, I would be free to . . .
If I handled money well, I could . . .

■ ■ ■

All too often organizing seems trivial and unimportant, but it can support your deeper purpose in life. Understanding this connection is vital; otherwise, you'll get organized sporadically with little impact, or it will become another "should" and you probably won't do it at all.

Some Purposes for Organizing

It's a new idea for many people that getting organized can serve a greater purpose in their lives. Those of us who are disorganized are that way in part because we don't value organization. It seems so trivial and mundane that it is hard to see how important it is. Here you find out how you could value getting organized, even though the actual activity might not be so pleasing to you. The key is to think of the big picture of how being organized could help you grow, live with greater impact, or allow you to achieve the life you want.

Organizing Can Help You Grow into Your Next Role

For many people, being disorganized is their biggest stumbling block to growing into their next role. They can't take their next natural step in life because they just can't get it together. Martin said, "I know I am the best social worker in my department. My supervisor would love to promote me, but she can't, because I just can't get through the paperwork. This is holding me back." Martin was committed to making a contribution in his agency. He was great with clients and a terrific mentor for the new professionals who were just out of graduate school. He was unable to create a system for staying on top of the reporting requirements, however. He was smart and capable but couldn't file the needed reports. He was ready to figure out how to organize himself to take care of this one issue, so that he could take on more responsibility.

It's hard to see that as terrific and talented as you are, something mundane like returning e-mails and phone calls in a timely way could be preventing you from growing professionally. Or perhaps you miss deadlines and people can't count on you. Learning organizing skills could help you move ahead.

Organizing Can Be a Spiritual Practice

For most of us, the good life includes friends, family, meaningful work, contact with nature, and good fun. Cleaning up after ourselves is not considered part of great living. We see cleaning up as an extra. If we could get someone else to do it for us, we would feel better. When we start to value our whole selves, however, we can see that through organizing, we can enter our whole lives, not just the "good parts." It is *all* good. Cleaning up and creating order are part of becoming present. Moment by moment, we can enter into our lives more fully.

Great spiritual teachers point to the potential for holiness in everything: "God is in the details." Rabbi Nachman of Breslov taught that we can find higher consciousness by addressing ourselves to the small things of everyday life with intentionality. He says that God is in everything, we have only to become aware of that, and through our attention, we can release the sparks of holiness in what seems like the ordinary secular world.

In the Zen tradition, there is the story of the young student who goes to his master and says, "Tell me how to reach enlightenment."

The master says, "Did you eat your porridge?" The student says yes.

"Well, then," says the master, "clean your bowl."

Over and over again, we get up, shower, eat, work, and play with the children. Over and over again, we have a bowl to clean at the end of our activities. What a blessing to clean up after ourselves. What a benefit to discover that we leave traces and can deal with them responsibly. The Vietnamese Buddhist monk Thich Nhat Hanh once wrote, "Washing the dishes and cooking are themselves the path to Buddhahood. . . . Only a person who has grasped the art of cooking, washing dishes, sweeping, and chopping wood, someone who is able to laugh at the world's weapons of money, fame, and power, can hope to transcend the mountain as a hero."

Chögyam Trungpa Rinpoche, a Tibetan Buddhist teacher, said, "The attitude of sacredness towards your environment will bring drala [magic]. You may live in a dirt hut with no floor and only one window, but if you regard that space as sacred, if you care for it with your heart and mind, then it will be a palace." You want to feel as if you live in a palace, not a dumping ground. From this perspective, mindful organizing could be as valuable a spiritual practice as meditation.

Organizing Can Increase Your Sense of Social Responsibility

It is so easy to get caught up in the race for success, the juggling act of family, work, play, and just staying one step ahead of everything. In the busyness, we can lose track of what we are doing. We forget to ask what is truly important to us, to our community, our society. Many of us don't have one extra minute to devote to considering the needs of people who have less than we do or to reaching out to our neighbors. Perhaps at one point in your life you decided to be a community leader, yet, now, you are just bogged down in the details. As you get organized, your values become clearer and you become more willing to make hard choices. You experience the preciousness of time and life more keenly.

The Indian teacher J. Krishnamurti, in *The Flame of Attention*, discussed the importance of creating order in one's life:

To find out what right action is we must understand the content of our consciousness. If one's consciousness is confused, uncertain, pressurized, driven from one corner to another, from one state to another, then one becomes more and more confused, uncertain and insecure; from that confusion one cannot act. . . . It is of primary importance to bring about order in ourselves; from inward order there will be outward order.

Organizing can be very closely linked to clarifying one's consciousness. This is not to say that all organized people have an easier time determining right action. It is to say that creating inner and outer order can significantly enhance our clarity as we explore our relationship to community and society.

Organizing Can Help You Be More Environmentally Aware

In his popular novel *Ishmael*, Daniel Quinn suggests that there are two types of peoples, Leavers and Takers. The Leavers leave their environment intact, and they travel without a trace. The Takers leave a mess behind them. There is no doubt that Americans are the biggest Takers of all, leading the planet in environmental waste and destruction. But in our individual lives, we can live more like Leavers. We can live with less harm. We can leave fewer traces. We can become aware of our impact. As we raise our consciousness in our daily lives, we can move toward more gentleness and graciousness in our own immediate environment. We'll start to consume less, because we find life more satisfying.

As you move your belongings around, you start to sense the amount of space they take up. As you see how you are squeezing yourself out of your space, you might ask, "Where can I throw these things away?" As we grow in environmental awareness, we begin to understand that there is no "away." We might get the stuff out of our house, but, then, where next? So, perhaps we can bring fewer things into the house in the first place.

Environmental activist Dana Meadows, who was a coauthor of *Limits to Growth* and a professor of environmental studies at Dartmouth College, wrote about moving her many belongings from her farm in Vermont.

I brought those books into the house, every one made of ground-up trees. I read them, yes, and loved them, but I have easy access to three good libraries. I didn't need to house a library of my own. I piled up those books because I am impatient; I want to look up a quote or a fact instantly. Because I fend off worries by escaping, and books are my escape mechanism. . . . The books are an expensive, troublesome, heavy, space-occupying fortress against having to confront my inner bugaboos. I guess that's also true of . . . the closets full of rarely worn clothes. Stuff taken from the earth to bolster fantasy or foist off fear, stuff our non-affluent household paid a fortune for, stuff I've housed for decades, stuff that occupied the space of real life.

Picture all that stuff wrested from the mines and forests and soils of the earth, and finally, unceremoniously, dumped. . . . The price we're paying for our stuff—in money and time and space and resources—is tremendous.

Most of us have too much stuff. But we can start practicing our environmental awareness right at home, by learning to consume less, recycling creatively, and treating our own "micro-environment" with the care that we want to bring to our larger environment.

Your Purpose May Evolve

As Mary began getting organized, all she wanted was to get home at a reasonable hour while staying current in her profession. She saw that her inability to make quick decisions about her reading and professional connections was eating into precious family time. Getting organized meant taking a stand for her family and home time. Later, she came to see that she suffered deeply from the constant pushing, and she needed to stop trying to do everything. She wanted breathing room for her innermost self.

Initially, Charles wanted to be more reliable and break fewer agreements so that his practice would have more integrity. The work habits that enabled him to be successful in college and during the early years of his practice were now driving him crazy. His last-minute heroics had gotten out of hand. He wanted to learn how to plan and follow through on each project so he could provide superb timely service to his clients. Then he started to realize that "service" had much deeper meaning for him, and that when he was truly serving his clients, he began to feel a much deeper sense of fulfillment in his work.

Your Beliefs Will Trump Your Purpose Every Time

No matter how good and strong your purpose is, if you hold contradictory beliefs, they will stop you in your tracks. For example, early on, my purpose was to get organized so that I could welcome people into my life and into my home. As I kept trying and failing to get organized, however, I discovered that I had some strong reservations about order. "Clutter is warm; neatness is cold," I thought. "Messiness is friendly and available; order is standoffish and formal. And lateness, though occasionally rude, is basically relaxed and flexible, while punctuality is oppressive." I was going to have to revise these strongly held beliefs if I was going to make progress.

I was also sure that messiness was a source of creativity. Not just my creativity, everyone's creativity. This was such a deep assumption that I thought it was just something true about life. Fact: Messy people are creative, creative people are messy. I was so sure that messiness and creativity were inextricably linked that I had never seen a creative neat person. I just screened them out.

Slowly, I began to notice that one of the most creative, artistic people I knew, a very successful painter, was impeccably neat. Then, I observed that a friend who writes children's stories has created a wonderful, serene, organized space for herself. Once I opened my mind to the possibility that orderliness and creativity could go together, I was soon flooded with examples of highly organized people who were extremely creative. I began to see that clutter has nothing to do with creativity, per se. You can be messy and creative, or orderly and creative. That surprised me. I started to separate notions that had been glued together in my mind. It also gave me more choices. Until then, I was scared to give up my mess, because I thought I would have to give up my creativity as well. I have since found that actually I am far more creative as a more organized person.

Reflect on your own beliefs. You might find it hard to get seriously engaged in organizing because you, too, believe that in some ways, orderliness will be detrimental to you. Organization and disorganization represent poles of a continuum. Once you have more choice in the matter, you can find a place on the continuum that works for you. Rachel shared with me her belief that "truly spiritual people don't care what their personal space looks like, it is only their inner life that is important." That was her deeply held conviction. In her view, organizing her life was going to take away from her spiritual development. There was one thing she did decide to do, however. Since she was a professional career counselor, she wanted to learn how to create a workable filing system for her client notes. She achieved that result and that was enough organizing for her. So, you can determine how organized you want to be. Complete order may not work for you, but stumbling over daily life probably isn't feasible for you either. Because beliefs are so important, we'll have another look at them in chapter 4.

Add Up What It's Costing You

You'll become more aware of your purpose for organizing when you acknowledge that your current way of life is costing you a lot. Adding up
the costs of your disorganization will help you clarify why you want to
get organized. People pay dearly for their disorganization with time, energy, self-esteem, success, relationships, and more. For years, you may
have said something like: "I'd like to get organized, but I don't have the
time." But when you look more seriously at your life, you see how
painful it is to be disorganized. When you see how much it hurts, you
can find the time.

Being disorganized can cost a lot. Yet, often you don't experience
how great the expense is because the costs are spread out over time.
Perhaps you lost a promotion or a good assignment because you missed
an important deadline, or perhaps you lost a friendship because you've
canceled dinner together one too many times. Unless you really look at
the costs in their totality, they don't add up to a commitment for change,
because we experience them separately over time. We have gotten used
to the pain. Hard as this may be, we need to deliberately cut through
our denial, so we can create the changes we want.

Perhaps you are like Sarah, who is a very sociable woman. She
deeply valued simplicity and friendship, yet she buried herself under old
newspapers and unopened mail. She couldn't invite people over because there was no place to sit. For years, she scheduled visits with her
friends in local coffee shops while saying to herself, "Next week, I'll go
through the newspapers and the piles." One day, she realized that she
had been saying that for fifteen years. This caused her such anguish that
she became ready to face the pain of cleaning up.

As you add up the pain that you cause yourself, don't minimize the
pain that you are causing other people. This is the point at which most
of us go into denial. We say, "I am trying and I didn't mean to. They
have to take into account that this is the way I am." Yet, there are some
contradictions that we have to face. We can't be both reliable and unreliable at the same time. If you pay attention, you might notice that you
are feeling pain yourself about letting people down. Allow yourself to
feel your anguish, instead of brushing it off. Pain can be a teacher. You
let the embarrassment of running late again crack through the armor of

your rationalizations, excuses, or hopelessness. Something in you says, "Enough!" Your pain can wake you up. When you develop the courage to stay with the pain, and you let go of your ten thousand excuses for why you can't change, you start to grow. It is then you can find the time to do the organizing that will make your life, and others' lives, more livable.

What are the costs of disorganization? Being disorganized can cost money. Lots of money. Think about all those lost, uncashed checks. Perhaps you don't return the catalog items you ordered because you lost the packing slip. Or the times when you finally just pay for the book club books that you wanted to return. Remember a time that you tried to return something you didn't need, and the store clerk wanted the receipt and you didn't have it? Perhaps there was an invoice that you never sent out. Or perhaps you paid your taxes late, and now you are paying the penalty. Think about all the times you paid the late fee on your credit card. Or perhaps you lost a chance for a good promotion. That's expensive. It starts to add up.

Being disorganized can cost time. Think about the time you spend looking for things, or the time needed for rework when you acted hastily and did a poor job the first time. Ponder the extra time spent doing errands that you might have grouped together. Add up the number of times you've had to return to the market because your shopping list wasn't complete. Relive the mistakes that you've made because you were hurrying and running late. Remember the extra time it took to make things right.

Another cost of disorganization is losing track of what you want in life. Many people are confused about their priorities. Trudy, a professor of mathematics, took a hard look into what her disorganization was costing her. She realized, "I'm so confused and disorganized that I might not do in my life what I most want to. There's a book that I want to write, and I think I'll never get to it. And now I am almost too tired to care." She wanted a way to stop, reorganize herself, and find relief from the burnout and stress of just too much. She wanted to scale way back so she could have the space to do what she deeply cared about.

Some people realize the stress of disorganization is costing them their health. Alex, a salesman, suffered from heart disease. His doctor warned him that he had to reduce the stress in his life. He, like others, tended to run late. He liked timing things to the second. "Never waste a minute," he liked to say. He often got to the train just as it was pulling into the track. But this habit meant that he often put a great deal of pressure on his heart as he ran from his car to the platform. And, then, all day long, he ran late, because he had so much to do. He began to notice the strain on his body after his doctor's warning. He got scared that his disorganization might cost him his life.

Being disorganized can cost relationships, too. When you lose phone numbers and don't return phone calls, it upsets people. There is a cost to canceling gatherings with good friends or colleagues because you double-booked yourself. There is a cost to the promises you make and don't keep. There is a cost to forgetting birthdays and anniversaries of people you love. If you do that regularly, they think you don't care. Sometimes, you lose your good reputation and the high regard of others because you let them down.

You may start to see that your family is paying part of the price of your disorganization. David's wife, Michal, told him that she could not live with such chaos any longer. He said, "The chaos never bothered me. I like it. It gives me the feeling of high risk—like I am in an action movie. It astonished me that Michal told me that she was moving out. She told me for years that she couldn't live with this, but it never mattered to me. We love each other." David finally accepted that his marriage could not bear the burden of his disorder any longer.

Margaret realized that her son was paying the price. "I realized major change was ahead when my son couldn't organize his homework. His role models were me and my husband, both of us successful but very disorganized. How could I say, 'Clean up your room' or 'Organize your homework' when the house was always such a mess? I realized I couldn't help him until I took my own problem seriously. I wanted to model something very different for him. My husband is slowly getting into the idea."

Our souls can also suffer from our disorganization. Cheryl said, "I'm a landscape designer and gardener. I create living art and I love it. Yet, the way I live doesn't reflect that at all. I just moved, and now I have a house and a barn that are chockablock full. I love art, beauty, design, color, and form, and I have created a whirlwind mess around me. I'm surrounded by the sludge of all this stuff. I suffer because when I look around me in my own home and office, I see ugliness. My reason for existence gets pushed into the back." The ugliness is offensive to her, but, so far, she has been unable to change it.

My turning point came when I became aware that I kept "cleaning up," and yet it had no impact. I realized that I could set aside every Sunday for the rest of my life to get organized, and I would still be a mess. I was Sisyphus, and every Sunday morning, I tried to push the boulder of my mess up the hill, and every Sunday night, it rolled back down. My disorganization was costing me my Sundays, my peace of mind, self-esteem, and sense of community. I could not have people over without creating more havoc. I started to move down the path of organizing when I got scared that I would live the rest of my life this way.

Are you willing to add up all the costs? The value of adding up all the costs at once is that you face the whole price you are paying for your disorganization. Hard? Yes. But worth it. Because when you add it all up, you are probably paying a lot for a way of living that you can change.

■ ■ ■ EXERCISE ■ ■ ■

This exercise will help you make the changes you want to make. Anthony Robbins, a specialist in personal change, says that one essential ingredient of creating change is to associate enormous pain with the way you are living now, and enormous pleasure with the way you want to live. So, here's the exercise. There are two parts to it.

1. Write everything that your disorganization is costing you. What is it costing you in terms of money? Family life and friendships? Time? Health? What is it costing you in your spiritual life? Your emotional life? Your life goals? Your soul's journey? What is it costing you in reputation? What is it costing you at work? How much leisure do you forgo because you are disorganized? What do you dislike about your current behavior? How does it make you feel?

Write down every cost that you can think of.

Now look at the price that you are paying and let yourself feel the pain of it. That is hard but essential to motivate you to make the changes that you want to make. Don't rush through this. Let yourself really face your suffering.

2. Next, write down everything that you will gain when you create the new, more organized behaviors that you want. What will you gain in terms of money? Time? Space? Love? Friendship? Spiritual life? Emotional life? Pleasure? How will it be with your family and friends? Describe in detail how good it will feel when you can locate what you need without a problem, deliver good work and pay your bills on time, do your taxes easily and routinely—or when you can walk into your home or office and it is pleasant and energizing (use the words that you want).

Now, stop and let the potential pleasure sink in. You can have this. It is possible.

■ ■ ■

Exploring the costs and benefits will help you get in touch with and strengthen your purpose for organizing. The potential pleasure will help pull you toward what you want, and the realization of the pain will help guide you away from what you don't want.

Make a Commitment

Now, ask yourself how much you really want to get organized. If you really want this, it is essential to make a commitment to yourself. When you make a commitment, you declare to yourself, and others, when you are ready, that you are going to stay the course. As Robin, a client, told me, "One night I came home around five-thirty and the house was a mess, I was a mess, everyone was upset, and I saw how I contributed to the madness. When I saw the mess I was making, I vowed to change my ways. It has taken time, but I have completely changed the way I live. I felt that vow living within me. I have been undeterred." It doesn't mean that she didn't have plenty of hard moments, but when she did, she recommitted to her purpose and to organizing.

Establishing your purpose for organizing is about deepening your sense of who you are and taking a stand for what you feel is important. As you set your purpose, take some time to look into your heart. Can you make a commitment to this purpose? Is this truly important to you? When you think about it, does your purpose give you energy? You will find that, as you learn about yourself and make a promise to pursue this path, you will feel stronger, better, and more capable, even before you see changes.

3

Visioning: It's Also About the Little Picture

As you become clearer about your purpose for organizing, you can turn to look at what your life would be like if you were actually living that purpose. Through visioning, you engage the power of your mind to imagine the results you want. Along with your purpose, visioning is essential for inspiration and direction. Without a picture of where you are going, it is very easy to get completely lost in daily pressures. What will your life be like when you are more organized? In visioning, you describe what you truly want in your day-to-day life, as if it were happening now.

Envision how these details will help you be successful in achieving your larger goals. If you can't get ahead at work because people see you as disorganized, your vision of your clean desk will be part of your vision of being a leader. If you are an artist at heart, but you rarely make time for your art, envision yourself in your studio, finding your materials easily. If you want to practice meditation but can't find time to sit, you can imagine yourself seated on your meditation pillow as relaxed as if you had all the time in the world.

At first, it will seem as if you are imagining the impossible. Call to mind this exchange between Alice and the White Queen from *Through the Looking-Glass*, by Lewis Carroll, when you feel doubt.

"One can't believe impossible things!"

"I daresay you haven't had much practice," said the Queen. "When I was your age, I always did it for half-an-hour a day. Why, sometimes I've believed as many as six impossible things before breakfast."

Through visioning, the impossible becomes possible. When Kristin was starting out as a coach, she just couldn't get her office (a disaster zone) ready for clients. She had buried herself in clutter, piles of old mail, and magazines from the past decade. She became infused with energy when she imagined feeling completely in charge and relaxed in her home office. She said, "I see a comfortable armchair for my clients and a white board for notes. I am sitting in my rocking chair. My desk is clear other than a phone, some standing files, and a computer. I have twenty clients a week." She wanted clear spaces and no clutter anywhere in her office or her apartment. Once she imagined her home free of clutter, she was enthusiastic. She threw out twelve boxes of clutter in two weeks. She said, "I am having a great time clearing out spaces. I am a clutter warrior. I can see my vision coming into reality."

Jonathan envisioned himself as a successful musician playing onstage. He imagined that people were very moved by his music. He was totally inspired as he let the music come through him. He also imagined taking excellent care of his sheet music. He dreamed of a filing system that was easy for him, and a reliable way to keep track of the many contacts he made on the road.

My goal was to create a successful consulting practice and to work with clients fully using my abilities. I wanted to work from an inner experience of calm competence, not wild frenzy covered by a thin gloss of ersatz confidence. In order to do that, I envisioned a clear desk and a filing system that helped me find client information easily. In my vision, I saw a vase of flowers on my desk. I imagined myself walking into my office and feeling energized, ready to work, not bogged down by the mess. I wanted colorful pictures hanging on my walls. I wanted the floor clear of piles. I started imagining this at a time when I had not really seen my floor for years and had seen my desktop only briefly (after the personal organizer had spent several hours with me).

Why Envision What You Want?

There are four reasons to envision what you want. First, imagining a different future helps you believe that it is possible. If you can imagine a clear desk, you are more likely to be able to create it. It is very hard to clear off your desk if you can't even think about it. The very act of imagining something different in your life starts to create new neural pathways. The new image prepares you for change. At first it seems impossible, then over time, step by step, visioning brings the impossible first into the realm of possibility and then into the realm of likelihood. Visioning is like tilling the soil; it prepares your heart and mind for something new.

Second, as you keep envisioning what you want, you identify your vision as something *you* want for *yourself*, rather than something dictated from the outside. In the middle of living your busy life, you are liable to say something like: "I don't have time for organizing right now." After visioning, there will be another voice that says, "It's worth the extra ten minutes to clear up the desk" or "It makes sense to fold the laundry." Knowing your purpose and clarifying your vision strengthens this second voice. People often identify this second voice as a voice of external authority that is telling them what to do. They don't want to obey that "bossy" voice, so they don't do what it is asking. But through visioning, you can reidentify that voice with your own inner strength and recognize that it is encouraging you to get what you really want in life. Making this shift is essential to increasing your sense of inner authority and well-being.

A third reason for envisioning what you want is that visioning helps you see where you are. You may be living more of your vision than you think, but you won't know that until you explore what your vision really is. Visioning shifts your mind-set. Since everyone is both organized and disorganized, visioning actually helps you recognize your current organizational skills.

Finally, once you imagine what you want, you'll start to see ways to go after it. Now you have an idea of where you are going with all of this organizing. Your vision helps you tap into your strengths and your goals. Your vision keeps you going on those days when you are bogged down in the mess, when you think this is all impossible and you'll never change.

How Do You Know What You Want?

For powerful visioning, you need to shift from avoiding what you don't want to describing what you do want. This is a fundamental shift from desperation to aspiration. Create a vision that inspires you, because you will need the inspiration when desperation sets in. There are a number of ways to do this, including the methods that follow.

Find a Role Model

A role model is someone we can directly relate to in external reality. He provides a touchstone or an anchor. She helps us see what we are trying to create. Early on, I spent some time with my friend the organized artist. She had a lovely style and an immaculate studio. She treated her paints and brushes with loving care, putting everything back at the end of the day. She did not seem tortured by this action at all. She loved returning things to their homes. She demonstrated to me how to put things away with love and care, without resentment and complaint. That became part of my vision for myself, putting things away with care.

Or perhaps you know someone who is always on time to meetings and seems completely prepared. This person has a calm air about him. Observe him and try to learn how he does it.

You may use anyone you want as a model. They don't have to know that you are learning from them. Don't disdain the people who seem neat and orderly, because they might have something to teach you. They probably aren't all rigid and boring. Look for someone who tends to arrive on time. Learn from someone who is completely reliable. I know a man, a senior professor who is known as enormously innovative in his field, whose word is solid. He is where he says he will be all the time. He sends the e-mail he says he will send. He calls when he says he will call. I wanted to experiment with that myself, and it helped to see someone else do it first.

When it is hard to clarify your vision, you can get inspiration by looking around and seeing whom you admire or what places attract you. Start to keep track of the people or spaces that you really appreciate. You may walk into someone's home and say to yourself, "That's it. That's what I want." Or you see someone's office that radiates a calm security, not frenzy. You can learn a lot from looking at the people who are doing things the way that you would like to. Copying is an age-old way of learning. Ask someone how she does it (just be aware that often she won't know). Watch her and learn from her.

■ ■ ■ EXERCISE ■ ■ ■

Part 1: Make a list of the people you admire and respect. Write down the qualities that each of these people embodies. Warmth? Keeping their word? Calm and thoughtful? Effective and accomplished? Organized but flexible? Ask them if they would be willing to talk with you about what their lives are like, what is important to them, and how they do what they do.

Part 2: Write down a list of the environments that you really love. Choose the three or four homes or work spaces that seem exemplary to you. Then write down the qualities that you admire about each. They may be modest in size and big in aesthetics. They may have beautiful inner spaces and lovely outer spaces. You may be surprised by what you find. It may not be beauty, per se, for you. It may be a sense of peacefulness, or a sense of tradition. It may be a feeling of action or liveliness. It may be a sense of the sacred. What qualities do you enjoy—the space, the energy, the color, the textures? You may be more visual, kinesthetic, or auditory. Note what appeals to you and why. You actually may be surprised by the essentials of what you like. Now look at your list. This list will be part of your vision.

■ ■ ■

When Kimberley made her list of places that she loved, she saw that they used natural materials, had spaces with beautiful wooden or tile floors, and included lovely handcrafted wall hangings. These places combined precision and play, elegance, simplicity, order, and creativity. (Imagine, she thought, precision *and* play, order *and* creativity???) She saw new combinations of qualities.

At the same time, she felt that her home was just too small to love and wasn't like any of the places she saw as models. Using her list of criteria, she looked for what was special about her own home. Her kitchen had beautiful woodwork with elegant molding, which was hidden by clutter and her son's artwork. She also had a large beautiful screened porch that was built in the 1930s that she currently used as a storage area. So, she decided to start there. As she sorted and discarded the piles of paper on the kitchen counters, found a new place for her son's artwork, and got rid of the boxes on the porch, she started to enjoy her small space. She now had two places in her house where she was manifesting her vision of elegant simplicity.

In your observations and conversations you may learn a new way of thinking or behaving that you can practice. Try it out. Do an experiment. See how this might work in your life.

Play with Metaphors

Metaphors are a powerful aspect of visioning because they appeal to the senses, engage the whole brain, and capture both facts and feelings. Using metaphors is like painting with words. These word pictures tap your brainpower.

Finding new metaphors for organizing helps to counterbalance the old metaphors that people often use to describe their lives. Cathy used to say, "I feel like things fly around and stick to me. I can't get unstuck." And Robert said, "I am sort of like Pig Pen. I can come into a pleasant, orderly space and within minutes, it's like a whirlwind hit it." Others have said, "It feels like living underwater." "I feel like a dancer with cement feet." "I feel like I am always just missing the bus, like I run and run and I never catch up." Holding negative images can be as powerful as holding positive images. Experiment with some new images so that you can let go of the old ones.

Charles used the metaphor of basketball to help him envision what he wanted. The image of players running in tandem, up and down the court, being totally in sync, was part of his vision. He wanted to be there for others, right there, when someone passed him the ball. He wanted to be a full participant in the game of his life. By contrast, he didn't want to arrive a half hour late for an appointment, too late to catch the ball, which, in a sense, someone had tossed in his direction a half hour earlier.

For Emily, imagining herself as a still lake in the middle of the wilderness nourished her vision for herself. This lake was deep, quiet, and extremely tranquil. Even under stormy conditions, it remained serene in its depths. Perhaps waves rippled across the surface of the lake. At times, the lake was blue, other times a deep green, but it was always extremely life-giving.

Alan pictured a frigate, a beautiful tall ship, as his metaphor for being organized. He imagined the frigate in full sail, catching the winds, mastering the high seas. Yet, he discovered that the most powerful image for him was the ship at night, anchored in the harbor, sails furled. He found that what he was really seeking was "deep anchorage." In his vision for getting organized, he was seeking a kind of security that he had rarely known because he had grown up in an alcoholic family.

For Karen, a powerful metaphor in her quest for organization was ice dancing. Ice dancers are extremely skilled athletes. They move with astonishing precision, grace, and style. They are elegant and strong; and command the whole rink. They move swiftly but are never rushed. They turn on a dime, executing very difficult moves with apparent ease. They seem to do all of this with joy. She could imagine herself going through her day as an ice dancer. It was also helpful for her to remember that skilled ice dancing requires hours of often tedious training. It reminded her that there was no way to avoid the tedium of organizing if she wanted to achieve that level of skill.

■ ■ ■ EXERCISE ■ ■ ■

Take a few moments to think of an image that speaks to how you would like to feel in relation to organizing. Close your eyes and relax. Take a few long, deep breaths. Perhaps listen to a piece of music that calls forth some of the qualities you are seeking. This will help open the metaphorical channels in your brain. Imagine your life the way you would like it to be. What are some of the qualities of the experience that you will have? What will your energy be like? Free-associate for a moment, let your mind go where it will. See if an image appears that captures the essence of your vision. Once you have that image, write it down, and keep it in a place where you can refer to it when you need a reminder of your vision.

■ ■ ■

Gain Clarity Through Conversation

Visioning is also a conversation. When we are visioning, we start talking about what we want in our world. In his book *The Fifth Discipline*, organizational learning expert Peter Senge tells this story: "Several years ago I was talking with a young woman about her vision for the planet. She said many lovely things about peace and harmony, about living in balance with nature. As beautiful as these ideas were, she spoke about them unemotionally, as if these were things that she should want. I asked her if there was anything else. After a pause, she said, 'I want to live on a green planet,' and started to cry." She had finally hit on what truly moved her. It may take time and conversation for you to discover what truly moves you about creating a more organized life. Start talking to people about what you want in your world. Ask them what is important to them. Sharing and supporting each other's visions helps us move toward them. Notice when you are touched or exhilarated; you may be on to something.

You Can Start with What You Don't Want

If you can't imagine what you do want, you may need to start with what you don't want. "I don't want the piles on the floor of the living room." Then, you can go on from there. Ask a few questions: What would it be like if you didn't have the piles? What would you get if you had clear spaces? What will you see or feel? You might then notice that what you really want is a living room where you can sit down, and that you want to clear the piles from the floor and the couch so that you can have a place to read after the children are asleep. So now your vision includes a clear floor, clear furniture, and you, sitting on the couch, fully absorbed in that book that you have wanted to read for a long time.

■ ■ ■ EXERCISE ■ ■ ■

Take one aspect of your disorganization that is bothering you, that you want to change. Begin by describing what you don't want. Then write down its opposite. Ask yourself what you would have in your life if you made that change. And, if you had that, what would you have then?

■ ■ ■

Create Your Vision

Set aside some time for visioning. Dream about your home and office. How would you like these spaces to be? Visioning gives you a rare opportunity to describe exactly what you want. Don't skimp on the juicy details: the colors, the sights, the sounds, or how it feels. The more detailed and vivid this vision, the more powerfully it will guide you during the hard work of creating new ways of acting and being.

Many studies have shown that the brain cannot recognize the difference between a well-imagined experience and the real thing. Try this experiment. Imagine that you have a beautiful juicy yellow lemon in your hand. Imagine yourself slicing the lemon in half and looking at the juicy circle of the lemon. Now, imagine yourself biting into the lemon. If you are like many people, you begin to salivate. You may feel some tightness in your throat from the sourness. But you can see that since there is no real lemon, you are having a physiological reaction to an imagined experience. So, too, with organizing; the more vividly you can imagine arriving on time in a calm, relaxed fashion, the more your body receives signals from your brain that it is a true experience. Through visualizing, you are practicing for reality.

Don't worry if you don't initially "see" anything. You can use the power of your mind to think about the details of what you want. Many people find that with practice, pictures begin to appear. For some people, their vision may be primarily kinesthetic or auditory; they'll feel it, or hear it, and won't "see" it. Like any other skill, the more you practice, the easier it gets.

■ ■ ■ EXERCISE ■ ■ ■

A short and powerful way of visioning includes three rounds of writing. You can do this by yourself or with a partner. Set aside about fifteen minutes. Make sure that you won't be interrupted. Don't answer the phone. For each round of writing, prepare yourself by relaxing and then reflecting on the question for a minute or so.

Round 1: Write for two minutes about what you really care about in your life as a whole. What's important to you in life? What really matters to you? What do you love and what do you love to do? What are you passionate about? Let your answers emerge from your heart.

Round 2: Write for two minutes about how you would like your life to be. Think about work, family, relationships, leisure, health, spiritual life, community. Play with possibility. Describe what you would like—even if it seems impossible. Write in the present tense as if it is already happening.

Round 3: Write for two minutes about the specific details of your life as you want to live it. How would your home or office look? What would it feel like for you to be there? What would it be like for you to arrive on time or to feel calm and relaxed? Write down your vision of the details in your life with as much vividness and precision as possible. You will use this description every day to remind yourself of where you are going.

Betty answered Round 1 this way: "I love my kids and my family. There's no doubt that I care about them deeply. I love my garden, I love just being in my garden and tending to it at each stage. I love my phone calls with friends. I love being in a community. I used to give big potluck dinners and I don't do that anymore, but I loved that feeling of bringing people together. That's really my passion."

Betty continued this way: "I want my kids to be healthy. I want at least five dinners a week where we sit down together as a family. I want the TV off after dinner, and I want to find new ways of just being. I want a beautiful garden. I can see a big harvest this year with enough tomatoes to freeze sauce for the year. I want to host a potluck dinner every quarter—mostly with old friends, but every time, I'd like to invite someone new."

Betty's description for Round 3 was: "To do all of this with some degree of calm, I would like my home office to be a place of ease and tranquility. I can't do that kind of entertaining from a whirlwind. I want a place for my phone list and my Rolodex. I want to be able to sit at a clear space and make notes and have a place to put them. I want organized home files so I can keep track of everyone's doctor visits. And I want to clear all the clutter from the kitchen. It's a piled-up place right now, and for all those dinners I want to make, I need to enjoy being in the kitchen. I can see the clear counters."

In your visioning, you can picture your office as a haven to get your work done, or meeting deadlines with ease. You can imagine being delighted when someone drops by to visit unannounced because your kitchen has become a warm, comfortable social place. You can picture yourself getting up in the morning and getting dressed in clean, attractive clothes (not pulling things out of the hamper and frantically figuring out which clothes are clean and unwrinkled enough to wear). Imagine yourself calm and centered under stress, leaving the house a few minutes early, instead of flying down the highway trying to shave or put your makeup on, late again.

See your attractive home as a sanctuary for family life. Pick a few details that capture your attention. It may be the image of your clear dining table, polished and gleaming, or an image of yourself taking a deep breath as you walk out the door, rather than running to your first meeting. Write your vision in the present tense, as if it is already happening. Then, immediately, tape it to the door of your office or the inside of your datebook before it disappears.

You might think that this level of detail is trivial, but it's not. These details accumulate to shape our lives. Annie Dillard once said, "How we spend our days is how we spend our years." As the little picture gets clearer, the big picture also comes into sharper focus.

■ ■ ■

Sustaining Your Vision

One way to sustain your vision is to create daily affirmations. As you keep affirming the possibility of something different, you get ready for change. That way, when you walk into your office one morning and find a clear desk surface with a vase of lovely flowers on it, you won't be shocked or back out, thinking that you're in somebody else's office. It will be your office, and you will love being there.

Affirmations are statements in the present tense that describe a reality that you would like to experience as if it is happening now. They sound like this:

I arrive at appointments prepared and relaxed.
I walk into my office and feel energized.
I move fast with grace.
My office is a haven; I am extremely productive there.
My office is a powerful work center. I am right on top of things.
My home is a sanctuary. I walk in and relax.
Our mornings are harmonious. We each know what to do and we do it.

You can group your affirmations into word pictures to repeat to yourself. Here are some examples.

I sleep easily knowing that my activity lists are complete and I am on top of things. I awaken refreshed. I have a good sense of my priorities for the day. I arrive at work on time. My work space is energizing and inviting. I can do the work that I am meant to do here. My work surfaces are clear. I can lay my hands on whatever I need, when I need it. I leave time to focus on my priorities. I say yes to what I can do, and no to what I cannot do. I am reliable and trustworthy. I feel great about being on top of things.

I have a good system for tracking my money. I know where my bills and invoices are. I know what I owe, and my money is under control. I sit down twice a month to pay my bills. I am powerful and responsible in relationship to my money. I care for the money I have, and I keep track of both the money that I bring in and the money that I spend. I am wise about my purchases and my choices. I feel calm and comfortable around money.

I walk into my home at the end of the day and I feel immediately refreshed and relaxed. Our home is a place of peace and love. It is a sanctuary, a haven. I love the beauty that surrounds me. I enter a space that completely supports me and my family to live and love well.

Affirmations can energize you. Tape yours to the bathroom mirror or to the dashboard as part of your vision. Keep saying them. Affirmations give your mind the boost it needs to create what you want. Affirming something alone does not do the work for you, but it paves the way. Moreover, affirmations contradict the running stream of negativity that most of us experience all day long. Affirmations help turn up the volume on possibility while simultaneously turning the volume down on your "gremlin," your negative self-sabotager.

The challenge with affirmations is to keep them going. You might say a couple of affirmations for a few days, then forget or let them go. If that happens, pick them up again. Make sure they have juice for you and you feel some excitement when you say them. Put them in your Palm Pilot or Outlook memo. Just keep conditioning your mind.

■ ■ ■ EXERCISE ■ ■ ■

Take a few minutes to write your affirmations on a piece of paper and post them where you will see them. Change them when they get stale.

■ ■ ■

Visions Evolve

Visioning is a process to help you stay in touch with what you really want. Your vision will naturally change as you change. Once a month or so, return to your vision and check to see if you still really want what you are describing. As you start to create more of what you said you wanted, what you want will change. You will start to discover more about what you would really like. As you change, you discover new insights about who you are. You get more in touch with your own authentic voice.

Trudy went on retreat at a Zen center. To her, the most beautiful part of the center was the burnished wood floors. There was something about the golden light and the smooth surface that she really wanted in her home. She imagined one room where she could create a similar feeling, so she pulled up the carpet and revealed the wood floor beneath it. She removed everything from the room and created a taste of what she loved. As time went on, she realized that what she really loved was the warm, comfortable uncluttered feeling. It wasn't just the golden quality of the wood floor that she loved, but the open spaciousness of a room that was clutter-free.

She discovered that she could create more of that feeling by keeping clutter out of two rooms. She kept picturing those rooms as clear open spaces. As time went on, she was able to remove the clutter from three rooms. But she struggled with clearing out her bedroom. There were clothes on the floor and on the bed, books and magazines scattered around, and nothing on the walls. She finally realized that a deep part of her dream was to have a very peaceful bedroom with a feeling of safety and comfort. She imagined pretty pillows on the bed and beautiful pictures on the walls. Since she had been sexually abused as a child, it was daunting work for her to imagine a bedroom that was safe and loving. So it was profoundly healing for her to remove the clutter from her bedroom. She was able to walk in, relax, and no longer feel assaulted.

You can see how her vision evolved. It started with revealing her wood floor, and it turned into creating a safe bedroom for herself. She did hang pictures on her walls, and finally found some beautiful pillows for her bed. Eventually, she not only loved how her bedroom looked, but she also was able to cultivate a sense of safety there.

Rechoosing Your Vision

One day I jumped into my car at 4:45 P.M. in a frazzled frame of mind. I had just remembered that my mortgage payment was due the next day. I hurried to the post office so that I could Express Mail the check before it closed at 5:00 P.M. The check was in the envelope, ready to go. When I got to the post office at 4:58, I discovered that I didn't have the address of the mortgage bank. Since it turned out that the post office closed at 5:30, I rushed home to get the address. I found it, and then raced back.

Mission accomplished. Yet, it seemed like my vision of calmly handling my financial responsibilities was far away.

What does this stressful story have to do with visioning? It was a chance for me to choose my vision again. In the middle of life's stressful moments, we can completely forget that we are trying to create something different for ourselves. When you have too much to do, your back hurts, or you're late again, it is easy to give up on this whole endeavor. Envisioning what you want, right in the middle of your descent, is a very skillful move. When you are in the middle of chaos, you can still remember what you want, and affirm it. In fact, you can take a strong stand for what you want. It is much more powerful than beating yourself up.

When I thought about my rush to the post office, I had a choice. I could say to myself, "You just spent an extra ten dollars on an idiotic expense like Express Mail when you could have mailed the check two weeks ago. But not only that (and here the inner exasperation increases), you just spent the last hour racing back and forth to the post office for no good reason at all!!! (You idiot!!!)." Or I could say something like: "I want to stand for responsibility and calm. This chaotic behavior is not what I choose for myself. I choose again to be calm and responsible. I can imagine paying my mortgage on the twenty-eighth day of the month, calmly. I can do this."

Does that seem so impossible? It is hard to do. But this, in the end, is what visioning is all about. It is not just about the pleasures of relaxing and imagining something wonderful in your life. It is a tool to keep making choices that are different than the ones that you are making now. When you are in the thick of the madness, you can say to yourself, "I really want something different from this, and I intend to make that happen." That is what it means to take a stand for yourself.

■ ■ ■ EXERCISE ■ ■ ■

Like the athlete who works out every day to stay in shape, you can do a daily visioning workout.

1. Practice every day. In the morning and evening, take your vision, your metaphor, and your affirmations and say them to yourself. Say them out loud. See if you want to change them. Choose your vision again. Choose it every day.

2. Then, mentally rehearse how your actions each day can help you bring your vision into reality and start making different choices.

4

Taking Stock

Even if you have great vision and purpose, it is still not enough. To get the results that you want, you need to understand where you are right now. One puzzle for me about being disorganized was this: Why couldn't I get organized despite the fact that I was trying so hard to change? I knew what I wanted and I had good reasons to change—so how come I couldn't get there?

I now know that I never accurately assessed the sources of my disorganization. I was so sure I knew what the problem was (I'm just a messy person) that I never took the time to really find out why I was so disorganized. There were unexplored aspects of my being that seemed to keep this whole chaotic system in place. I needed to ask some deeper questions. How did the mess get here? What was I contributing to it? What was the meaning of my mess? Why was I so attached to it, despite all my protests to the contrary? Was there anything scary for me about giving it up? And if my spiritual growth was so important to me, as I kept saying it was, why did I fill my life up to the brim, leaving little time for daily reflection or meditation? Could I look at the whole mess in a new way?

When we look into our disorganization with genuine interest, we go beneath untested assumptions to uncover what is really going on. We generate answers that are much more enlightening than: "Look, my office is just chaotic. There's nothing more to it. I've just got to bite the bullet and clean it up." Or, "Well, I'm just a slob," or "I've tried, but nothing works, it's hopeless," or "I'm just too busy to be organized." These labels and generalities obscure the actual data we need to understand ourselves. Usually, we can't see clearly. We jump to conclusions and make incorrect assumptions. Our self-criticism distorts our perception of what is happening. For example, think about an anorexic girl who believes she is fat and starves herself to extraordinary skinniness. She cannot tell how fat or thin she is because her judgment is faulty. Chronically disorganized people, too, often have trouble knowing what the reality of their situation is. You may assess that you are living in a disaster zone, when actually a few well-placed changes will bring you tremendous relief. You may keep thinking that all you need is one weekend to clean things up, when you actually need a long-term plan.

The Power of Witnessing Mind

You may have avoided getting to know more about your disorganization because you feel you have no time to look at how you behave. The surprising thing is that it actually doesn't take extra time. It takes a shift in focus. It takes a willingness to activate an inner witnessing part of the self. Or you may have avoided getting to know more about your disorganization because it makes you feel bad. You feel ashamed of the chaos and of how out-of-control and overwhelmed you feel, and you think everyone else is doing so much better. The witnessing self can help you look without the inner shaming and blaming that is so excruciating.

The great Indian teacher Krishnamurti said, "Start noticing how you actually live." There is a mindful part of everyone that can detach and observe the self in action, just looking with gentle appreciation. It is not easy to be present to your reality with compassion. The judgments flood in so quickly that you just cannot see what is going on. Yet, when you lift the veil of labels, judgments, and illusions, connecting with reality in an accepting way can be remarkably satisfying. For many people, it is very powerful to start simply observing and getting to know themselves without empowering the haranguing inner voices, without defending themselves, and without shame. You'll start seeing things that you hadn't seen before because witnessing is a perceptive and creative frame of mind.

Physicist David Bohm says, "It is a source of confusion to equate randomness with disorder, or even to say that disorder can exist in any context whatsoever. No matter what happens, it always has to happen in some kind of order, and what we have to do is describe and analyse the order rather than to avoid the question by calling it disorder." So now you'll start to see your own meaningful order in what might look like disorder on the surface.

Observing Takes Curiosity

The first step is to cultivate a level of pure curiosity. This is a process of "just looking, just noticing." You want to get around the mass of critical judgments. Think about a time when you have been genuinely curious about something. What were some of the qualities of your curiosity? Some people experience curiosity as openness, wonder, or discovery. Try on these frames of mind as you start to investigate your lateness or the messy piles. This time, study yourself and your environment compassionately without the barrage of inner criticism. If you notice the relentless inner critic, speak the words out loud, and listen to how mean you are being to yourself. Sometimes, this helps quiet the cacophony. What often happens, when you simply look with curiosity, is that you see your situation much more clearly. Sometimes, you will see a few steps that you can take that could make a big difference.

■ ■ ■ EXERCISE ■ ■ ■

Imagine that you are a visitor from another planet and that you are witnessing how this person (you) goes about their day with fresh eyes. You have no preconceptions about how things are supposed to be. Therefore you have no critical judgments, just curiosity and interest. (Hmm, this is interesting. . . .) What do you see? What patterns do you notice?

You might find it helpful to pick just a few minutes to observe this interesting creature with nonjudgmental attention or perhaps compassion for her or his dilemmas. (Oh, so that's how they do things here on Planet Earth. Remarkable. Fascinating.)

■ ■ ■

Observing Takes Courage

To look and see what is going on takes patience and courage, but will help stir your will and build your purpose. Once you start looking at your disorganization honestly, you'll start to see that the situation is far from hopeless. Difficult, yes, and maybe overwhelming. But the act of honest, respectful inquiry means that you are open and seeking, rather than closed and simply blaming yourself or others. You may find that much fresh thinking comes from getting interested in a genuine way. It's not that the racing around and frenzy disappear, but rather that you are facing into them. You are getting to know them. You are befriending them.

A key question that takes courage to answer is: "How am I contributing to this situation?" We usually think that disorganization results from outside pressures—too much mail, too many demands, too much stuff, an unrelenting boss. We may, in fact, have all of these challenges in our lives. While there are situations that we truly cannot change, much more than we think is under our influence. It is typically no use to think of ourselves as the helpless victims of external situations. We are often active participants in creating chaos. At the same time, looking into our contribution requires some delicacy. We shouldn't undertake this careful observation in order to blame ourselves again.

The purpose is to experience our impact and, oddly enough, our efficacy. We are effective in creating the chaos. As we begin to notice how we create some of this mess, we can see the consequences of our actions more clearly. We begin to discover with close observation that we're creating much of our current mess and disorganization by how we think. For example, we don't accurately assess how long a task will take. Or we don't think it is important to put things back when we are done with them. Once we can see how we are causing our own mess, even inadvertently, we can get traction for change. We see the difficult choices that we don't want to make. We see how our inaccurate thinking gets us into trouble.

Four Levels of Inquiry

There is more to current reality than meets the eye. So we include four levels of reality—the physical, emotional, mental, and spiritual—in our investigation. Each level represents an important part of the self. When we are seeking holistic change, we need to include our whole being.

Start on the Physical Level

When you encounter a messy space or chaotic set of behaviors that you want to organize, it is the physical reality that jumps out at you first. Initially, you ask, "What is taking place on the surface, the physical realm?" Let's say that there are piles of papers all over the floor in your office, or you are running late from place to place all afternoon. It's important to describe current physical reality with care and accuracy: "What papers are they?" "How long have they been there?" Or "Was I running late *all* afternoon, or was it only for a couple of hours?" You start with as accurate a physical description as possible. What would you see if you were looking at a video? In this way, you become acquainted with what you are currently doing. You observe with your five senses in order to raise your consciousness about what you are doing day to day.

Start your investigation with what is going well. What works for you? For example, you might always keep your keys in one place, or you may have one closet or drawer that you keep organized. You stay on top of your children's medical records. You may always be on time. Take some time to appreciate what works well in your life. You can build on what you already do well to make changes in what does not work for you. When you find a few examples of what is going well, you'll see that you do have some discipline in your life, and you can build on that.

Now, let's turn to what is not working for you. Be precise. Be as honest as you can without exaggerating or minimizing. You don't want to fix what isn't broken. And you want to work on the few places that can give you leverage for change.

Identify One Area

Focus in on one area and examine it with care. Choose a room, a time period, or a specific behavior, and try observing it with some detachment. See if you can relax and look with interest to see what your current situation is in this area. Perhaps you'll choose to have a look at your kitchen or your bathroom, or perhaps you are interested in the hour from 6:00 P.M. to 7:00 P.M., right when you get home from work. Or you can inquire into what happens when people make requests of you. Remember for now, you are not trying to fix anything, nor are you looking for a "problem." You are just trying to observe objectively what is going on.

Let's pick your bathroom as an example. This is not easy. You may walk in and just say to yourself, "I hate it in here! It's gross." Now, put that first reaction aside and look again. So, what *is* happening? What do you see, smell, or hear? Do you see the rows of shampoo bottles in the bathroom? Is the sink covered with debris, combs, old toothbrushes, or half-squeezed tubes of toothpaste? Do you have outdated prescription bottles around? Are there damp towels on the floor? Is the faucet dripping? Again, just observe what is there. Do your best to quiet the critical judgments that are flying in. For now, you are just getting to know your current situation.

Alternatively, you might begin with other parts of your home or office. Are you aware of the piles of newspapers, books, or articles? How many piles are there? How high? Did you spend ten minutes looking for your keys? Can you find the files you need? What items are in the car?

Or you might explore your punctuality. How many appointments did you postpone or cancel today or this week? Do you notice how often you are late? Did you make a promise that you couldn't keep? When did you become aware that you were going to be late? What are the excuses you make? What did you have to eliminate because you were late? This exploration is just to get to know what you are doing. Don't do too much. Just notice. For now, you are sensitizing yourself to the situation that you are living with. Don't rush in to fix the situation, see if you can just observe

However, you may see a few simple actions that you can take that might alter your whole experience. For example, Ted's experiment with his witnessing mind led to a small but important change. He noticed that a large part of his morning uproar was due to misplacing his keys and wallet. While he had been meaning to find a place for them, it only became important to him when he directly observed what this old habit was doing to his life. His unconsciousness in the evening led to havoc in the morning. It became totally obvious to him that he needed a wallet and key "depository." So he tried it out and began to deposit his keys and wallet there at night. They would be there in the morning, and he experienced much more peace in getting out of the house.

Erica observed that she often made appointments without checking her planner. She believed that she could keep track of her appointments in her head. This practice led to lots of double, even triple, booking. It became clear that she could save herself much embarrassment if she always carried her planner.

Donna noticed that she would never say no to requests. She might hem and haw, she might not return phone calls, but she never actually said no to people. She realized that a few well-placed nos might significantly reduce the havoc in her life.

It is important to do your own observing. Many people had suggested to Ted that he find a place to put his keys, but it was only when he saw for himself how he was creating his uproar that he was motivated to implement this "obvious" solution. Similarly, Erica's friends had suggested to her that she carry her planner with her. It was frustrating for them when she kept overbooking. She tended to laugh it off—she wasn't the "planner" type—until she became sensitized, through paying more attention to what she was doing and the costly outcomes.

For additional questions on organizing at the physical level, turn to the Self-Assessment Survey on page 289.

Discover the Story at the Emotional Level

The next level of inquiry is emotional, since it is so closely tied to the physical reality. You have feelings about the mess. You have feelings about the running around. Here, you try to accurately identify what your feelings are. In addition, you learn about the emotional influences on your organizing behavior. You ask, "What does this mess remind me of? Whose stories am I keeping alive in these piles? What are my emotional associations with order and chaos, punctuality and lateness?" You look at the intense personal meaning that may be buried in the mess. You begin to interpret the messages hidden in your chaos, your counterproductive behaviors, your lateness.

Organizing touches nearly every aspect of our lives—our time, our possessions, our clothes, our money, and our relationships. Most of us learned how to organize, or not to, from our families of origin. This history has left its emotional imprint on us and may be the source of some of our current patterns.

In exploring the emotional realm, you get to know the stories and the attachments that underlie your disorganization. What is your story? What do you remember about your home growing up? What messages did you receive about order, disorder, punctuality, lateness, or honoring your agreements? What was your room like when you were a child? What was the rest of your home like? Were you forced to clean up? Did you just leave things around? Did anyone teach you the basics of organizing or taking care of money? How did they teach you?

Answering these questions contributes to deepening your own understanding of the emotional roots of your disorder. Just as people probe memories from their childhood to heal the current damaging patterns in their lives, so, too, you can contribute to healing your disorganization by understanding your past history. It's important to bring the same compassionate nonjudging mind to your exploration of your history. Refrain from blaming your parents or anyone else. You are studying your past as a resource for understanding your present. Again, your nonjudgmental mind may see things that your blaming mind can't.

■ ■ ■ EXERCISE ■ ■ ■

Here's an exercise to do that can reveal some of the story line. The questions that follow will evoke lots of memories, so you may want to write down your answers.

■ Think back to your childhood home. What verbal and nonverbal messages did you receive about order and disorder? What messages did you receive about creating a sense of home? About cleanliness? About taking care of money? About what constitutes success? What were the messages that you received from how people behaved and from what people were saying? Notice if there were contradictions in what people said and how they behaved.

■ Do the same with your grandparents' homes. Are there other significant people in childhood (other relatives, family, friends, neighbors, teachers) that you learned from?

■ Take a particularly messy area of your home or office and ask, "Does this remind me of any earlier time in my life?"

■ Do the same with a chaotic part of your day. Does it remind you of an earlier time in your life?

■ ■ ■

When she answered these questions, Mallie said, "I really saw the connection with my mother and her perfectionism. I also remembered that my grandmother's more comfortably cluttered house felt warm and homey to me. Our immaculate home just felt sterile. My mother was always yelling at us to keep our hands off things. Now, I am overwhelmed by clutter. Perhaps it is my way to try to get that warm, homey feeling. But it's out of control."

The idea that there may be an emotional benefit to a painful chronic behavior honors our complexity as human beings. The emotional benefits of being disorganized can be hard to discern but are important to explore in order to allow you to evolve. It is often these unconscious emotional payoffs that keep us stuck in our old disorganizing patterns. The primary reason to surface these benefits is to reevaluate them in the adult light of day.

John started his inquiry by reflecting on his briefcase because it was was bursting with papers, books, pens, and reading glasses. He had tried to tame it, but it would overflow with papers within a day or two. When he unpacked it, it just seemed too quiet and controlled. He considered that this was his way of talking back to his very controlled, everything-in-its-place father. John's hidden message to his father was: "I am my own person, doing things my own way. I refuse to be over-controlled like you." The only problem was that his briefcase was driving him crazy.

Judith, a retired nurse in her sixties, had kept a reasonable level of order in her professional life. Her apartment, however, was chaotic and uncomfortable. Though she wanted to have an orderly, inviting home, she was drowning in years of saved newspapers and unopened mail. Judith remembered that her mother had been relentless about making her clean up her room when she was a child. She discovered that she maintained the mess in defiance of her mother, who had died years before.

Aisha had a different story to tell about her mother. Like Judith, she longed to create a welcoming home and truly enjoyed the harmonious feeling when everything was in its place. But her mother used to tell her, "Women who have neat homes don't have anything better to do with their time." Aisha said she had an instinctive fear of neatness, and her messy home was in honor of her mother's belief.

Some people notice that the mess itself may serve as a familiar, perhaps oddly comforting, presence. "Clutter is comforting to me," said Edward, a bachelor living alone. He grew up in a family with six children in a home that was full of life and busyness. "I like the piles of books and papers and belongings strewn around. It makes me feel that something is going on. The only thing is—there is no place for me to sit that's comfortable. I can't rest here. Nobody ever sat down in my home growing up. It was a place of action." The clutter had even taken over his reading chair. He recognized that it was against the family rules to sit and rest. This insight led him to clear off his most comfortable chair and protect that space for himself. "I get to sit and rest, even if no one else in my family does."

For others, the mess protects against intimacy: it's so uncomfortable at home that no one can come over to visit. Courteney said, "I want to get into a relationship, but I simply cannot bring a man to my house. When I get involved with someone, we always go to his place, and I can leave whenever I want to. I am far more comfortable taking my clothes off with someone than bringing him into my home. I would feel too exposed."

Robert found that his clutter was a way of knowing he existed. If he could see his clutter, if he could feel and maintain it, it gave him messages that he was present. He said, "When I first cleared out my clutter, I thought, 'I'm not here.' My living room had nothing on the floor. And I thought, 'Where am I in here,' as if I were the clutter."

Many people affirm their existence through the pressure they feel. This makes it challenging to release the pressure or to get rid of the stuff. People get used to a familiar level of discomfort. Often, when they clear up or reduce the external pressure, they find new ways of reestablishing a similar level of pressure or clutter. It is a kind of homeostasis. A life with less pressure can be more uncomfortable than the pressure itself. This is one of the ironies of becoming a more organized person. Some people feel most alive when they are up against an obstacle. "I struggle therefore I am" could be a good motto for many disorganized people. Life is hard and one way to ensure ongoing difficulty is to be disorganized.

Stella said, "I realized that I am very attached to my image as a busy, harried, overworked, overcommitted, just-barely-able-to-keep-it-together person because it is my sign that I am a martyr—that I am taking care of everybody else but myself and working so hard to make the world a better place that I sacrifice myself. It comes from old family patterns where I squashed my own needs to take care of the identified patient in our family—but I had to get kudos for that martyrdom, so I let everybody know about it. It was very interesting to see how my personal chaos and overscheduling is tied into that persona, which I realized years ago is not healthy for me or for anybody."

Telling our story allows some of the mystery to clear up, and we start to understand some of the roots of our disorganization. We have some more respect for how we got here, and perhaps some clues about how to step beyond the messes that we have created. In chapter 13 we take some of these themes and go deeper with them.

■ ■ ■ EXERCISE ■ ■ ■

Take a moment to think through the answers to the following questions: In what ways might my disorganization "help" me or protect me? If my disorganization is a statement about something, what is it saying? And, to whom?

Perhaps there are some messages in the mess, such as:

I'm like Mom or Dad.
I'll never be like Mom or Dad.
I have lots to do. I'm important.
Don't ask too much from me.
Please take care of me, I can't take care of myself.
Leave me alone, don't get close.
I don't count.

■ ■ ■

Investigate the Mental Level of Organizing

How we act and how we feel are often related to how we think. So let's explore how our thinking affects our disorganization. In particular, we'll look at three questions related to the mental aspects of organizing. What are you thinking each day that leads you to be disorganized? What are some of the deeper beliefs that lie under your disorganization? What are your thinking preferences or, to put it another way, what are some of your brain's preferred ways of operating? It's challenging to investigate our thinking and beliefs, because we are using our own thinking to observe our thought processes. But we can do that very task and in so doing, get some surprising and satisfying results.

The Surprising Consequences of Everyday Thinking

People are thinking all the time. These seemingly innocuous little thoughts can lead to actions that produce unintended results. Start with observing the running stream of consciousness that leads to your daily actions. At times, it takes patience to unearth these flickers of thought that influence our actions, but it is worth it because you start to see how your own unexamined thinking affects your everyday chaos.

For example, you can become aware of little thoughts like: "I'll just put the mail here and come back to it later." Maybe you received an interesting announcement for a theater production and think, "I don't know what to do about this," so you put it in a pile, and it stays there for a year. Or you think, "I like that person and she probably needs some help," so you make an offer you can't keep later. Or perhaps you think, "This mess is exhausting. I just can't deal with it."

When I was learning how to arrive on time, I started to become aware of how much I tried to do on the way to appointments. My thinking was completely unconcerned with real time. I noticed that I would think, "I'm passing the market. Maybe I'll just do a little grocery shopping. It will only take ten minutes." I didn't have a counterthought that might sound like " 'You don't have ten minutes," or "It will actually take fifteen minutes." I might think, "It doesn't matter if I am late, because this meeting often starts late." Then I would arrive even later than all of the other late people.

■ ■ ■ EXERCISE ■ ■ ■

Discovering our thinking patterns helps us understand why we take the actions we take. Then, testing our thoughts for accuracy and for their consequences can aid us in taking new actions. Answer the following questions.

What do you think when you look at your mess?
What are you thinking when you are running late or missing a deadline?
What are you telling yourself about it?

■ ■ ■

Observing thought can be surprising and extremely valuable. The mind is far from logical. The free-flowing thinking that we experience is often referred to as "monkey mind" because it seems so random and whimsical. At the same time, it can be very powerful to start acknowledging all the little thoughts that lead to some of your actions. "I don't have time for that right now." "I'm too tired to hang up my clothes." "I'll do the dishes later." By noticing her thoughts, Stephanie realized that one reason the sink was always full of dishes wasn't just that she was so tired at night. She realized, "No wonder I don't do housework. When I even start to do the dishes, I think, 'I just hate this. I refuse to be like my mom.' I can feel my blood pressure go up."

Becoming aware of our constant inner commentary is not easy. We talk at 100 words per minute, read at about 250 words per minute, and think at about 800 words per minute, so much of the time, we don't know what we are thinking. Some people become aware of how many good ideas they don't actualize because their thinking is ungrounded. A thought like: "I'll set aside an hour a day for filing" needs an accompanying thought like: "When would that be?"

Our unexamined stream of consciousness can lead to actions that are counterproductive. Let's look at Mary as she is trying to sort out a pile of articles on the floor of her office. She receives training magazines, business journals, and a stream of interesting articles from professional colleagues. When Mary receives an article, she thinks, "I want to read this soon, and then I'll file it. I'll leave it here [on the floor] so I won't forget to read it," and she adds it to her stack of articles on the floor.

Only when Mary observed herself in action quietly, without judgment, was she able to admit to herself that she was not reading the articles. Then was she able to change her actions. She became conscious that her thinking was "deceiving" her. She kept thinking that she could read those articles because she kept telling herself that she was going to. Only she never did. But she kept the illusion alive.

She realized that she had to reexamine the belief that "To be good at my job, I have to read *everything* and be completely up-to-date." She observed that while that may have been true in graduate school, it wasn't true now. She further recognized that she had to make a choice between trying to read everything and having family time. Therefore, Mary reframed her belief as: (1) Most articles do not increase my understanding of my field. (2) I cannot read everything and still have the time I want with my family. (3) I therefore need to be highly selective. She has developed a new system as a result—now she quickly looks at an article, determines its relevance to her in one minute, and then tosses it out if it is not truly important. As she tosses it out, she thinks another new thought: "I cannot afford to keep a library of material. I want time for the kids more than I want to read all the articles that come across my desk. If I ever need it, I can find it on the Internet."

Ultimately she is choosing between competing values that surface as thoughts. These are hard choices, but worth facing and making. As she consciously makes choices, she strengthens her sense of herself. Otherwise, she is just scattered and feels guilty all the time. Using her witnessing mind helped Mary to become more aware of her unconscious choices and actually select between family time and her fantasy of reading everything.

Uncover Your Beliefs About Organizing

In chapter 1, we learned that unacknowledged deeply held beliefs trump our purpose in getting organized. They also influence our everyday actions. Our beliefs also have a way of reinforcing themselves. It is an odd thing about thinking: we tend to think thoughts that we have already thought. It is as if the brain prefers old pathways. Once we believe something to be true, we tend to perceive selectively the very data that reinforce our "truth" and block out data that contradict this truth. The known world remains known and familiar. Yet, in order to change our organizing habits, we need to move from a known world to an as-yet-unknown world. In order to grow, we need to get smart about surfacing our beliefs so that we can consciously test them.

Andrew thought being messy gave him freedom, and that order and organizing were going to constrain him. Yet, when he looked at how he was actually living, he was at a point where his messiness and chronic lateness had become a trap. It puzzled him when he realized, "I'm genuinely constrained by my mess. I used to think that it was masochistic to create order. Now I think that it's masochistic to pile things up. I can't stand the piles anymore. Before they were the emblem of my freedom." He added, "If I can remember that 'In my discipline is my freedom,' then I can start feeling better about myself. It's exciting to make these changes and to see what is right for me."

Elaine had other fears about getting organized. She said, "I'm afraid that 'getting organized' will mean that I have bought into the whole success trip of this society. For me, 'getting organized' means being more productive, more white, straight, and male, and I'm proud of being different. I *want* to be less productive, if productive means being mainstream. I want to slow down, live from my heart, and to hell with planners and neatness. The only thing is, with my current way of handling things, I can't really achieve any of the goals that are meaningful to me. I don't write poetry, because I don't have the time and the space. And the truth is, I'm as frantic as anyone because I keep forgetting what I have scheduled for myself."

■ ■ ■ EXERCISE ■ ■ ■

One way of surfacing beliefs is sentence-completion exercises. Write five answers to each of the following sentence stems. Do this quickly, writing down the first thoughts that come to your mind. There are no right answers, just great information about some of your beliefs.

- People who are neat are————.
- People who are messy are————.
- Order means————.
- When I put things away, I feel————.
- When I see clutter, I think————.
- When I see a pile of papers on my desk, I feel————.
- A messy home is————.
- Cleaning up after myself means————.
- If only I had the time to do the things I want, I would————.
- Creative people are————.
- I save things because————.
- When I feel fully prepared,————.
- People who are savvy about money are————.
- If I got my finances under control, I would————.

Once you arrive at your answers, test your beliefs. Are they true? How do you know? Are you open to changing your beliefs?

■ ■ ■

Your Thinking Preferences

Research has shown that human brains are not all alike. People are wired differently from one another. Some brains love to think in association. We can think of these as branching brains: one idea leads to the next, which may only be minimally related to the first. Brains like this are highly creative. Often people with this kind of brain are very musical, they think in metaphors and pictures. They may be called right-brain dominant. Left-brain dominant people tend to love linearity, closure, order, numbers. They may have less trouble keeping "order" because they inherently like it. Our thinking preferences are part of our gifts. Let's not try to change our fundamental structures. However, since everyone has two sides of their brain, let's, as management consultant Ann McGee-Cooper puts it, learn to use both sides to our advantage. She says, you wouldn't try to live life on only one foot, don't try leaning too hard on only one side of the brain.

I have found two frameworks to be particularly helpful in understanding individual tendencies to be disorganized. I'll introduce each framework briefly and provide references for you so that you can follow up on them if you want.

The Myers-Briggs Type Indicator is a way of describing your personality type based on Jungian archetypes. The MBTI is a very practical tool for helping people learn about four dimensions of themselves: how we energize ourselves, how we learn about the world, how we make decisions, and our preferences with respect to closure and keeping our options open. These aspects of ourselves have a lot to do with how we get organized and are a good way to gain information about who we are. The Myers-Briggs Type Indicator distinguishes between people who have a strong preference for planning, decision-making, and closure and those who have a strong preference for keeping their options open, trying things out, and letting events emerge. If you are of the second type, you may enjoy changing plans at the last minute or waiting to see if something better comes along. You may have an aversion to completing tasks and projects because that just doesn't feel as comfortable as leaving things open. I like the MBTI because it turned my "problem" of avoiding commitments into a personality type that I could learn more about.

Your preferences are not fixed in stone. Indeed, Jung saw midlife as a time to expand one's repertoire to include the "shadow" side, the side of our personality that we are less familiar with. Getting detailed knowledge of your type will help you understand how to organize in a way that suits you. Getting to know other people's types will help you understand what their needs are so that you can work with them better. Have a look at *Type-talk*, by Otto Kroeger and Janet M. Thuesen, if this topic interests you.

The framework of attention deficit disorder (ADD) provides an understanding of how people who tend to be highly creative and distractible: It suggests a number of remedies for the person with ADD. This framework is another gateway toward understanding the brain and the self. ADD is considered a neurological condition; that is, it may be hardwired at birth. If you have ADD, you may have many or all of these symptoms.

- You don't focus well.
- You have trouble attending to one task at a time.
- You are easily distractible.
- You tend to be impulsive.
- You have lots of projects going on simultaneously.
- You are often scrambling to get things done.
- You tend to procrastinate.
- You tend to be moody.
- You thrive in high-stimulation situations.
- You enjoy novelty.
- You tend to need immediate reinforcement.

I have all of these symptoms. It was a great relief to learn that I most likely had ADD and I needed to take my distractibility much more seriously.

If you have ADD and were born with these tendencies, you may have developed some secondary challenges because you failed to fit many strongly held norms. One way to get a better sense if you have ADD is to read *Driven to Distraction* by Dr. Edward Hallowell. He describes twenty symptoms that indicate the likelihood of ADD. Children with ADD often develop problems with self-image and self-esteem. These problems tend to persist into adulthood and can make it very hard to get an accurate diagnosis of ADD.

People with ADD tend to resist structure. It does not feel natural to them and others who have similar brain patterns. Yet, basic organizing structures can be enormously helpful to these people once they overcome their resistance to them. Just the addition of a to-do list, a plan for the day, or an appointment book can decrease our inner chaos. The following chapters will show you how to do this.

Even if you are "organizationally challenged," it's not license to remain disorganized. No matter what your innate tendencies are, you can still run your life in a way that is less chaotic. Both of these frameworks will give you great information and some good direction on how to work well with the brain that you have.

Explore the Spiritual Level

The fourth level of inquiry is the spiritual level. In this level, you explore the soul experience of your home or office. You explore how alive and inspired you feel. You begin to tap into how you experience the sacred. You look to see if there is a place and time for you to meditate, to pray, or to simply sit and be yourself. Here you begin to explore how you experience a sense of place (whether at home or at work). You start to sense the energy of your space and time. Is it depressing to walk into your space? Do you have enough time to focus on what really matters to you? Do you feel open and receptive or closed and contracted?

Thomas Moore points out in *Care of the Soul* that "care for our actual houses, then, however humble, is also care of the soul." Our homes, work spaces, and our souls are deeply intertwined. Our work spaces are also part of the soul's journey. In some ways, the whole purpose of getting organized is to reconnect us with our soul's journey. In this fourth level, you explore the connection between the way you organize your life and how you express, or don't express, the life of your spirit and soul. We are often moving so fast that life's treasures get lost in the shuffle. Your disorganization may come from a lack of connection with your own sense of order, your intuition, or your deep calm. You may be disconnected from your spiritual journey and that may be reflected in how you live day to day.

■ ■ ■ EXERCISE ■ ■ ■

Examine what nourishes your spiritual life by asking the following questions.

- ■ Does your home invite you? Do you love being there? Do you have a sacred place in your home?
- ■ Does your work space support you in your deeper work? Does the way you conduct yourself at work nourish your soul? Can you listen for guidance even during the workday?
- ■ Do you have time to deeply connect with whatever you most care about?
- ■ Do you turn your daily tasks into acts of meaning?
- ■ Do you have time to listen to your intuition?
- ■ When are you present for yourself and others?
- ■ How do you connect with the life force? How do you experience blessing?
- ■ If you love spiritual life, does the rest of your life support your spiritual practice?

■ ■ ■

When Rafael began exploring these issues, he said, "I noticed two things as I asked myself these questions: First, every day I think to myself, I want to leave time for prayer before I go to sleep. And I never do it. I have an illusion of a prayer relationship with God. But it is in my head. I do not create space for actual spiritual contact with the Divine. Secondly, I often don't return phone calls. The impact on my sense of connection with others is devastating. I just let phone calls go. I lose the slips of paper that I write messages on. I am too tired to call people back at night. So I see how my connections with others and with the Divine are illusory for me. It's no wonder I feel frantic much of the time. I am so ungrounded. I try to sustain myself on very thin lines of connection."

Helen said, "I am starting to see that I am afraid of the realm of spirit. I sense the power of spirit in places and in time, in connections with others. But I use my mess to keep people out, to keep God out, to keep myself deaf to my inner voice. As long as I am running around, so busy, I don't have to listen to my inner voice of love or my intuition. I don't have to be powerful. I know that as long as I am anxious about being late or forgetting to return phone calls, I don't have to experience my deep awe. Sometimes, I can just taste the blessing there is for me when I stop driving myself crazy. I do taste it at times—I stop in the middle of my frenzy and I experience awe. I am alive, I am breathing, seeing, sensing. I love those moments. I am not alone. And, then, I put my head back down into my planner and start wondering what I am supposed to do next."

Marcia noted as she answered these questions, "There is one part of my home that is my sanctuary. I have an armchair that I keep clear. I sit there and think. I sit and drift. It's my one true pleasure in my house. Everything could be in wild disorder around me, but I keep this place for myself."

We will explore more of the spiritual aspects of organizing in chapter 11.

Questions to Apply on All Four Levels

We can take questions from our organizing challenges on the physical level, and pose them with respect to the emotional, intellectual, and spiritual levels. For example, if you find yourself looking for things a lot, it may be that you have transferred a search from one part of the self to another.

"What are you looking for?" can now be asked on the other levels.

What are you looking for emotionally?
What are you looking for intellectually?
What are you looking for spiritually?

If you keep cleaning up a messy pile or a messy room, you can do the same transfer of questions. What mess are you trying to clean up? Emotionally? Intellectually? Spiritually?

Try this: What are you late for? What have you missed? Emotionally? Intellectually? Spiritually?

You may find that switching levels can yield some insight into something that has been bothering you. Movement on one plane can often help to free you up on another.

Look for Unintended Consequences on All Four Levels

In your inquiry about your disorganization, ask this question: "What are some of the unintended consequences of my actions?" Or "What have I been unaware of?" Pema Chodron, a Buddhist teacher who heads an abbey in Nova Scotia, tells a story that illustrates how easy it is to be unconscious of the little traces that we leave behind. At the abbey, each person marks her own dishes with her initials. That way everyone takes care of her own dishes. Pema describes a time when she was really irritated with someone from her abbey for leaving her dishes and utensils all over the kitchen. She made up her mind to give that person feedback so that she wouldn't do it again. She went over to check who had left the mess and found that on each dish there was a P. C. The mess was hers.

Who would ever think that a simple thought like "I'll just save this article and put it in this pile" would lead to a stack of papers that is eight feet high and requires weeks of sorting? By then, it feels impossible to deal with. The huge pile stems from a little thought that at the time seems to have no consequences. Part of organizing is to internalize a sense of consequence so that you become aware that saving one piece of paper at one point in time could lead you to an overwhelming mountain of papers later on. See if you can begin to tell what were you thinking and doing that created your mountain. Note the differences between what you were trying to accomplish—accumulating information so that you could be on top of things—and what you did accomplish—burying yourself under a mountain of old articles that are difficult to access.

Who would think that dropping a wet towel on the floor would lead to a strenuous fight about respect and territory? Who would think that forgetting to return a borrowed book could ruin a friendship? We can become skillful at making the connection between the inconsequential actions of everyday life and the impactful consequences that result.

It's not easy to discover the negative consequences of your actions. The best way to find out is to pay attention to what happens when you mess up someone else's space, or someone else's plans, or don't keep your word. Right now, you may be in denial about the ways you injure others and you may find it valuable to interview people about their reactions to some of your behavior. Talk to someone whom you trust, and help them level with you.

Describe Your Current Reality

Writing can help you discover your current reality. When you are writing, keep looking and feeling for your truth. John Lee, author of *Writing From the Body*, suggests that you move your body and even shout out loud to connect with your physical energies in order to find your voice.

■ ■ ■ EXERCISE ■ ■ ■

Pull out your journal. Try writing for just five minutes. Sometimes, it is hard to do this, but writing can lead to many hours of joy and peace. Write about a compelling aspect of your current reality:

- A time that you were running late.
- A time that you were panicking.
- A time that you finally stopped rushing. A particular moment such as a vacation.
- A moment of deep connection with someone in the middle of the day.
- A time when you tried to sort a pile of financial papers and just couldn't.
- What it feels like when you have an overwhelming to-do list.
- Write about a time when you were late doing your taxes.
- Write about your life as if you lived on the seacoast in a simple village.
- Write about what it would be like if you were free of this burden of being disorganized.
- Write about a time when you just felt great.

■ ■ ■

When we are disorganized we rarely have time to attend to the basics we need. Although writing may seem like too much of a luxury, it can be a rich path to deepening your intimacy with yourself. It need not take long. You may be surprised at what emerges in just ten minutes at a time.

Helen used her journal to record her experience of disorganization.

January 12: I have translated my harsh inner life into a harsh outer life. Keeping the mess around me makes it difficult for me to ever really relax. It's not beautiful with clutter on all the surfaces. My eye can't rest, there are no pleasant forms. And that reflects my inner life, there is no place to rest and no space. . . .

I have made such a mess out of paying a simple set of bills. I take them out of envelopes, get them organized. Then, I lose them, or I try to take them with me to the library to do them. Under this is a sense of impatience. . . . Under the impatience is a longing to be taken care of.

February 12: Now the bathroom is neat. At first I didn't like it. Too neat. Now I like going into that room. Each room has its own energy. The bathroom can be for clearing, cleaning, and freshening. I never thought of it that way before.

February 23: I am so in touch with clutter as a barrier to doing what I want. I start to work on something, and then I can't find a particular file that I need. Or I have piled up little droppings from the mail and now I don't know where to put things. And, as I consider that, I am puzzled about how to move forward, what is truly important to me falls to the wayside as my scrambled brain tries to figure out where to put this little piece of paper.

March 1: I notice that I feel that clutter gives a place warmth and soul. That piles of things indicate dedicated action. But for me, I have to be honest, most of my piles are just mess, they have nothing to do with dedicated action, they have a lot to do with fear and confusion. I often simply do not know what to do with all the stuff that is coming at me.

As you observe and write, you will get a clearer sense of your current reality; you'll notice that there is probably quite a gap between what you have now and what you want. Author Robert Fritz says that this tension is the essence of the creative process. According to him, part of the work that artists do is holding the gap between where they are and what they want. As they hold the gap and take the actions that will bring their creative vision into reality, they often feel a great deal of creative tension. Fritz encourages people to develop a creative orientation in life, in which they experience themselves as a creator, not a victim of circumstances. As you move forward, try to view getting organized as learning to shift from a reactive to a creative orientation.

5

You Can't Go It Alone:
Choose True Support

Can you think of a time when you had reached a difficult moment while you were working on a big task, and someone came along to help? Perhaps you were weeding the garden or shoveling snow, or cleaning up after a big meal. Maybe you were working late at night on a presentation or had gotten stuck on the next phase of a project. At that time, didn't support make things go faster and the job easier, and you felt less alone? You can get that kind of help with organizing as well. Support is a vital force that relieves many of life's rougher moments, helps us live well and get where we want to go. Albert Schweitzer said, "In everyone's life, at some time, our inner fire goes out. It is then burst into flame by an encounter with another human being. We should all be thankful for those people who rekindle the inner spirit." When you know where you want to go and you know where you are, support is crucial for bridging the gap.

Support comes in many forms. You may find support in a colleague at work who creates a time line with you for a big project, or in a friend who comes over to help you clean a closet. It may come in the form of your spouse, who says, "If this pile is still here on Sunday, I am going to throw it out." Getting support when we are getting organized is essential for the changes we want to make—but it is also challenging because being disorganized can be embarrassing and not everybody understands.

For years, I couldn't talk to anyone about being disorganized. What would I say? "I can't keep track of my travel expenses? I lose folders with crucial data? I hate to hang up my clothes? My sink is always full of dishes? I'm incompetent when it comes to the small things in life?" No, I would conclude—it's better not to discuss it. When the administrative office would call for the third time to get my expense reports because I was delaying their client billing, I would be embarrassed. Still, I didn't know what to say—other than to make yet another promise that I would get them in.

I didn't know how to say, "I find it tough to fill out these expense reports. I'll need some help with this." And I most certainly couldn't say, "I can't seem to keep track of my travel receipts, and I panic when I sit down to send in my invoices." That would have been mortifying. But the reality of my situation was bad. I felt terrible, but I just couldn't talk about it or do anything about it either. It never occurred to me to ask for help.

The Road to Helpful Help

First, you have to accept the fact that you need help. Many people value the idea that they can face their difficulties alone. Our culture tends to glamorize such independence. Many feel that to need or ask for help is a sign of weakness. They might worry about sharing their vulnerabilities with others. Some feel that they just don't deserve help or fear burdening others. You may be like that. So, recognizing that you need and deserve support can be an act of courage. You come to a point where you stop thinking that you can do this alone. You become willing to face your vulnerability and frailty. That takes enormous heart and courage. It helps to realize that everyone has points of vulnerability—that this is yours, and it does not have to be a shameful experience.

It is a shame-based distortion that everyone else has it together and you are the most terrible mess. Many intelligent and effective people struggle with chronic personal disorganization. Why do you think that organizing books are on the best-seller lists? Shame leads you to feel that you are the worst one and the only one with this problem, but it is simply not true.

At first, I couldn't even imagine telling people what my life was really like. How could I dream of asking for support if I felt that my situation was too shameful to talk about? How could I tell people that I always lost my receipts, even when I kept trying to keep track of them. My shame led me to feel both bad and alone, which prevented me from getting the help I needed. Shame is not always a negative. Healthy shame is a deep, natural, and valuable feeling that we have done something wrong. Toxic shame is different, however. It is a feeling that we are fundamentally wrong, that there is something unworthy about our very being. Toxic shame leads us to hide ourselves from others, to hide our problems from others, and to try to solve them alone. You may be struggling with toxic shame when you feel that you can't let people into your office or home or if you feel that your messiness is further evidence of what a terrible person you are.

■ ■ ■ EXERCISE ■ ■ ■

One way to discover if you are dealing with shame is to ask yourself if you have ever talked with anyone about how disorganized you are. Can you imagine talking about it? Now, carefully choose a colleague or a friend and try to tell them about what your life is like.

■ ■ ■

Since secrecy enhances the power of shame, you can empower yourself by talking judiciously about your situation. If it is too much to tell someone about the extent of your disorganization, find a compassionate person and try saying one small thing like: "It is hard for me to clean up the kitchen at night" or "My office is so piled with paper that I can't find anything." Most likely this person won't keel over in horror and never talk to you again. They might say, "That sounds tough" or "You sound like my sister-in-law" or even "I have that problem, too."

It is also possible that you avoid seeking help because you don't recognize the need for deep change in yourself. I didn't seek support not only because I felt so ashamed but also because I thought if I just tried harder. I could fix the situation. "Next time," I would say to myself, "I'll get those invoices in on time. They won't have to chase after me next time." But, then, I would lose a restaurant receipt, or leave the airline ticket receipt in the back of the seat in front of me (again). And, then, instead of going after the data that I needed, I would worry. Then I would forget about it. The whole transaction would slip my mind. Every once in a while, I would remember with a flash of anxiety, but I wouldn't take action. Finally, pushed and prodded, I would swallow my angst and make myself finish the invoice. "You know," I would say to myself, "it's really not so hard. Next time, I think I can get this in on time." And the cycle would start again. So I remained mired in my ineffectiveness. I was smart, I was successful, yet I felt as if I were skating on very thin ice. I could fall through at any point.

■ ■ ■ EXERCISE ■ ■ ■

Review the costs of your disorganization from chapter 1. Honestly ask yourself, 'Have I been able to solve these problems on my own so far?' Use your journal to explore what is likely to happen to these problems if you continue to act the way you do now.

■ ■ ■

Receiving support is a courageous act, not a weakness. Stop telling yourself that you can get organized on your own. You cannot do this on your own. It's too hard. The fact that you need support for working through the chaos and the mess does not mean that you are a bad person or that you are lacking in strength or courage. It means that you are a human being and that you are in a tough situation. It takes strength and courage just to face your mess.

You may remember the story of a little girl who fell down a well in the Midwest. Nobody said to the little girl, "You have to get out of that well by yourself." When her rescuers pulled her out and discovered that she was okay, people all over the country wept with relief and joy. Similarly, you have fallen down a well. For some of you, as it was for me, it's a deep well. You are allowed your helpers and your rescuers, and you can get out.

Clarifying the Help You Need

When I finally recognized that I needed support, I didn't know exactly what kind I needed or from whom, and, as I mentioned earlier, my first stab at getting help, from Jane, the professional organizer, was a failure. I hired her to help clear my desk, but I didn't learn from her how to keep my desk clear. More importantly she couldn't help me with my fears. I started to realize I needed help with my anxiety about getting organized as much as I needed the actual organizing help. When I finally understood what kind of help I needed, things shifted much more quickly. I hired a professional organizer who organized my closets and office, and I found a therapist who could help me face my fears.

Support comes in many different ways, and each of us needs to know what is actually helpful. You can gain skill in recognizing what kinds of help you need. Does support come in the form of a compassionate friend who listens as you weep over the impossible state of your desk and how you paid the bills late again? Compassion may be helpful at some point, but perhaps the support you need is offered by a professional organizer who comes in and says, over and over again, "You don't need those papers anymore" and helps you throw them out. Perhaps you are like Sherry, who has a pile of files that she doesn't know where to put because her mind just does not work that way. She cannot set up file systems. So she needs the help of someone who can listen to her needs and set up the system for her. Perhaps true support for you is the colleague who lets you call in a panic, late at night, when you are pushing toward a deadline once again, and helps you calm down and focus on the essentials.

Learn from your experience. When Alice finally decided to get cleaning help, an efficient woman showed up and cleaned her apartment. At the end of the day, Alice was fuming. "She didn't do what I wanted her to do." Once she calmed down, she said to herself, "Wait, I didn't *tell* her what I wanted her to do, because I didn't know what it was. How was she to have known what I wanted?" So Alice learned what she wanted for next time.

It is wise to remember that you may need to turn to different people for different kinds of support. It is the rare person who can be emotionally supportive, know how to help organize your files, help you hold your vision for what you want, and be excited about cleaning out your closets. Diane said, "When I was finally ready to get help, I hired a professional organizer to help organize my office and home. And I found a disorganized friend to talk to. Every once in a while we just cry on each other's shoulders and then get back on our feet and remind each other of our purposes and visions. She's the one who truly understands how I feel. What's good is that we don't just commiserate, but that we encourage each other." Later in this chapter we will look at the range of people you can reach out to and the specific assistance you can request.

Asking for Support

Each of us has a very tough spot in our organizing, whether it's our finances, discarding the stash of stuff in the back room, or cleaning out the garage. It's often scary to tackle these tough spots. This is a good time to get someone to be with you. Carol called to tell her friend Sally that she was drowning in her taxes, but the good news was that she *was* doing them. She was panicking, but she was facing her panic. She wasn't running away. She asked Sally to talk her through a particularly tough calculation. Sally was glad to do it. Carol needed some hand-holding. It had been hard for her to sit down with her tax return, but also very hard to call Sally to get some help.

When asking for support, try to view your experience as a learning process. What did you need? What did you ask for? Did you get the help that you wanted? Learn to be specific about what you need. Make your requests of others clear. Make them time-limited. Try to figure out an exchange—perhaps there is something you can offer in return for the help that you want. Just remember: Good support can be a pivotal aspect of changing your life.

■ ■ ■ EXERCISE ■ ■ ■

This is an exercise to prepare you for asking for help when you need it. Close your eyes and imagine that you are in the middle of an activity that is difficult for you. You might have to sit down and pay bills or prepare a financial report, create a time line for a project, or choose among several alternatives. Or it is 9:00 P.M. and you are completely daunted by cleaning up the kitchen. Perhaps you feel anxious or overwhelmed. Perhaps you are confused. Imagine thinking, "I can connect with someone for help, learning, and encouragement. I can get through this in a new way." Next, think the old thought, "Oh, I don't need to call someone." Finally, see yourself changing your mind. Now think, "Yes. I am going to call someone this time. I am going to break new ground for myself. I know people who would be really glad to hear from me." Imagine that your friend is happy to hear from you and glad to be very supportive toward you.

■ ■ ■

Who Can Support You?

Many different people can support you. As you read the following passages, think about who can help you. If you are open to it, you might be surprised at the variety of help that is out there.

Friends

A good friend is someone who can be there for you. Yet, in the area of organizing, this requires a little discernment. Some people are more sensitive to the challenge of getting organized than others and are therefore better able to support you in this way. The ones who don't understand can still be your friends, but they won't provide organizing support. Ironically, some of your more organized friends might not have any idea of how they do it, and they won't be able to teach you.

Debbie tells a story about her organized friend Nancy. "One day, I screwed up my courage and called Nancy to see if she could help me deal with my frightening pile of bills. I revealed to her that I was a disorganized person and confessed to her that I had trouble paying and filing bills. She just couldn't believe it. She didn't know that people like me existed. To her, the solution was simple. She told me, 'Just put anything related to the house in the house file, and put work-related expenses in an expense file.' She made the answer seem so obvious, and me feel quite dumb. She did not realize that I was still in Bill Paying 101. She only reinforced my great sense of shame. For me, it was a significant accomplishment just to open the envelopes and put the bills in one place! I had to remind myself not to take her reaction personally."

By contrast, I have one organized friend who is tremendously sympathetic to my challenge. She has shown me that being organized can enhance one's creativity. She showed me that putting things away can enhance beauty, returning things to their proper place isn't just compulsive behavior. She gets immense satisfaction from producing results, and she has taught me how to focus on results rather than getting bogged down in the everyday details. She has been willing to show me her organizing systems so that I can see how they work.

A Peer Coach

Sometimes, you can develop a mutual coaching relationship with a fellow disorganized person. I call this peer coaching You may find a good friend or professional colleague who is in the same boat and is willing to devote time to a partnership that will get both of you out from under.

Here are a few guidelines to make it work. With peer coaching, you coach *each other* to make specific changes. Peer coaching works best when you follow clear guidelines and conscientiously take turns.

- Coaching can be on the phone or in person.
- You can set a specific time each week, or try to check in on an as-needed basis.
- Identify a time frame for the coaching session and then divide the time equally, using a timer to keep track.
- Have short coaching sessions where you focus on clarifying your current situation, describing what you want to create, and identifying a few strategies on how to get where you want to go.
- Set small doable goals, allow your coach to help you cut them down to a manageable size. Remember that small steps actually taken lead to more progress than great steps that never happen.
- Try a couple of coaching sessions first. See if you are compatible as coaches, then make a commitment for a longer period of time.
- Try coaching when you sort your backlog or set up a system.

You may be surprised at how good a coach you can be for someone else, even though you are so bogged down yourself. At minimum, you can be there for your partner in an encouraging, supportive way, helping them move through their mess. Then they'll help you with yours.

Here are some helpful coaching questions:

- What's going well right now?
- What is your organizing goal?
- What is your plan for getting there?
- How can I support you in achieving that goal?
- What do you think could get in your way?
- What are your best next steps?

One of the most effective and fun ways to work with a peer coach or friend is the organizing phone date. The organizing phone date takes place while each of you is in your own office or home. You'll communicate by phone. You set aside an hour, let's say, 8:00 to 9:00 in the evening, and each of you sets an organizing goal for yourself. Then, you plan a short coaching call every fifteen or twenty minutes. The goal-setting sounds like this:

Linda: For the next twenty minutes, I am going to go through my checkbook for business expenses for my tax return.

Cheryl: Okay, and for my twenty minutes, I am going to sort out the top shelf in the linen closet.

Then hang up and go to work, knowing that your buddy is in the background, waiting for the progress report. You call back in twenty minutes. "How did you do?"

Linda: I got halfway through the year. I need another twenty minutes.

Cheryl: I didn't even touch the top shelf, because I noticed that the bottom shelf was worse. I found two sets of decent sheets that we never use that I want to give to a homeless shelter. And I reorganized the bottom shelf. Now, I need twenty minutes for the top shelf.

Then you do your next twenty minutes. Then, you set another small goal for the next round.

The organizing phone date works with small, specific goals. Keep encouraging each other. Help each other stay focused. Celebrate your accomplishments. Stop while you're ahead. Set up another time soon so you can build on the momentum.

You can also do organizing dates in person. You take turns at each other's home or office. If you are the coach, you encourage your "client" to set doable goals, keep moving, and keep sorting and purging. Cheer your partner on as he takes some risks and lets some things go. Encourage your partner when he starts to get overwhelmed and help him set a smaller, doable goal. No shaming. Do not say, "I can't believe that you are still hanging on to that old moldy pair of shoes." Rather say, "In light of your purpose and vision, how can you let go of those shoes?" Let the "client" be in charge. When you are the "client," let your coach support you to get rid of some things that you have been hanging on to for too long. Tackle a difficult project that you haven't been able to get to by yourself.

Alternatively, you and your coach can set up a daily phone check-in. This is particularly helpful when you are just starting out. You check in once a day. Set a timer for three minutes each and just talk about how you are doing with your organizing goals. The "coach" just listens or asks a question as the "client" checks in, and then you switch. Good questions for a daily check-in are:

- How are you doing with your goal?
- What is getting in your way?
- What are your triumphs?
- What's next? What would you like to focus on tomorrow?

Organizing dates can be some of the most helpful ways to keep yourself moving toward your goals. Identify two or three people who can be your organizing buddies and call them frequently for a boost of inspiration. Make sure you find someone to whom you can tell your absolute truth. Even if you have twelve crazy days in a row, when you have a chance to check in, you will start to see openings for change. Your coach is there, cheering you on.

Family

As you increase your awareness of your impact on others, you may be able to create allies from the people who have suffered from the negative impact of your disorderliness. Give your family members this book. Tell them that you are committed to changing, that it will take time (we are talking months, or years, not days or weeks), and that you need their support (not ultimatums).

Perhaps your family can sit down together and begin to explore how to help each other, how to stop the yelling and fussing. Take your family members seriously when they tell you that you are causing them pain. It is all too easy to minimize the difficulty that you cause others. Try putting yourself in their shoes, seeing things from their perspective, listening to their complaints. If you pay attention and tell them that you are serious, your family may be able to provide genuine support for you.

Your family members often know more than anyone else what your life is really like. If you have been disorganized for a long time, you may have provoked some anger in them. (And no doubt they do things that annoy you, too.) So, it is doubly easy to become defensive and make excuses rather than change. Yet, if you want to change, your family can be a great source of support. For example, your kids can remind you to put your keys in one place. Or, as Gerry found, her kids helped her put things in perspective. As she and her two children were preparing to leave on vacation, she came into the living room with ten books that she wanted to take with her. Her daughter, Marina, said, "Mom, you're not going to read all those books. Take just two." In this situation, Marina knew better than Gerry what she needed.

If you are living with someone, your partner is probably more aware than you of the times you just drop your clothes on the floor. He or she can help raise your awareness. It takes great humility and trust to be open to this kind of support. In some cases, it can save your marriage or partnership. The conversation about how to create a pleasant and comfortable home environment is an essential couple conversation. It includes discussions about gender roles, standards of cleanliness and order, and what constitutes home. You should also review how you value (or don't) housework and what kind of space you will create together.

What is often challenging about these conversations is that they include tacit references to deeply held beliefs that are highly emotional and difficult to discuss. Building a home together can be a pleasure, a nightmare, or somewhere in between. At its best, it can be a time to learn about each other's beliefs and longings and thus strengthen the relationship. Many people consider conversations about "housework" and "decor" to be unimportant. They are serious, however, and can destroy relationships and bring a lot of unhappiness when poorly managed. When you and your partner communicate well, you move toward building a special dwelling place. Coming home to a place that feels like home can enhance life tremendously. Coming home to a place that is alien and uncomfortable can be very destructive.

Here are some guidelines for conversations with your partner or your children.

Rule 1: Scorn and labeling do not help. In your worst moments, your partner might be inclined to think of you as a slob or you might be inclined to think of him as compulsive. Speaking these judgmental thoughts *never* leads to a constructive conversation. Even more important, you will both benefit by learning to respect someone else's style.

Rule 2: Take the conversation about organizing seriously. Once you start to respect each other's innate preferences, you can negotiate with better results. Conversations about who does the dishes or the laundry or about who leaves their clothes strewn around can rapidly escalate to conversations about very emotional matters. When you engage the conversations with awareness and empathy, you often can avoid an unwanted conflagration.

Rule 3: Look for benefits in the very qualities that annoy you. The more organized partner's (or child's) concern for order may also mean that she is a great planner or stays on top of the finances. Your more relaxed style brings many spontaneous moments into your interactions. Appreciate each other's differences *and* be inventive about ways to create spaces that work for *both* of you.

There are lots of ways couples and families can have constructive conversations about their differences. In chapter 14, you will find strategies for these conversations, ideas about how family members can help you get organized, and activities that you can do together.

Work Colleagues

I finally confessed to a fellow management consultant that I couldn't get rid of the mess on my desk. I was surprised when he told me that he had the same problem. He didn't look disorganized. In fact, he looked polished and confident and well put-together. Yet he told me that he often raced around his house looking for his keys and invoiced clients up to six months late. Behind his impressive exterior was the same plaguing problem I had. He understood the overwhelming feeling of struggling to clear off a messy desk. It was very helpful to know that he was a fellow traveler.

To find those colleagues who might also be stuck in the disorganization boat, pay attention to who else tends to run late or miss deadlines. Give them this book and ask if you can have a conversation about how you might support each other. Let significant people whom you work with know that you could use some help staying organized. If you take charge of the situation, and you let work colleagues know that you are interested in changing your behavior, you may create some strategies that work for everyone.

You can ask for help in ways that are dignified. One executive dreaded doing her budget reports at the end of each quarter. She procrastinated until she was in a panic, but that didn't help her understand the software that she needed to use. Finally, she decided to ask someone from the financial department to help. She calmed herself down before calling, reminding herself that many people were having problems with the same software. She did have to reveal that she had procrastinated, but she did not have to explain how panicked she was.

Think hard about what kinds of help you need from fellow employees, and recognize that perhaps you can offer another kind of assistance in return. And see chapter 15 for more ideas on getting organized at work.

Hire or Barter for Help with Household Paperwork and Errands

Paper never stops coming in. There are bills, invoices, and lots of information. You have to handle them because putting it off just makes it worse. You can pay someone to help you. Get support from a local high school student in sorting and filing the mail. Alternatively, find a retired secretary or a stay-at-home parent who can come and work with you on billing, invoicing, and filing one day a week. Find a bookkeeper who can come in four hours a month to process the finances on your computer. You don't have to do it alone. This kind of help can free you up for work that is more meaningful to you. Alternatively, barter your services for theirs. If you love to cook, garden, or do home repair and they love to do paperwork, perhaps you can figure out a trade.

Barry discovered a different way of handling paperwork. "I struggled every week with the mail. I would get depressed just looking at it. I'd feel overwhelmed instantly. I heard from a friend that she never opens her own mail. Her secretary does it. I would never have thought of that because I don't have a secretary. But I liked the principle, and I looked around and found a high school student who lived down the street. I leave my mail in a basket, and once a week, Jean sorts it out for me. It is such a big relief."

Pamela, a single mom with two kids, often traveled on business. She said, "I hired a college student who comes in twice a week for two hours. She does all the errands, returns library books and videos, goes to the pharmacy, and picks up the dry cleaning. Sometimes, she does the ordering from catalogues."

Let's not forget about cleaning help. Professional cleaning help can make the difference between juggling successfully and dropping all the balls. Yes, it can be expensive, but the benefit is huge. Some people benefit from weekly help. Some people get great support from a monthly arrangement. Fred said, "I really appreciate once-a-month cleaning help and I use her visits as motivation for myself. When I know she's coming, I clean up and put things away so that she can really clean."

Professional Organizer

What do professional organizers do? They can help you set up systems for your files, your kitchen, your clothes, anything that needs organizing. They can help you bring order into your life. Some deal with everything, while others just work in time management. Some only work in homes and others only go to offices. Professional organizers can be enormously useful in getting you jump-started and keeping your momentum. You may feel that you only need a few sessions, although some people work with their organizer regularly for years.

Professional organizers have their own approaches, so make sure that what they offer is right for you. Some will sit with you while you throw things away, while others will come into your house when you're not there and create order without you. Look for someone whom you enjoy being with. Try to find someone who has a holistic approach to organizing and understands the personal growth challenges of truly becoming organized. At minimum, find someone who is upbeat, patient, and can help you create systems that really work. This is very personal work, and you want to feel good about it. You want to look forward to seeing your personal organizer, not dread the session.

Diane said, "I found someone who just loves to organize. She would come into my house almost with glee, because she got such satisfaction from putting things in order. She never embarrassed me. In fact, she made me feel as if I was giving her a gift with my mess because she enjoyed organizing so much. She rearranged my closets, kitchen drawers, spice rack, and the garage. At first, she came once a week, and the difference in our house was so palpable that I learned to maintain the order. She helped me unpack boxes that I hadn't touched for eight years. I actually found my iron—I still haven't used it, but I have it. Now, I ask her to come in every couple of months. She helps me with my 'to file' pile. If she didn't come, I would just never do my filing. Her help motivates me to do something that I would never do."

Paul said, "When I first got help from an organizer I hated letting go of things, I could barely breathe during the three hours that we worked together. Throwing things out was painful and my organizer was so patient. Now, she's too slow for me. I love throwing things out. I can actually see the difference in my home, and, more important, I feel different there. She has helped me so much."

A great time to hire an organizer is when you move. With good help, you can throw stuff out beforehand, which can often save you hundreds of dollars in moving costs. It's also a good time to find someone who can help you unpack and create systems when you arrive in your new home.

Make sure that you stay in charge of the process and that you feel comfortable and in control. It's your office or home. A good personal organizer won't talk down to you just because you are "organizationally challenged." To find someone to work with, call the National Association of Professional Organizers listed in appendix 3. This is a growing profession; if it doesn't work with the first person you call, find someone else. There is good help out there.

Professional Coach

A professional coach can help you look at the bigger picture. Sometimes, disorganized people lose track of what they really want in life. We get bogged down. Good coaches help people live more of the lives that they want to live. A coach can help you shape your mission and vision and then help you achieve what you really want. Some coaches understand that the way we conduct our daily lives has a big impact on the goals that we can achieve.

One of the best books to appear on the topic of changing the way we live is *Take Time for Your Life* by Cheryl Richardson, a professional coach and leader in this new field. The book provides a wealth of guidance on building a sound foundation for a good life. She has great ideas for organizing your time, your money, and for creating your life goals. A coach will help you overcome barriers, and this includes helping you face the bad news. Best of all, your coach is totally on your side. There are many good coaches out there. Even three or four sessions should help you to start making significant changes in your life.

Think of yourself as an athlete in training. You might have a workout program, and there are goals that you want to accomplish. Now you have a coach to work with every week who will help you through the rough spots, point out your weaknesses, and keep you moving and growing. Some coaches will work with you in person, others on the phone, or by e-mail. Call the International Federation of Coaches, listed in appendix 3 or check out professional coaching on your favorite Internet search engine.

An Organizing Support Group

You can form a small group that focuses on developing a purpose for getting organized, creating your vision, and developing a better understanding of your situation. Then you get help from the group for creating changes in your life. A good group will be fun, supportive, and will help you move forward. It should focus on changing and getting work done. Do not stay in a group if the focus is negative and on how hard it is to get organized. Do encourage each other to go to each others' homes and really help out.

Helen had resisted calling people in her organizing group for support. She said, "I don't have time for all this support. Really, I can do this organizing myself. And, anyway, no one will want to support me. Support doesn't work for me. It may for others, but not for me." She had a litany of reasons why support was not right for her. Finally, one Saturday morning, she called a fellow group member, Susan, to tell her that she was about to clean out a dreaded closet in her entryway. Susan reminded her of her vision for herself, which was to create a welcoming home and encouraged her: "You can do it!"

Helen said later, "The task was much easier than I had anticipated. I felt her help. I felt quite powerful while I was tossing things out and rearranging belongings. I was Warrior Woman. I didn't feel so alone, and I didn't go down that black hole that often happens when I try to clear up some of this mess. At the end, I could tell my group, 'I did do it! I cleared out that closet and it wasn't so bad.'"

What are some of the benefits of a group? First, you are with people who "get it." You don't have to hide, so you can tell the truth without being ashamed of it. In fact, you can laugh together. And, second, you can figure out ways to get organized together. You can experience a synergistic effect and learn from each other's growth. Third, you can cheer each other on. You can take extra risks knowing that your group is supporting you.

A Twelve-Step Recovery Program

Recovery groups are some of the best places to start with shame reduction. These are the Anonymous groups where people tell their stories to each other, support each other to forgo their addictions, and feel accepted for who they are. The recovery movement includes groups such as Alcoholics Anonymous and Al-Anon. Debtors Anonymous (DA) and Codependents Anonymous can provide particularly valuable help with setting limits and getting support for growing and changing. DA is valuable for people who have trouble with money, even if they aren't in debt. It also has excellent material on getting out if debt, managing your money, and "time debting." Time debting refers to the practice of consistently running late and not allowing yourself the time to do what you have to do. These groups have a powerful philosophy, and real healing takes place for people who are struggling with addictions and compulsive behavior. Some of us are addicted to our mess. Strong words, I know, but let me put it another way: For some of us, deciding to be organized does not mean that we are able to become organized.

The first two steps of the twelve-step program can be phrased for the disorganized person. Step one: "I admitted I was powerless over my chaos and that my life had become unmanageable." Step two: "I came to believe that a Power greater than myself could restore me to sanity." You may want to incorporate some of the twelve-step principles into your support group, as it can be very satisfying to sit with a group of people who also feel that they are out of control in their lives and who are seeking support to regain a sense of dignity.

Therapist

A therapist can help you work through some of the emotional issues that can surface as you organize. Make sure it feels likes a good match. Ask your friends for referrals, and be sure to talk to the therapist for a few minutes on the phone to describe the issues that you are dealing with. Listen to what they have to say about disorganization as an issue. You are looking for someone with whom you have rapport, and someone who can help you move through the challenges that you are facing.

■ ■ ■ EXERCISE ■ ■ ■

I call this exercise "The five C's of support." Think about someone who can help with each of these kinds of support. Write down their names and telephone numbers, then talk with them about how they can help you.

Celebration: A person to whom you can show off your newly cleared desk, and they will know that this is a time to celebrate.

Confrontation: The person who can give you the tough love of confrontation and help you face the consequences of your behaviors.

Compassion: The person you call when you are in despair.

Choice-making: Someone who can support you in making difficult choices, such as prioritizing and letting things go.

Clearing and cleaning: Someone who can do the work of clearing out and cleaning up with you or for you.

Carry your list of supporters with you so that you can call them when you need them.

■ ■ ■

Many people have vision, insight, and even a few good strategies for change. But when they don't recognize their need for support, they get stuck. Don't forget that getting support is an essential step on your path of organizing.

II

Drawing On Organizing Wisdom

6

The Rhythm of Organizing

The next six chapters constitute Step Five of the change cycle, drawing on the wisdom of organizing. Wisdom is what leads us to sane and balanced living. Organizing wisdom represents those principles of organizing that can help lead you back to this sanity and balance. We can think of the principles of organizing as a kind of aesthetics. Aesthetics are the principles of beauty. Our aesthetic is a deeply ingrained instinct about what is beautiful and what is not. It is influenced by culture, belief, and our own upbringing; it lies beneath many of our choices in life. We who are disorganized tend to believe that messy is beautiful, lateness is appealing, and frenzy has a pleasing element to it. This is the chaos aesthetic.

In order to develop our taste for the order aesthetic, we need to explore our deepest instincts around organizing and begin to find new principles to live by. I describe new organizing principles that will bring us farther on the path to a new understanding of beauty in our lives, identifying new principles for how we can take care of our possessions, navigate through time, make and keep agreements, and how we focus our powerful minds.

Let's turn now to the actual organizing itself. One reason why people resist getting organized is that they think it is a static condition. Yet, being "organized" is probably best described as a dynamic between a state of readiness for action and taking action. It is the rhythm of taking action, creating the natural disorder that comes with taking action, restoring order with helpful habits and useful systems, and thus returning to readiness for action. It looks like this:

Ready for action

Take action

Natural disorder

Restore order by engaging
• Habits
• Systems

Much of the disorder that we create is the natural consequence of our actions. When we create order, we are simply getting ready for our next actions. Here is an example:

Closet with clean clothes

Dress for the day

Clothes get dirty

Restore the clean clothes to the closet by
• Hanging up clothes
• Doing laundry

We can see the same pattern with a messy desk.

Orderly desk
(whatever order means to you)

Restore the desk to your order by
- **Putting things away**
- **Using your filing system**

Work during the day

Desk gets messy

The purpose of organizing is to be able to take effective action and live the life you want.

I have created a new term for what most people call getting organized—clearing out the excess, finding a place for everything, getting rid of the clutter and confusion, creating useful categories for their possessions. I call this "getting to ready" because these valuable activities are just the first part of getting truly organized. Unless you also build in the habits and create the systems that enable you to return to your newly organized state on a regular basis, you won't really be organized.

The three core elements of organizing are to be found in the restore order step.

1. **Getting to ready** is about clearing up your spaces and your calendar. You discard the clutter, organize your belongings, and arrange your calendar so that you can do what you need to do. You reduce the activities that are not essential to you.
2. **Creating new habits** are simple steps such as hanging things up and putting things away that return you to ready. New habits also make your organizing systems work for you.
3. **Building effective systems** identifies effective organizing routines that you can integrate into your life so that you can get back to ready through known pathways, including your laundry and filing systems.

Getting to Ready

The essence of getting to ready is that it prepares you for action, whether the action is cooking, writing a proposal, going to the gym, doing a presentation, taking care of a patient, meditating, or gardening. You can get to ready in time and in space. Once your desk is clear, your belongings and laundry put away, and your schedule is manageable, you feel ready to do what you want to do.

Getting to ready is a change of mind and focus. The martial arts teach that power comes from our "center" and you can keep coming back to center with your breath, body, and focused awareness. Coming from "center" can become a way of life. We don't have to go to an aikido studio to get back to center; we can learn to do this every day as we get to ready. As we put things away and finish off the day or the week, we can see that we are more available for what is to come.

How do you know that your space or calendar is at ready? You feel it. You feel good, energized, supported, uplifted, and ready for what life offers you. You like your space and your plans and you feel up for what you have to do.

Getting to Ready with Things and Places

Many people are buried in a backlog of mail, clothes, special mementos, or old furniture. Their backlog hangs over them as they live their lives. They are not at ready because they can't find things, don't feel comfortable at home or work, and don't use their space well. Too much of their home or office has become dead storage. They might be intimidated by the foot-high piles on the desk or the years of unsorted mail and piles of articles to read. The in-box that is flooding onto the floor is frightening. The drawers, the closets, the attic or garage that are filled with unusable clothes and old sporting equipment are daunting. It will take hours to get through it! (If not days! Weeks! Months! Years!)

"Getting back to ready" does not have to mean creating immaculate order. Far from it. It will be different for each of us. Some people will feel a sense of readiness when they know where their keys and glasses are. Others won't feel they are ready until the desk is totally clear, all previous work filed, and all phone calls returned. There is a feeling of fundamental ease at "ready," because you can find things and you're not overbooked.

Slow and Steady

You'll spend about one to four hours a week (maximum) on getting through the backlog in your home or office (or car or garage). Focus on one area at a time—your desk, your car, or one closet. If you do this slowly over time, one area a week, you'll be able to get used to it, value it, and maintain a sense of readiness. Instead of saying, "This weekend I am going to throw everything out," pick a small area and really clear it up. Now, having said this, every once in a while you may get the energy for a big push. Going with the energy, you may do half of the garage or a whole room in the basement. You will need to clear out the backlog initially, and then create a habit of doing a daily or weekly clearing up, getting back to ready every night or week.

Your Stuff Is Not You

Most of us have too much stuff. It makes sense to let the stuff go, yet it's hard, partly because we identify so strongly with it. Letting go of material possessions involves identifying less with them. How? Ironically, you begin by consciously making time for whom and what you love *before* cleaning up. Too often people don't enjoy their moments of leisure because they are thinking about the mess in their home or the things they have to do. Pedro said, "My wife and I live in San Diego, but we are so busy that we have to squeeze out time to get a little walk together on the beach. Even when we are walking on the beach, I feel stress because I should be cleaning out the basement." Let yourself enjoy some leisure moments first. You're committed to change now and true enjoyment will give you energy you need to tackle your backlog. So, read poetry, go to a movie, play basketball, or find a beautiful place in nature and take a walk. Create some quiet family time. Call a friend and go out together. Take a small excursion. Spend some time on a beloved, neglected hobby.

As you make time for these beloved connections and enjoyable activities, consciously build an inner conviction that you are more than your things. This strengthens your will to let go of belongings that are of no use to you.

Talk Back to Your Disorganizing Gremlin

When you are ready to discard, remember that your mind sometimes plays tricks on you to keep stuff you really don't need. Natalie had three large paper bags full of newspapers to sort through. She just couldn't throw them out. One day, her new cleaning help mistook them for garbage and took them to the dump. They were gone! "I was amazed that I felt so free," she said. "It helped me see that I could do that myself. I didn't need those papers at all."

Talk back to the part that wants to keep things. Karen said, "I find that I have to be ruthless in throwing things out. If I keep too big a 'to read' pile, I feel overwhelmed. I have to keep telling myself that a beautiful space and a clear mind are more important to me than reading everything that comes my way. I have an inner voice that says, 'But wait, I want to read that . . . and that . . . and that . . . and *that* looks interesting, and that other one is important . . . ' I have to remember that this voice has no sense of its own limits, and I can only provide appropriate limits by remembering what I want that is more important to me than reading everything." See chapter 7, which is about managing our possessions, for much more on this topic.

■ ■ ■ EXERCISE ■ ■ ■

Pick one area—a desk drawer, a closet shelf, a part of a kitchen counter, an area in the garage, and allow plenty of time to take all the action needed to bring it to ready. Note what you are thinking and feeling, but hold your goal in mind and finish the job.

A word about the "branching effect," which is what takes place when you start clearing out one area and discover that you now need to make space for things in another area. Focus on the first area and create a holding container for all of the items that need a new home. Get one small place to ready so that you can have and enjoy the experience of finishing your project. Then, go back to your holding container and find new homes for those things. Stay with it, the branching diminishes over time.

■ ■ ■

Getting to Ready in Time

This is about realistic scheduling. You are at ready when you look at your schedule for the next day and know that you can do what you have scheduled—including eating and taking care of yourself. When you look at your schedule for the week, make sure you have time for exercise and renewal.

Does this sound more basic than basic? Actually, many people set up impossible schedules for themselves. If they can do everything that they have scheduled, they do it in a way that is hair-raising, racing from one thing to the next. Matt often double-looks himself without knowing it and usually plans a stressful week even though he has a heart problem. "I often don't look at my schedule until the morning," he says, "and then I discover that I have two meetings back-to-back and a luncheon that I *have* to be at that I can only attend if I skip something else. This happens all the time. Then, if I miss the five twenty-three train, I am late for my daughters at their friend's house, and then dinner is tense. I have trouble sleeping, so I wake up late, which means I often miss the morning train and start my day late."

People's scheduling eyes are often far bigger than their accomplishing stomach, so to speak. In a gregarious mood, you might schedule everything you are interested in, without holding your wayward sense of time in check. Then, later, in a different mood, you might find yourself frenzied and tired and doing things you wish that you weren't. You then regret your earlier commitments. You probably have a strong urge to accomplish a lot and participate in many activities. Yet, you may be faced with the challenge that adding more things to your plate causes other things to fall off. If you have a lot to do, let something go or do it less perfectly. Ensure that you have allotted time to do what you have scheduled. Come down from the adrenaline rush of overbooking. You can find tips on how to do this in chapter 8.

Where time is concerned, getting to ready often starts with scheduling fewer things. Your first thought when you cut back on your schedule might be that you can't cut back. You might feel that you have no choice, that you are obligated. Here is some of the hardest work of all: to reflect on what is truly important to you. Some people have a hard time letting go of accumulated stuff, others of accumulated obligations. You may have to reassess your obligations in light of what is important to you now. The inner work is similar to letting go of your excess belongings—try to see that you are not your obligations. You may have taken on too many commitments and these are keeping you from reaching your true goals.

Ponder the notion that you are making choices about your scheduling. It is *you* who is overbooking yourself. Consider that lightening up your commitments may lead to some open time. When you are not running from one activity to the next, you can actually feel yourself, and that can be a little scary. You will have free moments. Even a moment of freedom can be challenging, since most of us are lost in the tyranny of our scheduling.

■ ■ ■ EXERCISE ■ ■ ■

Review your calendar from the past week and identify times when you were late, double-booked, or couldn't complete a task that you set out to do. What is one change that you could make in your calendar that might prevent a similar experience in your upcoming week?

■ ■ ■

Creating a Different Future

Keep in mind that your current decisions to keep things and maintain your excessive plans affect you in the future. Every decision you postpone today, you will still have to deal with tomorrow. You are, in effect, throwing unmade decisions (trash) into your future, since you don't want to deal with them today. But you are probably not very happy to have to deal with yesterday's leftover decisions or overcommitments. Remember, you will be even unhappier tomorrow when you have an even bigger pile of unmade decisions to deal with. Here is an image to illustrate the point.

Every time I save things I don't need or
make plans that I don't really want . . .

I TRASH MY FUTURE!

Every time I let go of things and activities I don't really need,
I create s p a c e for a new future.

Living with greater freedom, we can engage the messiness of life,
such as the surprise encounters and inner promptings. Perhaps, you are
currently so busy that you can't bump into someone and see where that
chance meeting takes you. You miss synchronicities. Bring at ready
means that there is time and space for quirks, mistakes, drop-ins, a call
from school when a child forgets lunch, or a call from a sick friend who
needs some chicken soup. There's an old saying: "Men make plans, God
laughs." For all our planning, there is some other Force in charge, and
much of the time, the best of life takes place when we haven't planned
for it.

Getting to ready is like rock climbing. Slowly and attentively, you
seek a handhold for yourself, then you pull yourself up a step. You're
now a little higher; you have a better view. And then you search out the
next handhold. Step by step, you get closer to the top, fighting gravity

all the way. You gain some altitude, then you maintain it with a new habit—which you'll learn about in the next section. As you climb, new habits will be the tools that will allow you to maintain your progress. After a while, you will be able to straighten up, look around, and enjoy a glorious new view.

The Discipline of Rhythm— Practicing New Habits

Your habits will help you return to ready on a regular basis. Habits let us perform highly complex actions routinely and smoothly, streamlining the workings of our powerful brains and bodies so that we perform many of our day-to-day tasks unconsciously. The more you can do routine activities on "autopilot," the more you can become aware of the truly important matters in life. There is a paradox here—the more daily tasks you do automatically, the more you can do with mindful awareness. When you stop fighting with yourself about doing the filing or washing the dishes, you can perform the task as a meditation.

We disorganized people tend to disdain the discipline of returning things to their places. We consider clearing up to be unproductive time. We say to ourselves, "It's a waste of precious time to be putting things back when I may need them later." Contrary to what we may think, this patient, respectful putting things away may be some of our most productive time, because we are setting up the playing field for the next time. Then, we can hit the ground running, instead of running around in confusion.

In order to create new habits, you'll need to rethink some of your beliefs about the importance of restoring order. Visit the kitchen of an outstanding restaurant, go backstage of a theater group, or view an operating room sometime. You will see that preparation and completion time is a serious part of life. Everything must be prepared carefully and then put away when done. Things have a place. I saw this when I visited an Israeli army base on a Friday morning before the Jewish Sabbath. The soldiers took the whole morning to clean tools, put them away, and sweep up and wash down the base. They were at ready when they went home for their family gatherings.

At the end of the workday, you might spend twenty-five minutes putting things back in order before leaving for home. Or at the end of the week, instead of squeezing in one more meeting, you might schedule a couple of hours just tying up loose ends: responding to e-mails, returning phone calls, filing loose papers, making notes for yourself for the next week, and putting materials away.

Mark, a technical writer said, "I started to see how much of my life was ruled by habits that created chaos. After many failed attempts to change all of my organizing patterns at once, I realized that I could change one or two chaos-creating habits at a time. I started with the car keys. I created a place for the keys and concentrated on returning them to the key rack. When I got used to that, and it felt natural, I went on to the next habit. I decided to hang up and put away all my clothes at the end of the day. It took me a while to break the habit of dropping things on the floor. Yet, I persisted just in hanging up my clothes until it became routine and unconscious. I find now that I have stopped thinking of myself as a slob. That has affected my life at work as well. I feel a greater sense of dignity."

At first, altering your habits can seem overwhelming. It seems harder than the "just do it" approach to organizing. Since "just do it" doesn't seem to work, however, slow change is essential. New actions will feel unfamiliar at first, as if it were not "you" acting in this different way. You'll get used to it, though, if you persist. You will also get better and longer-lasting results by creating a new habit than by "just doing it." Read through the following ten steps; they might look daunting, but they are the key to your new life. As you get a sense of how to do this, it becomes easier. The preparation time for creating a new habit can be as little as ten minutes and the daily practice time is short as well. Building new habits does not necessarily take extra time—it takes will, vision, and intention. The ten steps for creating a new habit are as follows.

1. Pick one small habit that is currently making your disorganization worse and that you'd really like to change.
2. Estimate what it costs you to keep this old habit
3. Become aware of your thoughts that accompany it.
4. Check your deeply held beliefs for validity. Look for disconfirming examples.

5. Create a picture of a new, better habit. Actually act it out. Part of learning a new habit is to enact it so that you know what the new habit feels like. You start creating some new neural pathways that you will go over and over again, creating neural grooves.
6. Remind yourself how your new habit will nurture your vision and purpose.
7. Interrupt the old habit with a shout, music, or a "No!"
8. Reinforce your new behavior with new thoughts.
9. Reward yourself for the new behavior.
10. Get lots of support; ask for help from all your support sources.

Mary wanted to build a habit of leaving her desk clear at the end of the workday. She was always resolving to clean it up, but she never did. Let's see what happened when she decided to go through the ten steps.

1. *Pick one small habit that you'd really like to change.* Mary's goal was to leave a clear work space on her desk every night. This may seem like a tiny step, but it was a huge change for her. In fact, leaving your desk clear is a *big* step. It changes many things.

2. *Estimate what it costs you to keep this habit.* She faced how expensive it was for her to get to the office in the morning and find a daunting pile of leftover work from the day before. It was a hard way to start because she couldn't start fresh. Rather, she had to sort things out, plowing through old work, before getting started on the day's work, and then she often felt exhausted by 10:00 A.M. In addition, she often lost things that were right on her desk, leaving her frantic. This old habit was stressful and tiring.

3. *Become aware of your thoughts that accompany this habit.* Mary paid attention to her thinking as she cleared off her desk. She noticed that every evening, she thought, "I just don't have time to put things away now, and, besides, I'll need them again in the morning. It's just too much work to put everything away. And I don't know where to put everything."

4. *Check your deeply held beliefs for validity.* She also asked herself the question: "What are my deeper beliefs about people with messy desks?" Several images occurred to her. "I love messes, messes are the stuff of life. Messes are creative. Order is deadly. My dad always had a messy desk, and I want to be like Dad." Well, that was helpful in under-

standing why she might cling to a messy desk. Was her belief about messes necessarily valid? Was her messiness actually creative? Honestly? No, she admitted to herself, this was not a creative kind of messiness. Did she know anyone creative who had a neat desk? Yes, in fact, she lived near a gifted cabinetmaker whose work space was very spacious and well organized.

5. *Create a picture of a new, better habit. Actually act it out.* Mary then imagined herself practicing the new habit of clearing off her desk before she went home in the evening. No more desperate searches for items lost under piles of unsorted papers. With a sympathetic colleague's help, she went on a marathon desk-cleaning purge, knowing that she was committed to a new habit. She didn't have to organize the whole office. The goal was to clear her desk and get used to clearing it off at the end of the day. She practiced leaving a clear desk surface so that she could see what it felt like.

6. *Remind yourself of how your new habit will nurture your vision and purpose.* Mary reminded herself frequently about why she was practicing her new habit. She revisited her vision of dignity and clear spaces. She imagined herself sitting at a cleared desk and working well, with great concentration and energy. She wanted to be powerful in her life, feeling much more ease and joy.

7. *Interrupt the old habit with a shout, music, or a "No!"* Mary noticed there were times when she was about to leave the desk a mess, as if she had totally forgotten her commitment to herself. As soon as she found herself doing this, she shouted (quietly), "No!" Then she stayed the extra time, even an hour, because this was important to her.

8. *Reinforce your new behavior with new thoughts.* She replaced distracting old thoughts with inspiring new ones, such as: "I love starting the workday with a clear desk. I can be so much more creative when I start off with some space. I am creating space for me."

9. *Reward yourself for the new behavior.* She kept track of how many times she cleared off her desk, and rewarded herself. Research shows that if you take a new action for twenty-one consecutive days, it will stick. She rewarded herself with a facial (an unheard-of luxury) after eight days; twenty-one was just too long. There were many times she despaired, and then she reminded herself that changing this habit would take time and concentration.

10. *Get lots of support. Ask for help from all your support sources.* Mary asked a friend at work for support and encouragement during the times she still left her desk a mess. She prayed for help.

"There were days, maybe weeks, in which I forgot that I wanted to clear my desk at the end of the day," she now says about the whole process. "It was as if I had no intention to do it at all. And then I would come back to clearing the desk at the end of the day. And, slowly, I would get used to this oddly clear space. It has gotten easier and easier. And it is a joy to start fresh in the morning with a clear desk. I am so much more productive now, and actually my office feels like a resource to me, not a drain. I am glad that I learned to be patient with myself. It was so worth it."

Changing habits is not linear and you can't force it. The ten steps are a useful framework. Yet, in reality, building new habits is a cycle of going for it, and then lying fallow and letting go of old ways of being. You commit, fall down, get up, and recommit. You can implement some basic habits for handling everyday items. This includes learning to:

- Put keys, glasses, hats, gloves in the same place every day.
- Clear off floors and countertops at the end of the day (or week).
- Hang up clothes and coats at the end of the day.
- Put things back immediately after you use them.
- Put your toothbrush back into the holder rather than on the sink.
- Bring everything in from the car when you arrive home from shopping, errands, carpools, trips. Bring everything in from the car at the end of the day.
- Empty your handbag or briefcase of the excess at the end of each week.

Don't try to implement all of these at once. Instead, use Helen's example. She worked on creating two new habits: hanging her coat up in the closet every day and replacing her sunglasses in her handbag. She picked these because they were highly impactful. She found that she was often spending ten to fifteen minutes a day looking for her sunglasses. And her coat might end up in one of four places, none of them being the closet. After a while, Helen said, "I was so surprised to find my coat in the closet, I couldn't remember putting it there. And I looked all over the house for my sunglasses, only to find them in my handbag. These were my two new habits. It seems so small, but it has helped a lot."

Remember the first weeks of practicing a new habit could be hard. Just keep going. Stick to it. Each time you practice your new habit, you are rewiring yourself. Give yourself a pep talk. The good news is that once your good new habit is in place, it will be hard to change, too.

■ ■ ■　EXERCISE　■ ■ ■

Pick one habit that you would like to change. Start with putting your keys in one place, finishing the dishes at night, making a schedule for the next day. Follow the ten steps outlined on pages 105–6.

It's best if you can do this with an organizing buddy. And track your progress in your organizing journal. It probably won't be linear, but over time, your new habit will become an easy part of your life.

■ ■ ■

The Structure of Rhythm— Build Systems That Work for You

Your new habits will take you a long way toward sustaining your organizing. The next step is building a few systems for the more complex tasks of your daily life. Systems entail a routine of two or more steps that enable you to reach an organizing goal regularly. You can create simple logical routines for most of your daily tasks: keeping track of phone calls, handling mail, tracking e-mail messages, scheduling meetings, shopping for the groceries, doing the laundry, tracking and handling car maintenance.

You may be saying to yourself, "Systems? Routines? Forget it! Boring! I don't do routines! I don't know how to create systems!" If you're worried that routines will make your life boring, ask yourself whether frantically looking for the keys or last year's tax returns is really that interesting. Trying to figure out which clothes are clean and which are dirty is not a fulfilling task. Your goal is to create routines to support a nonroutine life.

Guidelines for Effective Organizing Systems

As you create your own systems, keep these guidelines in mind:

1. Your organizing systems must make sense to you. They do not need to make sense to anyone else.
2. Your system should get you the results you want.
3. Systems should be as simple as possible. Don't create ten files where two will do. Be minimalist.
4. Systems should be accessible. A beautiful system that you won't use or that is too time-consuming is worthless.
5. Systems should be as low-maintenance as possible. Be realistic about how much time and energy you are willing and able to devote to maintaining your organizing systems.
6. Systems should build on your strengths. You need to like your system. If you love colors, use colorful systems.
7. For every system that you create, you need to consider how to manage the flow of items and:
   a. Keep what is coming in to a low minimum.
   b. Organize what you have simply and accessibly.
   c. Remove, discard, or delete items as quickly as possible.

Your goal with your systems is to get back to ready as simply and easily as possible.

As you create a workable system, keep these questions in mind:

1. What are your goals for a good system? What results would you like?
2. Note your current "system." What do you do now and what results do you get?
3. What steps might get you the results that you want?
4. Create a trial period when you experiment with your new system and determine if it works for you. Do these steps get you the results that you want?
5. If not, try again, until you get the results that you want.

The following systems are good examples of how different people came up with ideas to resolve a particular organizational issue. See if they work for you or inspire your own new system.

My New Mail System

I wanted to create a workable mail system since I often lost track of my credit card statements, phone bills, and ever checks. My old mail "system" was based on fear. Because of my disorganization, I was afraid that when I opened the mailbox, I would find an ominous note from the IRS, a bounced check, or a threatening letter from a creditor. Therefore, I left my mail in the mailbox as long as possible. When I finally got the armload of mail into the house, I would throw it in a pile on the kitchen counter or on the floor and avoid it, thus continuing the cycle of fear.

When I finally did open mail I'd start opening envelopes wherever I might be. I would leave the rest of the mail on my desk or chair and open it in stages, sometimes putting particularly interesting correspondence on my desk, other times reading it in the kitchen or bathroom. When it came time to pay taxes or bills, I would once again have to race around frantically in search of the necessary paperwork. My credit card receipts could be in my desk drawer, on my desk, in a pile in the kitchen, or under the couch. I might even have thrown them away. I was self-employed, so this was particularly distressing because I couldn't keep track of my business expenses.

Here is my new mail system: Every day, I collect the mail in a basket under my desk. I set aside a half hour every third day to open the mail—but *only at my desk*. I pull out the bills, the personal mail, the requests for money, and announcements, and I throw away everything else, including the catalogs. The bills go in a bill folder, all tax-related information goes in the tax folder, and the requests for charitable contributions go into another special basket. (I go through these once a year in late November. That keeps me from duplicating my annual contribution.) Then, I check out the announcements, and then I throw them out. If there is an upcoming event that I am interested in, I mark it in my calendar in pencil. And that's it. You can see that even if I don't open my mail for a week, there is no harm done. The mail stays in that basket until I open it. (And, okay, I do keep a couple of catalogues.)

The whole time I'm doing this sorting, I'm saying to my inner voice that wants to keep everything and leave everything on the desk, 'I have to be ruthless because I cannot waste my life horsing around with the

mail.' Today, my floors, counters, and bathrooms are free of old mail."
My work productivity has increased, since I can handle my mail with
confidence. I experimented with opening my mail once a week, but that
didn't work. The build-up daunted me.

Mary's Filing System

Mary's goals for her system were to see her folders and papers, and also
to keep them off her desk. As Mary organized the surface of her desk,
she noted that she left folders and papers out on her desk because she
wasn't sure where to put them. Her old "system" entailed keeping her
papers in sight, which meant that they were visible everywhere.

For her first trial, she created a very simple standing file system for
her current projects. She could still see the file folders. She put large,
simple labels on each folder. They were in order, and the piles were off
the desk. When she finished a project, she put the file in the file cabinet.
She tried to keep the standing files in alphabetical order, but it turned
out this didn't help her. So alphabetizing was not part of her system. In
order to make the system work, she had to learn to put papers in folders
and folders in the standing file. Finally, at the end of each week, she
took a half hour to weed out extra papers. Now, her desk was clear
for work.

Systems can be large or small, and can be structured on a daily, weekly,
or yearly rhythm. Systems create predictability and order. At first, you may
find it hard to tolerate predictability and order, but these things are well
worth getting used to.

A Simple Laundry System

A good laundry system gets you clothes that are put away ready for use.

1. Begin by placing all the dirty clothes in a hamper regularly.
2. When the dirty-clothes pile is big enough, put the clothes in the
   washing machine and then the dryer. Now here is where people's
   laundry systems often break down—you take the dry laundry and
   put it in a pile. That's it. You think, "I'm done." You're not, you've
   only gone halfway.

3. As you pull the clothes out of the dryer, iron what needs to be ironed. Ironing goes quickly when the clothes are freshly dried.
4. Fold the clothes.
5. Put the clothes back in the closet and drawers.

Your laundry system needs to include this last step of putting clothes back in drawers and closets, towels and sheets back in the linen closet. Make your system work within your life patterns and values. Lynn folded her laundry during her special TV shows. Matt got a headset phone and folded laundry while he spoke to his friends on the phone. Evelyn decided that laundry folding would suffice as her meditation time. She lit a candle and paid attention to her breath and her body, and she folded peacefully. Each of them then made sure to put the clean clothes away.

As good as your system is, it is only as good as your habits. Your new habit includes thinking, "I am not done with the laundry until all the laundry is put away," rather than "Why waste my time folding and putting things away when I can find them in this pile?" A good system is backed up by thoughts and beliefs that help you drive the new system. If the next step in your laundry system is to set aside time for folding and putting it away, think, "Folding and putting the laundry away helps me create sanity and saves me time. The time I take now to fold and put away laundry saves me double the time I waste later, when I am searching for clean, unwrinkled clothes or towels or rewash clothes because I can't tell which ones are clean."

A User-Friendly Bill-Paying System

1. Whenever your bills come in, put them in one pile for current bills only.
2. Set up a biweekly time to take bills out of the envelopes.
3. Take out your checkbook and pay the bills.
4. Print "Paid" on the paid bills.
5. Put all paid bill receipts in a box under your desk. You can sort these into categories immediately, or keep them in a box and sort them once a year for tax purposes.

Getting Through Your E-mail

1. Schedule a specific time to check your e-mail. For most people, two or three times a day is enough.
2. Immediately discard all impersonal, irrelevant messages. Discipline yourself—don't read them unless they are meant for you personally. If you have been copied on a large mailing, check to make sure it is relevant to you before you start reading and reacting. Reacting to situations that are out of your control can take up a lot of time and waste a lot of energy.
3. Briefly answer messages that require an immediate response. Then immediately discard the intial message.
4. Put all information-related e-mails into folders that you have created for that purpose. In Microsoft Outlook, you can set up folders for categories of e-mail that you do want to keep.
5. Keep only alive messages in your in-box.
6. Allocate time daily or weekly to deal with complex responses.
7. Empty your in-box every week, say, Friday afternoon. Do not collect e-mail messages in your in-box for weeks at a time.
8. Do not use e-mail for emotional correspondence. If a misunderstanding has taken place, schedule a face-to-face meeting or get on the phone. E-mail arguments tend to be huge time wasters. If you write a hasty irritated response to an annoying e-mail, don't send it. Wait! Jobs have been lost because of emotional electronic correspondence.

Remember that every time you are trying to get organized you need to get to ready, build a new system, and practice a new habit. These are the basics. You'll get better and better at this over time. You'll master a few habits, and then you'll go on to more. This is not an infinite task. Remember, being organized frees you to become the interesting, creative person you know you truly are inside.

■ ■ ■ EXERCISE ■ ■ ■

Part 1: Take a few minutes to review some of the systems that you are using in your home and work life. Even if it seems as if you have a random "no system," you must be doing something to arrive at your current results. Are your systems effective? Use the Guidelines for Effective Organizing Systems above to evaluate some of the organizing systems that you currently use.

Part 2: Choose one area where you'd like to create or improve an organizing system. Remember, it does not have to be large. Following the guidelines on page 110, create and implement a workable system for some aspect of your life.

■ ■ ■

Value Life Maintenance

Our habits and our systems are about life maintenance. According to Harriet Schechter's *Conquering Chaos at Work*, Michael Eisner, CEO of the Walt Disney Company and one of the highest-paid executives in the world, spends 75 percent of his time on maintenance tasks, including returning phone calls and keeping his desk clear, so that he can concentrate on the more creative work that he has to do. Note how much time you spend on all the small things you need to do to just keep your life together: paying bills, returning phone calls, answering e-mails, putting the laundry away, doing the dishes, repairing clothing and appliances, running errands to the pharmacy and the dry cleaner, picking up the groceries. These are not extras; these are the stuff of daily life. How can we possibly value these nitpicky, uninteresting, repetitive, uncreative, boring aspects of life? These are the things that when we don't do them, make our lives pretty miserable, pretty quickly So, let's start to look at them another way.

What happens to our lives when we don't do basic maintenance? Things start to fall apart: checks bounce, there are no clothes to wear, our home or office starts to be unpleasant, our appliances don't work. Maintenance is like oil in an engine. It enables all the various parts to work together. When the engine starts pouring smoke, you have to stop the car, no matter where you are, and take care of the problem. So planned maintenance helps you keep moving on your journey.

We have to learn to value maintenance tasks whether for their outcome or for the opportunity they allow us to increase our awareness and gratitude. First of all, keep in mind what the doing of the task will bring you. Doing dishes brings you a chance to serve the next meal. Paying bills brings you a good credit rating and peace of mind. Polishing your shoes makes you presentable and helps the leather endure. Maintenance tasks are excellent for spiritual practice. The Findhorn Community in Scotland is a group of people who are seeking to live in a more intentional, holy way who have developed methods of making their work sacred. One member who works in the dining hall explains that "before every work shift, we sit down, we light a candle, we check in with ourselves and each other, and acknowledge that we are whole people. This is key to being totally present and it has deepened my appreciation for the details. I can do each task with care."

Part of life is learning to do what needs to be done to maintain the very life you want. You probably have good reasons not to take care of things. But the challenge is that messes and breakdowns accumulate quickly. Then, what was an ordinary everyday task becomes a daunting mess. You need to think ahead and plan for the maintenance your life requires. As you implement this practice, keep in mind that your basic maintenance tasks need to include the following:

- Grocery shopping, cooking, and clearing up
- Laundry, dry cleaning, and clothing and shoe repair
- Personal hygiene, washing, tooth brushing
- Paying bills
- Paying attention to bank statements and other financial matters
- Car maintenance, including inspections and up-to-date car insurance
- Running errands—stocking medication and personal supplies
- Straightening up—the beds, tables, hanging up loose items
- Housecleaning
- Social and leisure planning
- Clearing off your desk
- Returning phone calls
- Medical and dental care
- Other personal care, including hair care
- Seasonal tasks in Northern climates—getting out and putting away clothes, boots, snow shovels, lawn furniture, hoses, etc.

Listed like this, it looks as if "maintenance" takes a lot of time. But when you pay attention to these aspects of your life, you will feel so much better in your "creative" moments. Ironically, Cheryl Richardson's very popular and valuable book *Take Time for Your Life* is largely about maintenance tasks. As you look around, you'll see that finding your own good reasons to cherish maintenance tasks and knowing what you need to make your life possible will also make it more livable and pleasurable.

■ ■ ■ EXERCISE ■ ■ ■

Take out your calendar and actually schedule in your maintenance time. During that time do things like return phone calls, open and read your mail, clear out your e-mail in-box, set up meetings, and put things away on your desk. Also use this time to arrange and schedule your major maintenance tasks, such as doctors' appointments or car inspections, so that you don't have to scramble to get them done at the last minute. This is not wasted time. You are doing the essentials when you are doing maintenance. If you find yourself resisting this process, tell yourself that you are taking care of details in ways that will enhance your life. And you will save time, money, and stress by reducing the amount of scrambling, reworking, paying overdue bills, reinstalling your phone service, or long conversations with people about why you didn't return their phone calls.

■ ■ ■

Now we'll take a deeper look at the challenge of managing our possessions.

7

Things: We Own Them,
They Don't Own Us

How do we become more skillful in our relationship to things? Much of our lives is spent purchasing, returning, taking care of, cleaning, putting away, moving, and getting rid of things. We acquire possessions through purchase, gifts, and inheritance. Once we are owners, possessions demand a large portion of our life energy. What do we do with the things we no longer use and the things that belonged to the people we loved dearly? Our choices about possessions shape our lives.

Most of us experience a complex range of intense emotions toward possessions. As Americans, we are trained consumers. We often purchase with mixed feelings, however. We know we have too much stuff. At the same time, we often feel, in fact are conditioned to feel, that we don't have enough.

Gaining a deeper understanding of your relationship to the material world can enhance your enjoyment of the things you have. It helps to recognize that you're conditioned to want more things. Unquenchable desires power our economy. An American Buddhist teacher, Sharon Salzberg, tells a story about a friend who said that when she was learning to talk, her favorite phrases were: "I need it! I want it! I have to have it!" For many of us, this is an ongoing mantra of our lives. Understanding both the will to own and the impact of owning can free us to let go of things we no longer want or need.

Desire does not by its nature have to become greed. It is a life force propelling us to move toward people, experiences, and things that we want. One great challenge of desire, however, is that it can slip into greed very easily. Greed is a passion that can blind us to reality and our true needs. Then, we might find that we are making huge decisions about our lives in order to fulfill our greed. Working skillfully with desire means learning to distinguish between need and greed, and learning to hold our desires more lightly, not take them quite so seriously.

We can use our possessions artfully to create places and spaces that nourish us. Traditionally, possessions represented years of savings and were passed on through generations. Yet, because we have become accustomed to the disposable nature of most things, we are less aware of how profoundly our possessions can shape our environment. Working skillfully with our possessions means that we can derive great benefit from each thing that we have and let go of the rest.

Pause Before You Purchase

One way to handle the overload of possessions is to keep things from coming through the door. "But I want things! Things make me happy," we say. We all know that it's true up to a point. Your fifteenth special memento T-shirt probably makes you happy for about a day, then it goes on a pile with fourteen others. On TV, radio, the Internet, and in magazines, we are offered pictures of how good things could be if only we purchased something. Americans consume an enormous amount of the world's resources, and there is no sign of diminishing demand. In fact, we are exporting our consumer-oriented lifestyle around the world.

What does this have to do with us? Even the prudent among us participate in overconsumption. There is a personal price to this. When our own desires for things are out of proportion to actual need, we cease to enjoy them as much. Then, old unused things collect. Even new unused things collect. Elizabeth's experience is not uncommon: "I'll go to the mall and see all kinds of things I think I need, and then I get them home and leave them unpacked in the corner of the living room. I don't have time to unpack them, let alone put them away. Later, I look at them and wonder what I was thinking. I don't really need this stuff. I have lost the receipts and now I'm stuck with things that I have no room for after all."

Does this mean no more shopping fun? No, it doesn't. You can still enjoy the sensuous pleasures of shopping, of choosing the colors and the textures. But shop with the awareness that it's just not fun to be snowed under by belongings. It's not economical or ecological to throw good products away when they aren't fully used. Buy fewer things of better quality. Truly savor the things you buy. Use them well. Allow them to shape your beautiful space.

Pausing before you purchase also means taking time to examine your underlying beliefs—beliefs about money and purchasing. We buy to look good. We shop to assuage hurt feelings. We spend our money to cover our fears. Take some time to sit with the anxiety of buying less. Mark said, "I go to the mall every week to check out the electronics. Most of the time I come back with something new. But I often don't open it. Sometimes I forget what I bought the week before, and I discover that I have two now. I decided to skip the mall run for a month to see what happened. A month seemed like a very long time. But I learned something. I realized that I go for the glamour and the sense of power that electronics seem to give me." Most of us have an area or two of buying addictions. It might be sports equipment, clothes, books, CDs, tools, or makeup.

As you take this challenge, you open a rich realm of learning about what's beneath the addiction. What are you covering up? What are you really longing for? When you give up an addiction, you can start to get what you really need. Go back to your vision of what you want in life, and slow down when you are buying things. Less is more. Buy something only if you absolutely love it, if it's been on your list for several weeks, and if you are sure that you have a place for it. Otherwise, let it go. Think of all those things that you thought you really wanted that you are now putting in the "give-away pile."

Tools to Help You Pause Before You Purchase

- Shop from a list. Remember, *you will want more than you need.* Wait a couple of days or a week before you buy something that seems very compelling. In a week, you may have forgotten about it. Buy it if it's been on your list for several weeks.
- Buy it only if you really love it, not sort of love it.
- Buy it only if you have a place for it. Whether you are buying clothes, toys, books, tools, or kitchen equipment, remind yourself that everything you bring into your home or office needs a place. It's best to identify the place for this purchase beforehand. If you don't have space for it, either don't buy it or choose something else to get rid of.
- Make a list of things that you really want but think you can't afford. Include a special vacation or a beautiful piece of artwork. Perhaps you want to take a workshop or course.
- Keep that list with you when you shop.
- Put the money you don't spend on the clothes or equipment that you don't really need into a savings account. Save the money for something that you really want.
- Get skillful at comparing the allure of the new thing with the piles of unused belongings in your house.
- Examine your beliefs about ownership. What does ownership mean to you?

Create an "Alive" Place for Everything

Once you bring things home, you have to put them somewhere. This is where your new aesthetic comes to life. All the organizing advice supports the traditional wisdom: "A place for everything and everything in its place." I used to think that was a terrible idea. It was so routine and uncreative. Finally, though, after many years of looking for misplaced items, I could admit that this practice helped me find my keys, shoes, and sunglasses, because I had learned to put objects back when I was done using them.

Finding an "alive" place for everything takes this idea one step farther. It means making sure that the things you own are in use. It means that when they are in place, they are in place for a purpose. The purpose may be aesthetic or sentimental, but the things have a specific meaning. When everything you own is actually in use in this sense, your office or house comes alive. You don't feel the deadweight of unused things around you.

Creating an alive environment around you enhances your own daily energy. As you think about finding alive spaces for your possessions, you'll begin to see which things have a purpose and which drain your energy. You'll realize that the twenty bottles of shampoo and conditioner on the shelves in the tub can be reduced to eight and then to two. The suit you have not worn for three years is no longer "alive" for you. You don't like it. You're not going to wear it. It could be alive for someone else, though, if you gave it away. Those training manuals from ten years ago are useless to you. You're not using them. They are creating dead space.

The harder questions may concern your twenty beautiful vases, bowls, artwork, special books—some perhaps were presents, while others you picked up traveling. They take up space, and chances are you don't use all of them. Start to prune them. Let go. You'll start to feel better and better as you are using the things you have rather than using your home as a storage facility.

An "alive" place for everything means that you store the things that you use frequently within easy reach. You have enough to meet your needs, but not too much. You love or use the things that you have. The energy in your home will feel fresh when you live like this because you are not maintaining unused, unappreciated items. When the things around you are in use, you have a sense of true elegance, a sense of fit between yourself, your things, and your environment. You are in relationship to the things you have. They become special because you are living your life with them

■ ■ ■ EXERCISE ■ ■ ■

The unused things in your space are like energy leaks. In *Clear Your Clutter with Feng Shui*, Karen Kingston suggests that you ask three questions about the things that you own:

1. Does it lift my energy when I think about it or look at it?
2. Do I absolutely love it?
3. Is it genuinely useful and do I use it?

Set aside a short amount of time, say ten minutes. Walk around a room in your home or try this in your office. Look at five items in your space and ask the three questions about each one. Kingston says, "If the answer is not a resounding yes to question 1, and an equally resounding yes to either question 2 or 3, then what is it doing in your life?" Let it go.

If you decide to keep it, now ask, "Is it in a place where I can access it easily?" If not, find a better place for it. Sometimes finding a better place for something means creating that space. Papers tend to be more useful and aesthetic when placed in file drawers. Books also benefit from being stored in bookshelves rather than on floors and other surfaces. After you decide what you want to keep, make sure you have sufficient, attractive space to store it.

■ ■ ■

Love What You Own

As you clear away your clutter and excess possessions, you start to discover some spaciousness in your home and workplace. You are creating space through letting go. Now, perhaps you have fewer things. The less you have, the more that the things you own can truly enhance your life through their beauty and usefulness. When we truly appreciate our things, we get much more satisfaction from them. Then, in turn, we need fewer things. Our possessions can bring us art, beauty, knowledge, utility, and pleasure.

As you let go of what you don't need, your true treasures can emerge. Recently, Deborah went on a search through her house for a special pair of shoes that she loves. "These are from Italy, and I love them, but I have so many pairs of shoes that I completely forgot about them for a while. Last year, I found them in their shoebox at the top of a closet. They are my favorite shoes, but I barely wear them."

Holding on to things can be a way of connecting to your history. You might have heard stories from people about a particular chair or a table, and how their grandfather carried that special table across the country. Or how this beautiful set of dishes belonged to "your great-grandmother in Hungary." And these things evoke our families and our past. Something extraordinary can happen when the spirits of our forebears join with us in our own present-day lives. They are treasures.

Slowly over time, you can fill your spaces with things that have special meaning for you. These items help tell your story. In Hebrew, the word for "thing" and "word" is the same. Thus, our things could be our words, and our words are part of our story. Loving your things helps you tell your story. Your special treasures then contribute to a place to live that is alive with meaning for you. Your things contribute to what we could call your landscape, and your personal landscape influences how you experience life. If your environment is meager in meaning, you'll experience that meagerness in your soul. When your environment is rich in meaning, not overfull of possessions, you'll feel that richness in your soul as well.

■ ■ ■ EXERCISE ■ ■ ■

Select one of your favorite possessions. If it is small, take it in your hands. If it is large, such as a piece of furniture, sit on or near it. Now, tell the story. You can tell the story to yourself, a child, a friend, or write it in your journal. Notice how much a treasured possession can enrich your life. Now notice the difference between this and something that is not important to you.

■ ■ ■

Care for the Possessions You Decide to Keep

Caring for your things is a practice of seeing life energy, or God, or the Buddha, in everything. Things themselves have energy. When we treat our belongings with care, we become aware that the caring energy returns to us. Our personal environment reflects a high quality of consciousness. How you care for your things is a way of caring for the self.

There are several ways to care for possessions. Some of them are purely technical, such as keeping them repaired. Others are aesthetic, such as ironing shirts or tablecloths. Or it extends the life of an object, such as oiling wood and leather. Each type of care is time-consuming and can be valuable. I remember a time when at about ten o'clock at night, I was wiping off the dining table. I thought, "I hate this. Why do I always have to be the one who clears off the dining table?" Suddenly, I noticed the grain of the wood. And I started actually looking at the table. The grain was beautiful, and I noticed that looking at it made me feel peaceful. I thought, "I am revealing beauty" I realized that, in caring for the table, I was also caring for myself and my husband. I not only suddenly felt relaxed, but I took care of the task much more quickly. I was not wasting time, I was doing something worthwhile. My resentful thoughts were brakes on the activity. Now I could set those aside.

Caring for the things you have is a special category of "valuing maintenance time" which you read about in chapter 5. When we take care of our belongings, not obsessively, but with an attitude of appreciation, we bring a sense of care to our homes. When you are wiping down the table, making the bed, or washing the tub, try doing so in a spirit of caring. Appreciate your blessings and your possessions as you give them the care they need. Think about this teaching that comes from the intentional community of Findhorn: "You can do it positively and really enjoy seeing a lovely shine come up as you rub, or you can do it negatively and just feel it is another job that must be done. When you start on a job, whatever it may be, see that your attitude toward it is right, and how very different an experience you will have. Your attitude makes it one thing or the other."

Determined Discarding

Determined discarding takes the actions of moving belongings out of your house seriously. You might have begun this work in chapter 6. Now you can take it farther. Create standards for your determination. Whether you are clearing office files, computer disks, bookshelves, or closets, apply these principles. You will get rid of something if:

- You haven't used it for a year.
- You don't actually *require* it for record-keeping.
- You don't *love* it (just liking it isn't enough) or think it is beautiful.

■ It doesn't have deep significance for you (not a little nostalgia but deep significance).

Alternatively you might set standards for being very discriminating. I find it much easier to look for the few things that I will keep rather than identify what I have to let go of. It's a completely different experience to identify and keep the things that:

■ You use regularly.
■ You require for bookkeeping.
■ You love or think are beautiful.
■ Have deep meaning for you.

Deborah decided to keep only the clothes that she loved and felt great in. If she had passed up an outfit for a whole year, it would go out—even if it was cute and she only had to lose ten pounds to fit into it. At the end, she had a closet full of great clothes, and none of the things that made her feel bad, fat, or ugly. She had a self-acceptance closet. When she opened it, she felt great.

Create a memory box for storing a few things that still release a flood of special memories. Keep a few of your treasures, just not all of them. A small carton, basket, or small suitcase could be enough for your special things.

Kimberley used her move overseas for a year to discard as much as she could. "When we were packing, I would load up the car every week and bring a load to the Salvation Army bin. When we were finally ready to leave, there was nothing extra upstairs. It is now beautifully and simply furnished. I had given most things away, and what is left is in the basement. I felt unencumbered. The house felt light. Now, I think, when I come back, I don't want to bring anything up from the basement. I like this feeling of freedom."

Notice that when you keep things, you have to deal with them. Instead of doing something that you love, you will be sorting through paperwork and unused belongings. You'll be moving them, trying to organize them, cleaning them, figuring out where to store them—and you won't be doing what is important to you. So, watch how you talk to yourself, when discarding, the unnecessary things you keep will come back to haunt you.

Sometimes, we hold on to things to avoid the grief of acknowledging that we are at a crossroads. When we let go, we are forced to recognize that we have made a choice, that we can't do everything in life. We are always making choices, letting go of the path that we won't follow. That is the nature of life. Keeping our possessions is often a way of trying to keep our many choices alive. We think, "I still can go that route. I still have the things that allow me to take that path." We do this with our size-six clothes, or our notes from the botany class that we loved. We still mean to take nature walks and pull out our notes. And, yet, years go by and we haven't looked at them once. So what is going on here? If we keep those notes, we can imagine that we are still interested in botany. But we never touch them. So, is it botany that we are interested in? Or is it retaining the memory of a wonderful teacher? Or do we want the feel of earth on our hands as we work in the garden? Or was it those moments of pure curiosity that we loved, the pure exploration of something new?

When you look more deeply to see what it is that you are wanting when you keep these things, you may find something pure and inspiring. The botany notes may mean that you want to plant a tray full of geraniums, and to dive into the earth, and you can do this as well as let go of the notes. Can you see how keeping all the options alive can deaden your current life? There's too much swirling around in you. It's hard to focus. Yet, as you make those hard choices, you might have to grieve. And yet you can free parts of yourself that linger, undeveloped, giving you a chance to follow up on what you really desire instead of simply maintaining all that old stuff.

■ ■ ■ EXERCISE ■ ■ ■

You can do this exercise by imagining a specific pile, mess, or drawer in detail. Alternatively, approach the actual mess and find a place to sit facing it or, if it is a very messy area or room, in it.

Feel your way into this messy spot. What does it feel like? Where is the feeling in your body? Allow yourself to stay with that feeling in your body and explore where you learned to feel this way. How do you feel about the backlog?

Write about those feelings.

Now notice that you created it. You are the source of this. You are the king or queen of the backlog. It's yours. Write about creating the mess. Own it. Revel in it perhaps.

Now imagine that the backlog is gone. Imagine life without your piles and excess. All the mess is gone, you can see the floors, desk, couch, dining table. You have a lot more space. Your calendar is manageable. You feel exhilarated each day because you are doing enough, and no more than you can do. Your surfaces are clear, your mind is clear, your heart is open. From this place, write about what your backlog has been doing for you. As you write, consider the following benefits.

- Protecting
- Isolating
- Keeping you from what you really want
- Keeping you at home
- Keeping you out of the house
- Keeping you close to someone
- Keeping you far away from someone
- Covering anxiety
- Keeping you from feeling your loneliness
- Keeping you from feeling your feelings
- Keeping your inner critic alive and close to you
- Helping you be like someone you love

Once you have identified a benefit of the mess, ask yourself if this benefit is what you really want. And, if so, is maintaining your backlog the best way to get it? Explore whether there are other ways to get this benefit and give up your backlog.

■ ■ ■

The Special Case of Sorting and Discarding Piles of Paper

Here is what some people say as they try to sort through their backlog of paper.

"I just get close to my pile, and I start to get confused. I could have been having a great day, and I can ruin it by sorting piles."

"Every time I try to sort out my pile, it seems that I create almost exactly the same pile next to it. I can't seem to get anywhere."

"I get bogged down so easily. I find myself reading through catalogs or old unsent letters. Or I get hung up on these outdated refund checks that I thought I had lost. I don't know what to do with them. Can they be reissued?"

Do these comments about those plaguing piles of paper sound familiar? The fact is, sorting piles is one of the great challenges of getting organized. The problem is that most of us re-create our piles over and over again rather than diminishing and then getting rid of them. Remember, if you go through the same thinking when you first created that pile, you will re-create the same pile. The trick is to think different thoughts than those that you were thinking when you created it.

Your old way of sorting piles might have included thinking like: "I don't know where this [insurance form, bank statement, invoice] goes, so I'll put it here until I figure it out." Or you might think, "I don't know if I want to engage in this activity [theater, lessons, community group] . . ." Or "I'll probably need this information for something, but I am not sure what, so I'll leave it here in case I need it."

You can begin to see that your pile is a collection of unmade decisions, a pile of confusion, emotional stuckness, and perhaps insecurity. In order to get rid of your pile, you need to be thinking thoughts such as:

- "I am going to take the time right now to figure this out."
- "I am going to create a folder for bank statements right now."
- "This is confusing. I'll call and get help, now."
- "It is important to completely deal with this item."
- "I'll make this decision now. Even if it is not perfect, it's done."
- "The faster I completely work through this pile, the sooner I can get out and do something that I love. I deserve that."

One of the challenges for imaginative people is that they can think of lots of things to do with some of the papers in their piles: send it to someone, write an essay about it, use it as an idea for an event they might want to hold someday, save it for later, or create a new file for it (but they are not sure what file). The whole time that you are sorting piles remind yourself to use your creativity to *get through* the sorting, not make the sorting more complicated. Do not sit in a comfortable chair rereading old letters, and don't interpret why it is amazing that you found this item now. Recognize that your piles of papers may include a wide range of items that are unrelated to each other, and be prepared to think about many different things one after the other. That takes creativity and flexibility of mind.

Once you have prepared yourself to think differently about the task ahead, you are ready to begin sorting through a paper pile.

1. **Set a short time limit.** Twenty minutes of real sorting is much more effective than an hour of horsing around, getting distracted, depressed, or bogged down. Use a timer. Set your timer for ten minutes. And then set it for ten minutes more. This will help you stay aware of time. Then, reset the timer if you have the energy to continue.

2. **Consciously energize yourself.** Remind yourself of your purpose and vision. Put on good music with a beat. Tell yourself that this is a moment of truth. You are a clutter warrior. Pull out your sword of clarity and sort.

3. **Remind yourself of your purpose in sorting the pile.** You are looking for current financial papers, you need current health records, you might want to keep a few letters. Everything that you do not need goes out. Be ruthlessly realistic. This is the path to your vision.

4. **Take a short stack of papers:** no more than an inch high away from the main pile. Now, your energy is bigger than the pile. You can handle an inch of paper.

5. **Take care of each item completely.** Either file it, take action on it, delegate it, or throw it away. *Do not put it in another pile because you don't know what to do with it.* This is the time to find out. Even if you spend the whole twenty minutes trying to figure out what to do with it, take the time. Then it's over.

Your pile may be full of things that have nothing to do with each other. You might find a fifteen-year-old article, or an uncashed check, dated 1993, a letter from a colleague that you never answered, and then some old insurance forms that you thought you had lost. Aauugh!!! As Charlie Brown would say.

Libby said, "I have checks that are refund checks. They expired 12/15/00 and it is now 1/15/01. I just don't know if they are valid are not, so I don't know what to do.

This is a perfect time to call someone up, and say, I have three items that I don't know what to do with. She might say, "I don't know either, but let's think of someone whom you can ask. You might say, "I got this refund check for $7.00, I didn't put it into the bank soon enough, and now it has expired." You can say, "I forgive myself." You can replace the check or you can give yourself a $7.00 gift. It could be worth $7.00 to you to practice letting go of this. In fact, you could pay $100.00 even $200.00 for a workshop on letting go and getting perspective and here you are paying only $7.00 for this exercise. Now—remember this and use this memory as a way to help yourself get the check into the bank next time.

When Frank, a senior marketing executive, got bogged down in his e-mail backlog, he used the same tools. He would not open his in-box until he had established that he was an e-mail samurai. He was focused, mighty, and swift. Sometimes he even felt tough, most unlike him, but it helped him set boundaries and blast through his e-mail mountain. That image worked for him. He wouldn't even try to get through his in-box if he was on the run; rather, when he had ten minutes or more he would ground himself in his vision, his purpose, and his warrior stance.

The Special Case of Discarding Our Deceased Parents' Belongings

When our parents die, we often have to deal both with losing them and letting go of their possessions, which can represent a whole world to us. This is a sad topic; letting go of the beautiful shoes and dresses that were worn by a beloved mother, the books she loved, the cherished coffee cup, or the special casserole dish, can be painful. Pick a few special things that remind you of her essence. Pick out the china or the necklace that have value to you, and let the rest go. All those belongings won't bring your Mom back. Giving or throwing them away does not make you a bad person. It doesn't mean that you didn't love her. It just means that you can distinguish between things and feelings and that is good.

Sandra's parents had passed away and she had thirty-five boxes of their belongings in the basement. She had no idea what to do next. She had no need for the things, yet she was reluctant to just give it all to the Salvation Army. That seemed disrespectful of her parents' well-lived lives. In addition, when she opened the boxes, she was overwhelmed by the sense of an era that had passed, that would never come again, and she grieved anew, not just for her parents, but for herself as well. "I open those boxes and I feel like an orphan. Then, I just can't do anything. I am paralyzed with grief, longing, memories."

She decided to hold a special ritual for letting go of her parents' belongings. She wanted to create an event that was special, respectful, and honoring of her parents and of her need to move on. She found an organization for the homeless that desperately needed the things that she could not use. She selected a few things to keep that really mattered to her, that would represent her parents. She wrote a letter to her parents describing the special things that she had with her. She invited two good friends to witness the letting go of her parents' belongings, and in tears, she watched as the volunteers picked up the things.

She almost said, "Wait, don't go. I want those things, I can't let them go. It's too hard to say good-bye." She knew that she was weeping for her parents, not for the belongings, but she felt another tearing away, another leaving. Her friends helped her let the things go. Later, she felt that she could claim more of her space and her life, and she created a practice of communicating with her deceased parents once a week to keep them updated on her life.

Practicing the Wisdom of Things

Mastering the wisdom of things in a consumer society can be as powerful as mastering a martial art. Take it seriously and you will be well rewarded. You will develop your character by affirming what you truly want and need, and saying no to the rest. You will develop a sense of your limits, deepen your knowledge of who you are, and enjoy the courage of not getting too caught up in limitless desire. This is the power of organizing as a journey. You can use your developing skill with possessions—very concrete and physical—to master some of the inner qualities that help make your purpose for organizing meaningful to you.

8

Master Your Time and Your Tasks

J ust as we can cultivate a wisdom of things, we can cultivate a wisdom of time. We can get better and better at knowing what we can and can't do. A friend of mine tells me that she rarely feels rushed, almost never feels squeezed. She has an important job, travels overseas for work, has a husband and child, friends and extended family. "How do you do it?" I asked. "I hate to feel overwhelmed," she said. "I plan my life so that I experience as little overwhelm as possible. My priorities are work and family right now. That will change as my daughter grows up, but I know what is important."

Many of us schedule our time as if overwhelm were a requirement for modern living. Some people like to be overwhelmed, some not. Part of developing the wisdom of time and tasks is deepening your understanding of your preferences, rhythms, and cycles. You begin to get a sense of what the appropriate rhythms in your life are, both temporally and physically. You can think about the rhythm around a task—beginning a task, being engaged in the task, and then completing it. There's also a rhythm about the tasks of the day—beginning a day, engaging in the day's work, and ending the day. You can become more aware of what times are appropriate for what tasks for you. Some people are buoyant early risers and love to take action first thing. Some people really wake up in the evening and find their best energy at night. There's a weekly rhythm, as well. Know your own rhythm and relate it to what you have to do. Know what kind of energy you need for each kind of activity. Become a better judge of what kind of energy is good for what kinds of tasks. You'll know your own body's energy better over time.

You may begin to notice that "hurrying" and "moving very quickly" are two different experiences. Hurrying can, paradoxically, slow you down because in your rush, you start to get clumsy and forget things. On the other hand, moving quickly increases your focus. You can become more centered as you learn how your actions take place in time. You become much clearer about what you really can and cannot do. You bring more awareness to your life.

It's also extremely helpful to learn the basic approaches to time that are covered in the next five sections. These will help you develop your own aesthetic of time.

Match Your Energy to the Whole Task

What is a "whole task"? It is one that leaves no wake. When you complete it, you are back to ready. By contrast, incomplete tasks leave loose ends that we have to face later. Many of us are great at starting tasks with a surge of energy, but then we lose momentum or interest before finishing the task. Sometimes, we are not even aware that we aren't finished, yet we feel that the task is "done." When I write a letter on my computer, for example, I often feel a sense of completion when I finish writing—even though the letter is still sitting in the computer. (I wrote the letter, didn't I?) Sometimes, I'll print it out and then forget to put it in an envelope. I often feel that bill paying is "done" when I sort the bills into piles. I have felt "done" when I get out of the shower, dry myself off, and drop the towel on the floor. Sometimes I feel "done" when I look up a number in the phone book and then leave the book out on the table. I let my energy drop before the whole task is done.

Matching energy to the whole task means internally allocating enough energy to actually complete the task. To do this, you need to be aware of the full scope of the task and learn to feel finished only when the whole task is truly done—down to the last loose end.

All tasks have three phases:

1. Preparation
2. Implementation
3. Completion

Whether the phases last a minute or several hours, they each have their own rhythm. Preparation is always about setting something up. Implementation is the action itself. Completion is putting things away and attending to the details of finishing. It's about closure. Once you experience the whole task as including all three phases, you see that completing a whole task now is easier than coming back to finish it later, because it lets you follow momentum. Leaving a task incomplete, by contrast, takes extra energy because, when you come back later to finish the loose ends, you have to take on the hard work of refocusing.

What's the whole task of writing a memo? Reading e-mail? Planning a business trip? Going for a job interview? Shopping for groceries? Making a cup of tea? Some whole tasks are more complex than we think. Grocery shopping includes making the list, selecting the items, paying for your purchases, putting the food away. I used to allow for enough energy to get the groceries into the car, and sometimes into the house, but often I would forget that I wasn't done until everything was put away. This tendency led to more than my share of melted quarts of ice cream.

Valuing preparation time does not come easily, but it is essential. This lesson, that creating a strong foundation for action is as important as the action itself, is vital. Artists know this as much as anyone else. For painters, much time is spent in caring for brushes and organizing colors. Chefs spend their time in selecting fine ingredients, setting them up, and cleaning the space for food preparation. Dancers warm up. Yet, even the most minor of setup time gets howls of internal protest from disorganized people.

So, how can you value preparation time when you are just terribly bored by setup and cleanup? Perhaps you can learn to value preparation by noticing the price you pay when you plunge into action without getting ready. What is it like for you to try to take action with clutter scattered around you? Perhaps you could say to yourself something like: "In order to accomplish this task, I need to be able to focus. It's hard for me to focus when I am not sure which bills I have paid, or if there are papers scattered about." Use your frustration when you can't find what you need to reinforce the value of preparation for concentration and focus.

Completion is as essential as preparation time. It allows you a sense of accomplishment and closure. Completion includes putting everything away, which in turn helps ease preparation. When you finish the day, take the time to put things back and savor the day's work. As you put the last dish in the dishwasher, consider taking a split second to say, "Ahhh . . . that's done, and I feel good about it," even if you have to rush on to the next thing. Give yourself little cues When you've cleared the clutter and newspapers off the dining table, admire the spaciousness for a moment. When you finally get the bills all paid, take a moment to appreciate that you have done something difficult. After a while, it gets easier to complete things.

Marjorie noted, "I have to say that I don't like putting things away. I don't like finishing things. I just don't. I love to keep my options open. I like the rushing around; I don't mind leaving a shambles in my wake. However, I also strongly dislike dealing with leftover work—work that I should have completed yesterday, but didn't for so many reasons. I also don't like loose papers lying around the floor or desk. What to do? In my judgment, it was worth clearing up at the end of the day. I try to end my work a little early to put things away. I have come to appreciate closure because it enables me to open to the next activity.

"Sometimes I play my favorite music as I am putting away a writing project or filing notes at the end of the day. I learned that I have to discipline myself to complete things. It is not my nature, but I am learning to appreciate a true sense of 'doneness' when I am done. And I love starting fresh in the morning."

There's another aspect of completion that Larry Rosenberg, a Buddhist master, describes as "a certain joy at being able to finish something, to do it effectively. You know the feeling from other aspects of your life—some art form you've mastered, or a meal you cooked particularly well, even a simple household task. It's the feeling of taking something from the beginning through the middle to the end, thoroughly applying yourself and coming through it."

Charles noticed that he tended to avoid completion and carry his work around with him. Even though it felt awful to carry his work around with him, he had trouble leaving it at his office. He experimented with completion one evening. "I was at work late. I still had some paperwork to do, and I wanted to get home. Normally, I would take the paperwork home in my briefcase, telling myself that I would do it after dinner. Then I wouldn't do it, and I would feel burdened by it all night. But this time I thought, 'If I stay here and do this now, really focus, I can get the major part done in twenty-five minutes.' I didn't rush, I got it done, and then I had a more relaxed evening."

One way that many of us have handled our aversion to completion is to start something new. Then we have lots of new projects, along with many that we haven't finished. One trick that can help with this tendency is to start a new project *and* consciously leave time to finish the old one, which can help with the sense of loss you may feel at having to move on. So you can start something new *and* finish a prior project in the same time period.

Marshaling your energy to match the whole task means that it will be much easier for you to come to completion and to move on to the next thing. Allow yourself to enjoy completions. As you come to the end of a task, say to yourself, "There, that's done. Good." And then keep going.

Learn How Much Time Things Take

We have highly flexible minds, so it's easy to imagine that things take less time than they really do. We often tell ourselves, "This conversation will only take a few minutes." "I can eat my lunch in ten." "I can put the groceries away in five." When we imagine that things take less time than they do, we leave loose ends or run late. Learning how much time things take can help you match your energy to the whole task. Diane's seven-year-old daughter was always late to school partly because Diane just couldn't believe that it took more than an hour for them both to get up, get dressed, have breakfast, make lunch, and leave the house. But that's how long it always took.

It's also easy to miscalculate time in the other direction and assume that certain tasks take more time than they really do. I was surprised to discover that it took only seconds to replace papers in a file folder or put receipts in an envelope (after all those years of struggle). I was equally surprised to find that it required only about twenty minutes to put everything away at the end of the day and restore a sense of peace to my office. You may neglect to hang your clothes up at the end of the day because you think it would take too long, and you're tired. You might be surprised to learn that folding your sweater and putting it away probably takes just fifteen seconds, and hanging up a skirt or slacks takes another fifteen seconds. Try timing it.

Learning how much time it takes to do common activities is like ending a lifelong argument. You might say, "It shouldn't take that long." And Life says, "But it does take that long." And as it turns out, Life is always right. You can find a sense of relief and peace in recognizing the real nature of time. There is a settling into the real rhythm of real moments. Of course, you can still argue with Life about time and scheduling, but probably with less and less outrage.

▪ ▪ ▪ EXERCISE ▪ ▪ ▪

This is a good way to start getting better time estimates for activities. Pick an activity that you do frequently and also frequently misjudge the time it takes. Then, predict how long it will take. If you are setting out to go to the grocery store and the pharmacy, do you think it will take a half hour? An hour? At the end of the activity, check to see how long it actually took. Try timing the following activities you perform regularly.

- How long does it actually take you to get out the door from the time you get out of bed?
- How long does it takes to do the dishes at night?
- How long does it take to walk to your office from the bus stop, the subway stop, the parking garage?
- How long does it take you to get out of the house starting from when you start putting on your coat, looking for your sunglasses, filling your water bottle, and putting things in your briefcase or handbag?

You will get better and better at time estimates, and this will help you plan your tasks and your day more accurately. When you get an accurate idea of how long things take, you'll be less surprised and become much more astute at making good choices for yourself.

▪ ▪ ▪

Allow for Transition Time

In his book *Time Shifting*, Stephan Rechtschaffan tells this story: An admirer once asked the great pianist Arthur Rubinstein, "How do you handle the notes as well as you do?" He answered, "I handle the notes no better than many others, but the pauses—ah! That is where the art resides." In making music, and in creating a life, what is between the notes is as important as the notes themselves. Transitions between our activities can be as essential as the activities themselves—for in our transitions, we are absorbing, learning, completing, preparing, and moving toward our next activity. Allocating time for transitions declares that the "trans," the moving across, the time between the notes, has value.

Many of us schedule meetings back-to-back. There right in your schedule, you might see "1:00 to 2:00, meet with Cheryl" and "2:00 to 3:30, meet with planning team." You can't do it. This reflects an all-too-common human tendency to forget the importance of transition time. When you schedule meetings or other events without planning for transitions, you end up having to rush to stay on schedule. You also risk being late, struggling to focus once you arrive at an event, or otherwise failing to fulfill your commitments.

Activities end; others begin—all are part of the ceaseless flow of time and events. How transitions take place influences the quality of that flow. Allocating transition time helps you absorb experience and refocus. Daily transitions include:

- Putting things away after you've completed an activity. Look back as you leave a room. Does it look the way you would like it to be when you return?
- Preparing for the next task.
- Traveling from one appointment to another.
- Making a mental shift from one activity to another.
- Refocusing your energy on a new task.
- Allowing for personal needs, bathroom breaks, makeup.
- Taking moments of refreshment—closing your eyes for a few minutes.
- Eating, drinking, and other nourishment can be part of transition time.
- Returning important phone calls that came in during the previous activity.

At the core of transition time is checking in with yourself: Where am I? What did I just experience? What's next? What do I need right now to be present with this situation?

"Backcast" for Ample Transition Time

Backcasting is a tool that lets you work backward from appointments and build in transitional time. For example, if you have to lead a non-profit board meeting at 4:30 in the next town over, you work backward from 4:30 to accurately assess how much time you need to be punctual. In order for you to be seated, sorted out, and ready to lead the meeting at 4:30, you need to be in the parking lot of the nonprofit by 4:20. This means you have to leave your office parking lot at 4:00, which in turn means you need to leave your office at 3:55, which means putting things away at 3:40, and so on. You get the idea. The upshot is that you cannot schedule anything else during the transition time required for you to arrive at the board meeting promptly and in a focused frame of mind.

Before you learn to use backcasting, you might say to yourself, "My board meeting isn't until four-thirty, so I can work until four." You might blithely schedule other meetings for the hours just before the board meeting, and end up racing to make the 4:30 commitment, coming in late, apologizing, and starting with an unpleasant flurry. A powerful shift in creating saner workplaces is to consciously schedule transition time instead of racing from meeting to meeting. People often say that they do not have time for transition time. Remind them that meetings in which people are tired, distracted, confused, and unprepared are usually not that productive.

Write in your transition time when you schedule any meeting. This creates a time buffer in your calendar. It really helps provide a much more realistic picture of your day. So, when you have a 1:00 lunch, write in "12:30—leave for lunch." That allows you ten minutes to file a few things away, check your afternoon schedule, comb your hair, get your coat, and walk out the door by 12:40. You'll be on time, refreshed and ready for this lunch meeting.

Even when you are in your office and could schedule meetings back-to-back, add fifteen minutes to your planning so you can truly finish the meeting. Todd, a financial services provider, said, "I now plan for ten minutes after every client meeting to take notes, put away their material, and add the follow-up items to my to-do list. Instead of extending my meetings with my client (my old way of showing them how much I cared), I close the sessions a little early, and I tell them that I need to take notes and track administrative details. By the end of the day, my office is still in decent shape, and it gives me extra time at the end of the day to wrap things up."

Plan for transition time in your big picture as well. If you are taking a vacation, leave time at either end for getting ready and for unpacking and reentry. Transition time during household moves is also important. Allow for double the time that you think you will need to unpack, then double that again. I include myself among the many people who have lived with unfurnished rooms filled with unpacked boxes because they didn't leave the extra days to unpack, put things away, and make themselves at home. Harry said, "After our last big move, I gave myself three days to unpack. That was excruciatingly unrealistic, and so during this past year, I have wasted hours going through packed boxes and moving them around, because I never took the time to unpack them in the first place. I also hate the way the place looks, so unfinished. Yet, I have trouble allocating the time to unpack; there is always something else I would rather do." Now I have learned for myself that unpacking from a move is a huge project that takes time, extra help, focus, and for me, the goal of a housewarming party at the end.

Allowing for transition time seems expensive to people, yet transition time is just part of life. Learn from your transitions, and you, like Arthur Rubinstein, will have a much better feeling for the music in your life.

■ ■ ■ EXERCISE ■ ■ ■

At the end of each day, make it a practice to take a look at what you have planned for tomorrow. Pull out your calendar and make sure that you have established ample transition time between activities. Notice that you may need to reschedule or curtail certain meetings to incorporate transition time into your plans. At first, it may seem that you are doing less, yet pay attention to your overall energy and effectiveness. Over time, you will be able to do more.

■ ■ ■

Don't Use Lateness to Get Your Adrenaline Rush

There is a thrill in running late, postponing something to the last minute, or meeting a deadline by minutes. If you're in your car, rushing to an appointment, you experience the exhilaration of trying to get through each traffic light. Then, there's also the adventure of trying to maneuver around the inevitable slow-moving car right in front of you. If you're on the highway, there's the challenge of speeding and shaving or putting on your makeup at the same time. And now that you are officially late, there's the drumming up of excuses—that can charge you up, too. Finally, you launch into the inner arguments with your internal critic: "Why can't you ever be on time?" "I tried! I really tried! But I had to take that last phone call!"

This kind of stimulation feels exciting. It gives you the illusion that there is a lot going on, and that you're accomplishing something. It makes you feel that you are making the best use of your time. Because cutting things close is so intense, it can mask other anxieties you may have about deeper issues. When you're running late, you're probably not thinking about why your home life is so strained, whether you are putting adequate money aside for retirement, or how to find a better job that really uses your talents. This addiction to daily intensity can keep you from addressing those deeper issues because you consume all your energy handling the small crises. This doesn't mean that you have to give up stimulation. In fact, seeking other sources of intensity may lead to some real adventures instead of these phony ones.

To rechannel that addictive adrenaline rush, start by noticing how you like to create intensity. Joe, for instance, liked to let his car run on empty. The last sixty miles were a guessing game to see if he would get to a gas station before he ran out. This gave him several good doses of adrenaline in the few days before he gave up and got the tank filled, but for no good purpose. As he started to take better care of his car and pay his mortgage on time, his adrenaline dance could shift to something much more important to him. He began to cultivate the courage to face another demanding and potentially exciting part of his life. He was still single, and while he was terrified about actually looking for a partner, he began to explore what he might need to do to get married.

Eve, on the other hand, recognized that chaos was familiar to her because of growing up in an alcoholic family. "I do little things to make myself run a little late, so that I can ramp up my anxiety to familiar levels. If things are too calm, I'm not totally sure that I exist. I generate little crises. I do that with my husband, if we're getting along really well, and having a nice time, I think 'Am I in a relationship? It's not familiar.' It's the same way with being organized. If I'm on time for too many days in a row, or if the dining table has been cleared off every night for too long, I will find ways to create agitation. The heightened intensity helps me feel alive."

Losing things and running late are the old ways of living with fear. The new way will be to take on greater challenges and, possibly, to allow your life to quiet down. You might experience more peace. After a while, you will notice that your life has a different quality to it. That quality could initially feel like boredom. When I let go of some of my disorganization, my life quieted down. At first I thought I was bored, then I realized that I was calm. We can reeducate ourselves.

Adrenaline is addictive, but you can unhook yourself. Work on one pattern to see how you can shift it. Give yourself other thrills instead of the customary self-sabotaging ones. What else thrills you that is more healthy and satisfying? Try joining a basketball team, go to more thrillers at the movies, try an outdoor adventure, or learn a new skill.

Postpone Procrastination

Charles came to believe that he was at his most effective under enormous pressure. He prepares legal briefs at the last minute, countering the pain of worrying with the rush of victory at the end. He experiences a distinct thrill in postponing things to the last possible minute. After all, each time he "pulls it off," he's a hero, at least to himself.

Yet, there is also a dark side to this: there's the anguish of feeling stuck in so much quicksand that "I can't seem to get this done." There's the embarrassment of having to tell a colleague or client that you can't keep the agreement you made, the pain of continually feeling behind, and the chaotic feeling of not trusting yourself when you make agreements with yourself.

Most of us have our own unique procrastination patterns. Below are some common reasons for chronically putting things off until the last minute. You may have different reasons or a blend of the ones listed.

- You dread the thought of doing the task.
- You are used to the chronic worry that procrastination brings.
- You're a perfectionist, and you want to wait until you can do it right.
- You're not sure how to proceed.
- You don't understand how much time the task will take.
- You're a rebel, thinking, "I'll do things in my own way, on my own terms."
- You're drawn to the heroic moment, the thrill of pulling off an unlikely victory.
- You feel that the task just isn't important.
- You just don't want to do it.
- You want to enjoy yourself now, and forget the arduous tasks.

Sometimes we procrastinate because we have the wrong next step in mind. Pat had to buy a water filter for his kitchen. So, he added "Buy water filter" to his to-do list. Then, he didn't do it. Every time he thought about buying the water filter, he couldn't do it because he didn't have the phone number. So, he put it off. Finally, he rewrote the task as "Find phone number for ordering water filter." He then was addressing himself to the right task. He found the phone number and made the order. Richard got stuck filling out the refinancing papers for his mortgage because he didn't have a copy of the deed. He put off refinancing for a year because he didn't know where to get a copy of the deed.

Procrastination is a rich zone for exploring your dance with yourself. How you procrastinate is a unique experience. If you are willing to investigate with kindness and awareness, you will discover treasures. Don't try to fix your procrastination right off. Learn about it. Mine it. Watch it. Some of it may resolve with your kind attention.

When Beth looked at how she procrastinated, she realized, "I imagine that things are going to be very difficult for me, and I get scared to do them, so I avoid them. I tell myself that I need a whole day, say, to do my financial report. But I never get a whole day, so I don't do anything. I keep waiting until I have the kind of time I think I need. Then, I get people angry at me. Finally, I do get things done. Rarely are things as terrible as I think they are going to be. Often, things go pretty quickly. But I do need uninterrupted time. I suppose I could bar the door for two hours at a stretch and just not take phone calls. I never thought of doing that because I thought I needed a whole day. I'm sort of an all-or-nothing thinker."

Take a look at what your procrastination is like for the people around you. Mary began to see that her procrastination affected everyone else. Not calling the plumber in a timely way was sure to result in arguments and inconveniences. And while Mary didn't mind leaving things to the last minute, her secretary hated the moments of franticness. It was not her style. By becoming aware of her impact on others, Mary began changing her own behavior to improve her relationships and ended up accomplishing a great deal at the same time.

Here are a few tangible actions you can take that will help you get things done in a more timely way:

- Make sure you have the right tasks on your to-do list.
- Know why the task is important to you (not just to someone else).
- Identify the repercussions if you don't do it.
- Use a timer to get started.
- Identify why you are stuck:
  1. Ask: what is making this hard and what would make it easier?
  2. Break it into smaller tasks.
  3. Take the smallest possible next step.
  4. Get support if you need it.
  5. Set a deadline.
  6. Be accountable to someone; this is where a peer coach can help.
  7. Reward yourself.

Each time you approach a task you have been putting off, tell yourself how good you will feel when you have completed it. The more you do in a timely way, the more present you will be. Your energy will improve. You'll feel better about yourself and you'll be more on top of things.

■ ■ ■ EXERCISE ■ ■ ■

Start to know what your patterns are. Next time you procrastinate, pay attention to the experience. What are you doing? Do you know why?

How do you feel when you put something off? Do you feel a burst of relief, dread, or a sense of burden? What's the impact when you put it off? Be very specific. Now, ask yourself what you need so that you can take the next step. Do you need to break the big job into smaller tasks? Do you need support?

■ ■ ■

The Learning as Leadership group, a leadership training organization based in San Raphael, California, identifies what they call *diversions* as one of the most subtle and powerful ways that we get off track. When faced with taking an action that is challenging or anxiety producing, we often launch a diversion. This is an activity that can appear to be very real and important and yet completely diverts us from our goals. We might unconsciously launch a diversion when we start to feel that we are not up for the task ahead. It may be time for a diversion when we receive difficult feedback or hard emotional news; we might rather go into a tailspin over the news, than constructively face it and work harder toward our meaningful goals. The critical aspect of diversions is that, as a way to avoid feeling bad about ourselves, we will start an activity that is familiar but irrelevant to what we really want in life.

Often diversions become crises and therefore take up a lot of space and attention, which make them a unique and powerful form of procrastination. In fact, it won't seem like procrastination at all. We are totally unaware of our diversion; what we engage in seems like a really important topic, even though it is not the important issue that will help us move toward our meaningful goals. Asking myself what this emergency/crisis allows me to avoid helps to figure out if I am in a diversion. Once I realize that I am in a diversion and that I am avoiding something challenging but important, I can turn my attention back to the difficult but constructive activity.

Practicing the Wisdom of Time and Tasks

As you develop your wisdom about time, you may become more like my nonoverwhelmed friend—present, committed, and focused. Ironically you will be able to accomplish more of what's important to you and have more energy to do it, and you may do much less of what is less important to you.

There is no lack of things to want to do. As you refine your ability to choose where to put your precious life energy, you can deepen your appreciation of the bittersweetness of limits, of the limit of life itself. No, we can't do everything we want to do, but we can still put our hearts into our experiences, knowing that being fully present with whatever is happening is a powerful path to growth and well-being. Mastering the wisdom of time is a valuable step toward making sure your word is good, the next stage in the organizing wisdom journey.

9

Make Sure Your Word Is Good

Keeping our word may seem like an odd chapter in an organizing book. But think about it for a moment. What happens when you are counting on a friend to show up and they are half an hour late? What's the impact when you are expecting a colleague to meet a deadline and they fail to deliver? How we make and break our agreements contributes to everyone's sense of coherence or chaos. To reduce the chaos, we need to make agreements that we can keep and follow up on our promises. In this chapter, therefore, we consider reliability as an important aspect of organizing wisdom.

We make agreements all the time. We agree to do work assignments, show up for meetings, send out information, cover child care, do the grocery shopping, and make that phone call to the electrician. Our lives consist of a fine web of verbal commitments. When that web is strong, we, and the people around us, feel confident that we can count on each other. When the web is weak, we don't know which agreements to trust. The lack of trust in ourselves and our word increases the stress in our lives. We're not sure if we can be counted on, and other people consider us unreliable. Giving our word can be powerful, or it can mean nothing. The power potential depends on how we treat our commitments. Notice how you feel when you say words that you know you can stand by, and by contrast, pay attention to the times when you say something that you aren't completely committed to. This exercise in awareness can help your word become stronger.

So, let's talk about making good agreements and keeping them. When your agreements mean something, you become someone to respect. In addition, you can relax because you don't have to create a list of excuses for why you couldn't keep them.

Value Your Word

At some point, you may start realizing that when you make a commitment, people don't believe you. You start recognizing that your free-wheeling ways cost you a great deal. Charles remembers that when he was always running late, "I became aware that I would say to myself, 'It doesn't matter if I'm five minutes late, or even ten. I'll just make this call or do this errand.' I realized that I didn't value my own agreements. I thought that being precise about time was silly and petty. I'm a free spirit. I didn't care about things like that. I just didn't realize that people didn't like being kept waiting. I never thought about it."

This is a challenging area because everyone, at some point, cannot keep his or her word. The first question is: "Does it matter to you whether or not you keep your word? Or are your promises and commitments empty—lovely, perhaps—but empty?" This is a great area of investigation. Begin to notice what happens when you don't keep an agreement. What happens to you? How do you feel about it? Are you forgetting or simply ignoring the agreement that you made? Do you make excuses for yourself? Or do you just blow the agreement off? What is it like for you when someone else doesn't keep an agreement with you? No matter how good your intentions are, or how wonderful your excuses, it creates chaos in other people's lives when you say that you will do something and don't. You might not want to disappoint people, so you say that you will do something, but when you don't follow up, you disappoint them even more.

Begin to consider what it is like to believe what you yourself say. We all know that lying is wrong, and we believe telling the truth is important, yet we often think nothing of loose talk such as: "I'll give you a call later today." "I can get that report to you by Tuesday." "Sure, I can mail that package for you, no problem." Then our communications become slippery, and we are not sure what to believe. It may be tempting as you read this to think about the other people whose word is a little shaky. The best use of this chapter is to focus on yourself and the value of your own word.

Keeping agreements with ourselves would be a good place to start. We promise ourselves that we will get out of the house in the morning at 8:00, and yet we leave at 8:30. We make a commitment to call the dentist, but then we let it go. Start with learning to build trust in your own word to yourself, and the rest will be much easier.

Be Consistent: Hold Yourself to the Same Standards You Have for Others

Often people are very sensitive to how other people's disorganization affects them, yet very insensitive to how their disorganization affects other people. People don't like being let down, but they have a raft of excuses ready when they let others down. Diane would start getting upset with her colleagues when they didn't return a call or an e-mail within twenty-four hours. After two days, she would be waiting for an apology. If, heaven forbid, someone got back to her after three days, she'd be livid, and they would have to discuss it.

In the high-tech world that she lived and worked in, all this made sense. A manager in a fast-paced thriving company has to stay on top of things. There was one small problem, however. Diane often lost track of who had been in touch with her, sometimes not getting back to people for days. From her perspective, it was never serious, never personal. "What can I do? I am swamped." Yet, she often forgot to give others the same benefit of the doubt she gave herself.

If you consider call-return-time important then set up a system whereby you can track your important calls and the e-mails and faxes that you need to send. Refer back to chapter 6 for general guidelines on setting up systems and for a specific example of a system for managing e-mail. Track the calls you have to make, when you returned a call, and who owes you a call. One way to track calls is to keep a small notebook that you always use when you check your messages. Once I have logged the call I delete the message from voice mail. If the call needs to be returned, put a box ❑ by it and check the box ☑ when you have returned the call. Let people know when you think your message is urgent. If the message is not urgent, give them a time frame within which you will look for a return call. Don't make people guess what your expectations are.

Set Good Boundaries

We cannot do everything, we cannot be everything to everyone, and, in the end, we cannot create healthy connections with others through overreaching ourselves to please them. Yet, some of us believe that saying no, setting limits, and expressing our own limitations is risky or selfish. So, often people set their limits, say no, or express their dislike with a situation not through an intentional statement, but through their disorganization.

Running late, being overbooked, forgetting promises, not returning phone calls or e-mails, being incredibly harried, *having* to cancel at the last minute, having a desk that is piled high with work, all of these can be ways of being unavailable, without directly saying no. Yet, this indirect kind of communication might prevent you from doing the difficult emotional work of setting appropriate boundaries intentionally. It takes work to know where you begin and end, what you want to do and don't want to do. It is hard, hard work to set clear boundaries and risk the disapproval or disappointment of others. You might feel that you are putting relationships at risk by being direct about what you can, cannot, or don't want to do. Yet, you are putting relationships at risk anyway, with your high-stress "Now you see me, now you don't" disappearing act.

Maintaining personal boundaries involves making clear requests as well as clear responses to requests. It is an entry point to a much more satisfying sense of adulthood. You have a perception of safety within yourself. You do not need to stretch yourself beyond recognition to serve others. Your yes is a yes and your no is a no.

Assertiveness training can be a very powerful and practical step toward saying appropriate yeses and nos. Assertiveness includes the capacity to be clear about what you want, to ask for it respectfully and firmly, to believe that you are worthy of what you want, and to take responsibility for your actions. The literature on codependency can also be an invaluable resource for people who discover that they find it too frightening to set appropriate boundaries for themselves. A large part of getting organized is learning to act from a place of self-esteem, knowing what we want and don't want to do, knowing what we can and can't do, not taking on more than we can do, and taking good care of ourselves.

Practice Saying No

When someone makes a request, don't say yes immediately. Try saying, "Can I get back to you on that?" This is hard when you feel that tug to say, "Yes, I'll do it." Then make sure that you do get back to that person within a reasonable amount of time. Don't say no by disappearing. Make a practice of imagining how exactly you will do what you promised. Consider if the deadline is reasonable. Check your calendar to see if you have time to keep your agreement. Learn what a manageable deadline is.

Next, get to know why you have trouble with saying no. Are you afraid that you won't be valued if you set limits? Are you concerned that you won't be seen as a team player? Are you nervous that others might see you as selfish or weak? Often our reasons for taking on too much are not tested. We just load up our schedules and then pay a very heavy price on the other end. Sometimes, you think you can't say no to things, but you might start to recognize that your busyness may be an indirect way of saying no, or of trying to substitute action for a sense of identity.

If you work where saying no is not "allowed," or the dominant style is one of working nights and weekends, you may find that setting limits is very difficult. Yet, in many cases, people work nights and weekends, only to find that their productivity goes down. You can try pointing out to your boss that this kind of pace is enormously costly in the long run. One way to handle too many work demands is to offer your colleagues or boss a few alternatives. Try saying, "I can do this or that. But I am unable to do both. Which do you think is the most important?"

People will adjust when you learn to say no more often. And, miracle of miracles, you will start to discover who is really for you in your life. There is nothing better. You will start saying those difficult nos, and some people won't like it, won't be nice to you and they won't be your friend anymore, which was probably what you feared. But if the friendship was based on your giving more than you genuinely were able to, it may be time to let go. But other people will say, "Great! You are sticking up for yourself."

Sarah gave this example: "I recently had an experience when I had to stand up for my own space with my son and ask him to stay somewhere other than my house when he came to St. Louis for a visit, because he was setting conditions that were impossible for me. It was very hard, I thought, 'Let's see what happens.' He has been so much warmer and more appreciative of me, because he understood that I was not going to be pushed around anymore. And it has been so much easier for me. It was scary as hell, because if I count on anyone's love, it's my kids'."

As you consider whether or not to say yes to a new project, remember to double the time you think something will take. If, for example, you figure that a project will take two days, double that, since most of us are very bad at estimating project time lines. Then really think about whether you can fit it into your schedule. If you can't say no with dignity, or if someone offers you a deadline that seems tight, negotiate up front to lengthen the time horizon. Try to avoid letting yourself and them down when you can't get the project done on the time line that you knew was unrealistic from the start. If someone keeps pressuring you, you can say, "I will make a good effort to deliver what you need, but I cannot promise because I think this time frame is unrealistic." Or say, "I'd rather turn you down, than let you down." Yes, that's courageous, but it can also save upset and bad feelings later.

Find good, courteous, but direct ways to say no when someone has a request for you. Here are some examples:

"Thank you for asking me, but I am unable to do this task at this point."

"I appreciate your thinking of me as someone who could help out on the *X* campaign. And I support your ideas, but I cannot commit any time to that right now."

"You know, I enjoy you and appreciate your work. I'd love to collaborate with you in some way, but right now I cannot commit to doing one more thing. I am sorry about that."

View saying no as a practice. As with decision-making, you can get better at saying no over time. You do not owe your life to other people.

As you say no, you can give up blaming people for making requests and take responsibility for your answers. If you do make agreements, you will find that your life goes much better because you are more likely to keep them.

Say Yes Only When You Really Want To

The converse of saying no effectively is to say yes only when you really want to. Once you have paused before saying yes or no, try this. Check to see if you want to do it. Do you want to—really? Yes, we have obligations. Someone has to do the grocery shopping and someone has to be there when the kids get home. Many of our obligations are negotiable, however, and with some creativity, you can find ways to share, trade, or drop something that you thought was a must.

The next question is: "Have you identified the trade-offs?" Be clear that if you say yes to one thing, it inevitably means you will have to say no at some point in the future to something else. Think ahead before you make agreements, and check to see if you will be thwarting deeper desires later. How do you evaluate what you really want to say yes to? Say yes to what enhances your values. Think about your deeper purpose for organizing and remind yourself what you are trying to create in your life. Sometimes, we say yes to people to satisfy our ego needs, we want to look good or be seen as a giving person, yet we can overload our lives with such things, and egos tend to be insatiable. Try to get in touch with more satisfying reasons for your commitments. For people who want to do everything or are burdened by a sense of obligation, try asking the following questions:

- Does it give me energy?
- Am I excited about doing it?
- Does it bring me joy?
- Does it connect me to the people I most care about?
- Does it help me manifest my most valued goals?

Say yes to what you are already committed to. Beyond that, only say yes to something new when you really mean it. This alone can change your life.

Lower Your Sights When the Stresses Increase

After Sandrine had her third child, she realized, "Right now, it's important that we eat and sleep and my two older children keep to their regular schedule. We are back to the basics. I've cut back on work. My husband is home every night. We plan to be this way for months until we all adjust."

Becky, by contrast, tried to go sailing through her regular life during her difficult divorce. She tried to keep all the same balls in the air while consulting with lawyers, grieving deeply, selling her beloved home in a beautiful suburb, and looking for a decent condominium to buy. "I tried to keep it all going just as before. I wanted to feel that nothing was changing. I booked the same evening activities. I kept the same level of clients. I just tried to keep up, but I started breaking all kinds of agreements. I let a lot of people down. I thought people would understand, but many people had no idea what I was going through."

There are times in life when demands naturally increase: right before and after a move, having a child, taking on a new job, the start of the school year, caring for aging parents, visits from relatives and friends, the death of a family member. Even getting ready to go on vacation is a kind of extra stress. At these times, the best thing to do is to lower your sights. *Plan* to do less. Make fewer promises. Ask for more help. Tell people when your stresses are increasing. Reduce the number of commitments that you make. If you are generally overcommitted, this is the time to cut *way* back. Difficult times need your attention and presence. If you ever needed permission to say no to things, this is the time. Try a time-out. Take a week when you just come home from work and do the minimum. Take two weeks. Read a novel. Go to a movie. Take lots of baths. At these times of greater stress, it is even more important to make commitments that you can really come through on. You are under enough stress without making others mad at you because you are failing them.

Restrain Your Desire to Make Offers

For the extroverted soul, making offers to do things for other people is energizing. It feels great just to make the offer: "Sure, I'll take the lead on the Somerville Project." "I'd love to do the backup on the marketing study." "I'd like to make the main dish for the community potluck." "Can I take your kids skating with us?" Offers are like the sugar of connection, they sweeten the feeling and they feel great to make. The catch with offers is that you have to come through on them to keep your relationships strong. When you make offers, and then forget, or double-book yourself and have to cancel, you do damage to relationships.

There are a lot of people like Lucy, an excellent hairstylist who thrives on offers to her friends: "Let me take you to lunch . . . I'd love to color your hair . . . Let's catch up with a long walk . . . I thought of the perfect birthday present for you." But she generally doesn't follow through on any of these great ideas. This, of course, has affected the quality of her relationships. She is wonderful, effervescent and fun. But she is also unreliable and untrustworthy. She is unaware of her unfilled offers.

If you are like Lucy, you may have a number of offers outstanding that you have forgotten about or dropped off your to-do list. You may see yourself as enthusiastic and generous. Chances are you are not aware of the ill effects of your behavior. People often won't tell you directly that they think you are unreliable and that they don't like it. Lucy's friends don't tell her that she has disappointed them, they just don't believe her offers and don't take her seriously.

Let's say that you do have a habit of making offers and promises that you can't keep up with later. The first thing to do is to become aware that you do this. Do you find yourself calling to cancel plans with people frequently? Do you have to apologize for promises that you forgot to keep? Do you find yourself making excuses for yourself? Do you blame people for expecting too much from you? All of these could be indications that you offer more than you can follow through on.

After you increase your awareness, get in the habit of checking yourself before the offer comes out of your mouth. Stop for a moment and consider whether or not you can really do what you are offering. Even though you might feel a strong pull to make the offer, you can tell yourself that you need to wait. Ask yourself why you want to make the offer and if it is realistic. Pausing before making an offer does not mean that you are not generous or supportive or kind. It means that you are starting to take your offers seriously, because you recognize that it is not generous, supportive, or kind not to show up. You realize that your presence matters to people.

Make Your Calendar Work for You

Skilled calendar use can help you keep your word. Make sure that your personal calendar is coordinated with others'. For some families, it makes sense to have a family calendar and a work calendar. The family calendar is in a public place—the kitchen or the main hallway—and everyone writes their activities on that calendar well in advance. This way, your son's basketball game that conflicts with your daughter's soccer game doesn't surprise you, and you all can work out the scheduling in advance. Keep your family calendar where everyone can see it, and your private calendar in your Palm Pilot or your day planner. Make sure your own calendar is your master calendar. Get into the habit of checking the family calendar every day and writing all your commitments in your own calendar. Do not rely on more than one calendar for your own commitments.

Schedule "Unscheduled Time" in Your Calendar

Don't fill in every empty space in your calendar. Block off chunks of time that you just won't schedule at all. Not all "open space" in your calendar can be available for scheduled appointments. Now you know you need "transition time," but you also need to allow for planning time, time to put things away, time for following up on conversations, and time to complete administrative tasks that you may need to do.

Try blocking off ten minutes in the morning for goal-setting and list-making. This does not have to be first thing, but by noon it is a good idea to know what you want to accomplish that day, otherwise chances are you won't accomplish it. Block off the last hour of the workday to complete the day's work. Block off at least a half a day a week for loose ends, details, and setting weekly goals. Block off a day a month for catching up, filing, returning phone calls, and setting monthly goals.

Guard this blocked-off time tenaciously. Don't give it up. Don't tell yourself that it is available for appointments. When asked, tell people that you have a prior obligation. Only you need to know that it is a commitment to yourself. You will find that guarding white space makes your life much easier and your commitments to others more realistic.

Check Your Calendar Three Times A Day

This seems like a no-brainer. How could you forget a 2:00 o'clock appointment that you noted first thing in the day? Yet, it's a good habit to get into. Check your calendar and your to-do list several times a day. This allows you to acknowledge that things do slip your mind. This can also be an easy habit to learn and one that will gain you a lot of good results.

Managing Broken Agreements

Stephanie spent a year studying art in Florence. She asked her roommate to send her an art book she had on her shelf in their apartment in Pittsburgh and that she couldn't locate in Italy. "Sure, no problem, I'm happy to help," said Marie. "I'll be able to send it in a couple of days." What a relief for Stephanie, since it was important material that she needed for her work. A month went by, no book. Stephanie, after ranting and raving about how bad the Italian mail system was, finally realized that Marie had never sent the book. Evidently, Marie had written it on her list but had promptly forgotten about it. It created havoc for Stephanie. Marie was apologetic, but seemed to think that it was no big deal: "I just forgot to mail something. But I'll Express Mail it to you, if you want to pay the extra charge. "This is not the way to rebuild trust.

People often won't tell you how mad they are at you or how bad they feel when you let them down. It is actually quite stylish to convey to those who break agreements that whatever they did was fine: "No problem, life is hard, we are all busy, it's too much to expect, etc., etc." (I think the idea is that if don't I expect you to keep your word, you won't expect me to keep mine.) It would be rare for someone to say how they *actually* feel. Meanwhile, you might be thinking, "I am making all these promises, I am so generous, I am really a wonderful person." You might think that you are present for all these people, and it might be quite a surprise to discover that many people think that your word is not good.

You might not realize that you weren't keeping agreements. Others may decide, however, that they don't need to keep their agreements with you. You then may have no idea why you are experiencing distance from others or why you are feeling lonely.

No matter how fabulous a person you are, if you make a habit of running late, postponing or canceling meetings, it will harm your relationships with others. The best way to manage this problem is to prevent it from occurring in the first place. Stay aware of the offers that you make, and the meetings that you postpone or cancel, and the ways in which you keep leaning on other people to bail you out. If you do have to cancel or postpone (and this happens to all of us at some point), advise the other person as soon as you can. Don't wait to see if maybe somehow you can make it. If your schedule is generally in flux, advise people in advance that you may have to cancel. Ask them how far in advance of a scheduled meeting you will need to let them know that you can't make it. It's not that canceling or running late is so terrible, it's that you pay attention to your impact on others. You can minimize the harm done by being conscious and staying in contact.

Whatever you do, when you are about to break an agreement, or just did, *don't disappear*. Stay in touch and let the other person know what is going on. Don't make them run after you, and don't get mad at them because you broke an agreement. Feel your remorse if necessary and then repair the damage.

Apologies are important, even about small things. Apologize face-to-face if you can or on the phone. Make your apology heartfelt and keep your excuses out of it. If you are defensive and apologetic, your listener will primarily hear the defensiveness and your apology will seem insincere. If you apologize by voice mail, follow up with a reiteration when you talk with the person you have offended; check with them to make sure that your bond with them is restored and that they know that you understand you violated a trust.

You can repair the damage of breaking agreements, but it will take some work. Maimonides, a twelfth-century Jewish scholar, described what was required when relationships broke down. He wrote that the injured party had a right to expect someone to say that they were sorry, but that was not enough to repair the relationship. The person who broke the agreement needed to:

- Make amends.
- Take responsibility for any harm done.
- Express real remorse.
- Resolve to change.

If the injured party refused to accept the apology, it was to be repeated three times, in public if necessary.

Don't neglect apologies, but don't rely solely on them either. Try to figure out how you can make things right between you and the other person. And learn from your experience so you are less likely to break future agreements. If you do this consistently and you see the great benefit of maintaining solid relationships, it will help dissolve your pattern of breaking agreements.

Trusting Yourself

One of the biggest costs of not having your word be good is that you can't count on yourself. Even you don't know if you can be trusted or not. The ultimate wisdom of being reliable is that your words have weight—you and others can take you seriously. You stop hoping that people will give you the benefit of the doubt, and you start behaving as if you respect your own word. Trusting yourself comes from knowing yourself well, loving yourself, and knowing and understanding the world that we live in. It is one of your most precious benefits of the wisdom of organizing.

Focus Your Powerful Mind

The fourth area of organizing wisdom is the wisdom of attention. We who tend to be disorganized have wonderful gifts. We often have artistic sensibilities, and we like music and metaphor. We are also often highly curious and "distractible," which means we can pay attention to many things at once. Not everyone can do that. But we are often not so great at figuring out where everything goes or planning accurately. For many of us, distractibility is at the heart of our disorganization. We forget what we are doing or what we meant to do next. It is the opposite of being fully present. We are not there. Sometimes, we're plain confused. Managing distractibility means moving toward a much more powerful frame of mind in which we are clear, present, alive, and can pay attention to what we want to.

Your distractibility may be hardwired—but it may be amplified by a number of sources, such as fear, poor planning, overstimulation, overscheduling, and not enough sleep. You may have attention deficit disorder. You may be a survivor of a traumatic experience. You may be the parent of young children. No matter what the reason, managing distractibility takes skill. You need to know when you are distracted. You must value your clarity and focus and learn the steps to take to ensure your presence of mind. Let's explore a few practices that can help you focus when you need to and accomplish what you set out to do.

Focus Your Attention

Our attention is like a powerful light. We can illuminate what we focus on. Yet with so much to do, so many options, so many goals, it is easy to scatter your energies to the winds and get overwhelmed. You can learn to focus on what you truly want, which begins with knowing what is important to you. This task is lifework. Managing your attention, learning to focus, is a big part of accomplishing what you truly want.

Part of learning to be present is defining your priorities and then staying with them. There are good reasons not to define your priorities. Perhaps you pile on tasks in order to avoid getting to know yourself and your deepest aspirations. Sherry said, "I am completely busy, I am never home. My schedule is full to bursting. But I am too busy to feel much or to think about the things that are bothering me. Sometimes, I think that's a good thing, but other times I am vaguely aware of a deep fear that is driving me."

Prioritizing strengthens your sense of who you are and what you value. It also sets a virtuous cycle in motion. As you get to know yourself, you find it easier to set priorities. You are not spread so thin, and you see more clearly what has meaning for you.

Sometimes people don't focus when they are working because they feel they don't have the time to concentrate. It's hard to focus because there is so much to do. However, lack of focus leads to poor quality work, which then needs to be redone, which increases the feeling of pressure

Stress

Lack of focus

More work

Poor Quality
of Work

Errors

by adding more to your to-do list. This is a vicious cycle that can be interrupted by learning to focus on doing what you are doing well.

Give Up Those Little Slips of Paper— Create a Reminders System

Many of us are tempted by little pieces of paper. We write good ideas on Post-it notes or jot reminders on napkins. We put grocery lists on the back of birthday cards or school flyers. As a result, we often lose the bits of paper, forget which pocket they are in, or accidentally run them through the laundry. Or we write down the number we need in order to return a phone call on the margin of the nearest newspaper. Then when we need it, we often remember that we wrote it on the top margin of the front section. But which day? And where did it go?

Put notes and reminders in one place, and life will become so much easier. Carry a day planner, a small notebook, or an electronic data assistant and "collect" your ideas and notes to yourself. For some people, moving from the "little pieces of paper" system to the "daily collection list" system—although it's not easy at first—can be the most powerful new habit they cultivate. (Reminder: see chapter 6 for general guidelines on building new habits and systems.) You capture your spontaneous thoughts about actions that you want to take in one easy place. Then, you can move your new action items into a reliable place—a master to-do list—that you will check frequently when you want to take action.

There are several places to keep one master to-do list. You can keep it in the back of your planner, set it up on your computer or in your electronic data assistant. The critical thing is to have a process whereby a "to-do" goes from your head onto a reliable "spontaneous ideas" collection list, then onto a master list, then from the master list onto a daily to-do list, where you check off the action item once it gets done. Your master list will probably be long.

Now, instead of writing your notes randomly, you decide to build a habit of writing things down on a daily "collection" list. When your hand strays to the back of the envelope, you say out loud, "Nope, I'm writing this in my planner or on my little notepad, where I will find it again." Or you tell yourself, "It will be much easier if I take a minute now and write this on my collection list, and forgo the pleasure of writ-ing it on the back of this envelope." Then, you get up and find your collection list and write the note. At the beginning, it will feel as if it takes an hour to find your collection list (I carry mine with me all the time), as opposed to the one second it takes to write the note on the back of the envelope. But that is an illusion generated by an old habit. More likely, you will save hours by learning the habit of keeping a daily collection list and a master list.

Stephanie Culp and David Allen, both master organizers, suggest that as you get organized you take some time to write down everything that you can think of that needs to be done: unfinished projects, letters, repairs, communications, or whatever feels incomplete. Your master to-do list will get unwieldy very quickly. It can be helpful then to break your master list down into several distinct categories, such as: to buy, to call, errands, household repair, kids. Try keeping a master grocery list on the refrigerator. You can get a magnetic pad and keep a felt-tip pen nearby.

Once you have broken your little-bits-of-paper habit and replaced it with a collection list habit, you need to do one more thing. You need to build in a weekly review when you look at your various lists and make sure that you write your action items into your calendar, so that you do them. Then, as you create your daily list, pull items from the master you generated. Here's what the path of a to-do item looks like:

Your head → daily "collection" list → master to-do list →
weekly review → daily to-do list → action!

Sometimes, of course, you'll go from your daily collection list to taking action. Thus, this is *not* a rigid system; the main idea is to collect your to-do's regularly and then do them. Experiment with how to make this work for you.

Create an Energizing Daily To-Do List

Your to-do list is a tool to help you get things done. How you structure your list can give you energy or it can drain you. A good to-do list guides you through the day. A disorganized to-do list only adds to the confusion.

An energizing daily to-do list is doable. That sounds ridiculously obvious, yet many people carry long lists of tasks that they can't possibly do that day (or even that week or month), or they have lists that they can't read, have outdated items on them, or aren't broken down into manageable tasks. Here are some basics for your to-do list.

- You can read it. It is really legible, i.e., you haven't scribbled in mystery scrawl and it isn't totally cryptic.
- It is in one place in your planner or your electronic data assistant. It is not spread out on Post-it notes all over your desk.
- Only today's to-dos are on it. Not all of this week's, not this month's, not this year's.
- Each item is a manageable task.
- You have identified the tasks that are absolute priorities for the day.

Think for a moment about how much time you spend during the day not knowing what to do next. You can cut through this confusion when you have a to-do list that helps you focus. Your list should be relatively short and should feel like a friend, not a boss. In fact, on good days, you'll feel psyched when you look at it. Your to-do list gives you information about where to allocate your energy.

When I first started working with her, Jenna's to-do list had every single thing she could think of on it. She carried a list that was many pages long wherever she went. Whenever she looked at it, she felt drained, confused, and overwhelmed. Now, she creates a list for each day. It takes her a few minutes the night before. It is short and she knows what she has to do that day. She still maintains her long master list, but she looks at it only once a week, and only in order to select a few things to add to her daily to-do list.

Removing action items that you concede you will never do is as important as building a good to-do list. Helen used to carry around old action items and make herself feel bad about them. "Write thank you note to Cousin John" had been on her list for three months. Another action item, "Write out check to Susan," had been on her list for five months. Mary's action items included sending journal articles to colleagues: one month, six months, a year on her to-do list. Old action items start to get moldy. They only go away when you take action on them, delegate them, or you let them go. The sooner you acknowledge that you just aren't going to take action on something, the better. It reduces the time that you feel bad about not doing it. Life is hard enough without an old smelly, confusing to-do list.

George explained why he had so many old, undone action items on his list. "Once I put an item on my to-do list, I think it's done. I often forget that this is only the beginning." It is not uncommon to forget what is on your list; get into the habit of checking your to-do list several times a day.

■ ■ ■ EXERCISE ■ ■ ■

What do you need to do tomorrow? Create an energizing to-do list by listing your items as follows:

1. State them in action language. Use a verb. Don't just write "Cousin John." Say "Write thank you note to Cousin John." Don't just say "Plumber," write "Call plumber." Add the phone number. If you don't have the phone number, write "Get plumber's phone number." People often write shorthand to save time, but it takes about a second to write a whole phrase and it will help create clarity for you.
2. Write down how long you think that each item will take.
3. Identify a time when you will do each thing on your list.
4. Write down only those tasks that you know you must do or want to do that day. Do not get into the habit of littering your to-do list with items that you can't or won't do. Being hopeful really doesn't help in this case.

When you have created your list (and it is an act of creativity), take a few seconds to imagine yourself doing everything on your list with grace and presence.

Here's Anna's list:

Call Martha	10 min.	9:45 A.M.
Return book to Luke	10 min.	11:45 A.M.
Schedule FedEx pickup	10 min.	12:00 P.M.
Order supplies (add specific list)	30 min.	3:30 P.M.
Pick up groceries—grocery list attached	30 min.	5:15 P.M.
Drop Alan off at baseball	30 min.	6:00 P.M.

Enjoy checking things off your list and the energized feeling that you get when your actions match your aspirations.

■ ■ ■

Today's Priorities

As part of your to-do list, you must learn to identify your absolute priorities for the day. It is very easy to lose track of even the few burning priorities, so ask yourself, "What three actions are top priority for me today? What must I do by the end of the day to reach my goals?" Write them down in a quiet early moment, or even the night before. It may help to carve out time at the end of the day to connect with what is important for the next day. Try limiting the top priority list to three items, four at the most. Later in the day, refer to this list when you get tired and unfocused, and when you start feeling the tug of too many demands.

Prioritizing takes place all day long. When you are in a moment of confusion and don't know what to do next, you can read your list of priorities. Prioritizing isn't easy. Yet, it is the most important work of our lives. With practice, it helps you get better and better at wisely investing your precious time and energy. Keep asking, "What is really important?" Professional coach Cheryl Richardson says, "Sometimes you have to say no to what is really important, in order to experience what is really, really important."

Create Replanning Time

In almost everyone's day, there is a moment when you feel your day has gotten out of control. You may realize right before lunch or in the middle of the afternoon that you are just not going to get done what you wanted to do. For instance, it is 11:40 A.M.—almost lunchtime—and you have not been able to start to work. There is one phone call after the next and an onslaught of e-mails; time is slipping away. Your true goals are receding into the distance as you struggle with the immediate demands of the moment. You may start to become resentful. You notice that your stress increases. "This shouldn't be happening!!! I had other plans for the day!! I have deadlines to meet and appointments to keep!"

Or you may be facing the "world of ten thousand things." You are dealing with five issues at once. You get flustered. Another hour goes by. You were on a long phone call and you haven't done anything that was a priority. You can see that precious time for your workout slipping away. Meanwhile, there are calls and e-mails to be returned. Children to be picked up. You need to make something for dinner.

What to do? You now know that you cannot do everything you have to do. It's tempting to try to move faster and give in to the inner critic: "Do more! You didn't do enough!" You might even resort to eliminating meals or giving up on your workout to make more time.

Instead, take two to five minutes in the middle of the day to reassess your goals and plans. This is replanning time: a moment to "fall back and regroup" that comes out of sitting quietly. It fosters a different kind of inner conversation. When you take a few minutes for replanning, you look at the hours you have left in your day, you look at what you wanted to accomplish, and you *consciously* make the trade-offs. And you use some time reallocation strategies. You consciously ask several questions:

- How can I sustain my energy and presence of mind today?
- Do I see any way of accomplishing all of my goals, or do I have to deliberately say, "I can't do it"?
- Do I see any clear trade-offs?
- What can I delegate?
- What can I say no to?
- Where can I change the time line?
- What could I do less of and less perfectly and still derive value?
- Revisit your top three priorities for the day and ask, "Given my current constraints, what are my priorities now?"

You may realize that you can work out or you can finish a case write-up, but you cannot do both. You realize that you need to choose. Or, instead of going to the gym, you can speed walk for twenty minutes. It's still better than no exercise at all. You need to negotiate your day's plan with yourself.

The challenge is to sustain your energy and your presence of mind all day long. Use replanning as a learning process. Do you always eliminate your workout? Do you consistently overbook yourself? Cultivate these questions as an inquiry, not an inquisition. You can't criticize yourself and learn about yourself at the same time. When Helen first tried replanning, she said, "I would say to myself, 'You're not exercising again, you'll never get fit, you didn't clean off your desk again, you didn't respond to e-mails again.' But now I can see that when I replan, it's best not to badger myself about it. I use scheduling as a learning process. I see how I consistently overbook myself. I also see how to make some good changes."

Keep your week in mind when you make your trade-offs. If you haven't responded to a few key phone calls for two days, then they become the priority. On the other hand, if you have worked out for the past three days, then maybe you can give that up this evening.

You can use your vision as a helpful tool here. Every day you are faced with choices about how to spend your time. Different choices have different pulls to them. And some are quite difficult. Do you want to take a forty-five minute walk or comfort a friend who is calling for help? Not easy. Do you want to pick up your children at school or finish a report before the deadline? Our lives are full of trade-offs. There is no way around that. We are always making trade-offs. We can't do everything. However, when you are faced with a choice, you ask yourself, "How important is this to me? Is this truly part of what I want to create for myself?" Your vision is a guide to making choices in the present moment. You create a new future for yourself by making new choices in the present.

The Hourly To-Do List

It's easy to lose track of what you want to do even in the next hour. If you have an "open" stretch of time, create a short list of what you want to do as a way of reminding yourself what is important in that hour. Take a blank, brightly colored index card and simply write down what you would like to accomplish in that hour. Keep that card in front of you. This can help you stay on track for the next small amount of time. When phone calls or e-mails come in, you can remind yourself of your priority for this hour. Remember, we are very easily distracted from what is important to us.

Structure Your Time with a Timer

A timer can be your most valuable tool for organizing. Set it for fifteen minutes, and plunge into a task that you have been postponing. Even the most odious job is tolerable if you know it's just for a limited time. Once you get started, it may not even seem so bad. Mary uses a timer to get herself started on sorting her piles. She says to herself, "I can do this for ten minutes." She often finds that once she gets started, she can continue her task for much longer.

You can also use your timer to manage distractibility while you're doing a task. If you tend to get distracted by phone calls or other work demands, the timer can remind you to go back to the initial task. A timer can help you keep track of multiple activities. Set your timer when you put the water on to boil for tea; otherwise, you may go on to the next thing and discover an hour later that the teakettle has boiled dry.

You can use a timer to let you become fully absorbed in a project without being afraid that you will forget to stop when you have to. If you know that you need to leave the house at noon, you can set the timer for 11:50. This will give you time to collect what you need, comb your hair, check your datebook, close the computer, put on your coat, and walk out of the door right at noon.

Using a timer can help with structuring an "open" morning or afternoon with a great deal to accomplish. Yacub, a freelance consultant who works out of his house, described his morning: "I would plan to write for two hours. I would get myself seated in front of the computer at nine. I would check my e-mail, then make another cup of coffee. Then I would remember a few phone calls that I had to make. Then I might receive a phone call or two. Soon, the morning would disappear, and I would be very unhappy and frustrated. I couldn't show any significant accomplishment for the morning." Detailed time structuring is almost essential if you are working out of your home office, but it's also valuable at any workplace.

So, instead of leaving large blocks of "free" open time, you structure your time instead. Here is the basic idea. Take a large block of time, say, two hours, and divide it up into, six twenty-minute segments. Instead of telling yourself, like Yacub "I am going to write for the next two hours," you say, "I have six blocks of twenty minutes each." Now you have smaller, more manageable blocks of time to plan. You plan each block of time, and you work through one smaller block at a time. Use your timer as you go through the morning so that you keep track of where you are. You can get a lot done in twenty minutes when you have a goal and are focused. You start with a list of "must-dos" for the two-hour block of time, and then you plan the rest of the time accordingly.

Instead of "write for two hours," Yacub's morning now looks like this:

9:00–9:20. Make coffee, check e-mails for anything urgent.

This acknowledges that making coffee is an important ritual for him. And he needs to check e-mail for messages. He sets his timer to go off at 9:15. That gives him a five-minute buffer before 9:20, when he will start working on his writing project.

9:20–9:40. Review yesterday's work and start the second section.
9:40–10:00. Write the first two paragraphs for the conclusion.
10:00–10:20. Write the concluding paragraph.
10:20–10:40. Make follow-up phone calls, five minutes of yoga. (The few minutes of yoga provide a change of pace.)
10:40–11:00. Edit the introduction. (At 11:00, he will acknowledge the morning's work and block out another hour or two.)

Once he got used to this detailed way of planning his time, Yacub realized that "one reason it was hard for me to settle down is that I was intimidated by what I had to do. Even though writing is a big aspect of my work, there are times when I am daunted by what I have to produce. So, I'll make phone calls, pay bills, anything not to have to face it. Now, I just have to work for twenty minutes. I am willing to tackle the hardest writing problem, if it is only for twenty minutes. But, usually, I get started and I enjoy the challenge that I face."

Structuring your time like this helps you learn about managing distractibility as well as your own work habits. Here are some pointers for making this time-block system work for you.

1. Be aware that you may plan to do too much. Keep noticing how much you actually do in any given time frame. The more accurately you understand how you use time, the more effective your planning.
2. You may need to replan frequently. That's part of the way this system works.
3. Take tiny two- to five-minute mind breaks to get oxygen to your brain. Five minutes of quiet, gentle stretching, a walk down the hall, or sitting meditation can be enormously refreshing to your tired brain.
4. Celebrate even the smallest accomplishments. You may be so used to keeping your eye on what you haven't done that you may forget to acknowledge your victories. This is essential.
5. You will learn to be more aware of trade-offs. You'll start to see that if you do *this,* you cannot do *that.* You cannot do everything.

Structuring your time helps you know where you are in your work. It gives you a very clear picture of how well you are focusing and what you are achieving in relation to how much time you have.

Stop and Think

In the middle of the rush of the day, pause for a moment to ask:

- "Do I have everything I need for the next meeting or activity?"
- "Is there anything I might forget?"
- "What do I want to accomplish in this hour (or in this conversation or meeting)?"
- "What do I need for the day?"

Do this every day like a discipline. Before you walk out of the house, stop and think. Say, "Stop. Do not go through this door. Do I have my wallet? Do I have the shopping list? Do I have directions? Do I have my gym bag? Do I have the folders (library books, items to return) I need?" A thirty-second pause allows you to collect your thinking even if you are running late again. Give yourself time to think it all the way through.

It won't take that long. Stopping and thinking help you arrive at the airport with your tickets, or show up at a meeting with the right information, or get to the swimming pool with your swimsuit, towel, and goggles. You can practice "stop and think" right now with a little dry run. Go to your door and say "Stop!" What will I need . . . ?"

"Stop and think" at any transition during the day. Check that you have everything with you when you leave a store, restaurant, or client site. Make it a habit to mentally review that you are leaving with everything, so that you don't get home and discover that you left your umbrella on the airplane or your grocery shopping list on the pharmacy counter.

Deal with Panic—It's Only Temporary!

Panic is an acute fear response that is accompanied by physiological flooding of adrenaline into your system. It can both cause and result from disorganization. Just when you are facing a deadline, trying to find receipts so that you can figure out your taxes, or when you discover that you can't find your car registration, panic sets in. For many of us, this happens far more than we would ever admit, even to ourselves. So, often we suffer panic attacks alone. There are the awakenings at night in fear; the forgetting to put the check in the mail; the running late to a very important meeting. Some people suffer from serious chronic anxiety and some people have occasional panic attacks.

I remember one of my moments of panic. It was a day when I had an important meeting, and I was trying to get a lot done beforehand. My heart was racing. I was doing too many things at once. I had to leave my office to get to the meeting on time, but I needed to do one more thing. I was trying to print something out, and the printer jammed. I was in a hurry, so I pulled the paper out too fast, and thus broke the printer. I left in a state of agitation. I rushed off, and of course I got lost and missed this very important meeting entirely. A few hours later, I went to pick someone up at the airport, and I misplaced the ticket for the airport parking lot. Panic often breeds more panic.

I reviewed what led to my panic attack. I just wanted to get a few things done before I left. I wanted to fax a couple of items, make a phone call, and print something out. I lost track of the time and started to realize that I was cutting things very close. And here is the important point: I couldn't seem to let go of any of the calls or faxes. I kept saying to myself, "I just have to get this one thing out the door" rather than "I think that it is time to quit so that I can allow for traffic and get there a few minutes early." I was pushing my limit and I started to lose my focus. I got out of touch with time. Then I got scared that I would miss the meeting, and I did.

Get to know what leads you to panic. Sometimes, we panic over seemingly small things, or because our day is just unraveling and we have planned too much. Sometimes, our pattern of frenzy just goes over the top, and now we are in a full-fledged anxiety attack. At other times, something else altogether is bothering us, and we will only discover this by taking a little time for a gentle conversation with ourselves. Many people try to do too much in any given period of time. Pushing too hard and failing can lead to panic.

A key to dealing with panic is to plan for it in advance. Create some calming phrases for yourself at a time when you are in good shape. Practice them for the times when you are overwhelmed. In particular, if you tend to create jams for yourself, such as losing the keys to the company car right before an important presentation, learn how to remove self-blame for the moment. Talk to yourself: "It's going to be all right. This is a small matter in the larger scheme of things. . . ." Once you calm down, you will find that you can think again. You'll remember where you put the keys.

At these chaotic and frightening times, it helps to remember that panic is basically a *temporary* chemical reaction. See if you can stop for a minute and take some deep breaths. Unless there is a true emergency and you are on the way to the hospital, you can take the time to get some oxygen to your brain. Pay attention to the feeling in your body. Don't label it, just feel the feeling. Chances are you are feeling a lot. This is the result of the adrenaline that is coursing through your veins. Interrupt your thoughts. You may be frightening yourself with what you are thinking.

If you can be patient and not fight the nervousness, the adrenaline will be reabsorbed by your liver in a matter of minutes. You don't have to stay in the panic zone. You can tell yourself something like: "I'm nervous now, but in a few minutes, if I don't fight this and breathe normally, I'll start feeling better."

When you get disorganized and panicky, it might be a sign that it is time to face something difficult. Consider that you may be like an alcoholic who drinks when under stress, or a compulsive overeater who eats when things are overwhelming. We create extra messes and stresses for ourselves when overwhelmed and upset about something else.

Once you recover from the immediate fear, you can explore what might be an underlying source of the panic. Ask yourself the following questions:

- What's bothering me?
- What else could be going on?
- What does this remind me of?
- Whom can I talk to about this?
- What do I need?
- Can I see that making messes or chaos is painful but not lethal?
- Can I calm myself down and start again?

You can gain control over your panic. Keep reminding yourself that it is only temporary and that you will be back in charge soon. Quiet yourself so that the chemical imbalances can drain out of your system. The panic will pass.

Take Care of Your Physical Needs

Rest

Rest. What a concept. Close your eyes and breathe deeply for a few minutes. Do this once an hour and allow your body to refresh itself. Rest is wonderful for helping to focus your tired, distracted brain. Pause—let the events of the day sink in. Thomas Moore suggests that pausing provides a "period of non-doing that is essential nourishment to the soul."

If you are rested and focused, you will be able to get more done in four hours than you can in eight when you are fragmented and burned out. You may need rest periods. Plan rest in your days. Put rest into your weeks. Turn off the phone. Read poetry. Turn off the TV (it is not restful). Play music. Breathe. Sit and watch the ants. Play with your dog or cat. Don't do anything. It's easier to rest if you find a comfortable place. If you work at home, sit in your favorite chair for a few minutes after lunch. If you work outside the home, perhaps there is a park or a coffee shop nearby where you can rest for a little bit.

Get Enough Sleep

Sometimes you are just too tired to clean up. You just can't face the dishes in the sink or the mess on the dining table. Okay, that's part of life. But, then, go to bed. Don't watch TV in a stupor. It won't refresh you. And don't read. Put the magazines and catalogs down. Do not answer the telephone either. Give yourself permission to go to sleep. Climb into your bed and enjoy the sweet feeling of letting the fatigue wash over you. You did enough for one day.

Most Americans are sleep-deprived. One consequence of not getting enough sleep is difficulty paying attention. Sleep deprivation contributes to distractibility. Since you're distracted, you don't get done what you wanted to, and you stay up late trying to finish everything. Then you don't get enough sleep. It can turn into another vicious cycle.

Some people can't sleep because they are up worrying about what they need to do or didn't get done. Others don't sleep because the only time they have to themselves is late at night. It is the precious moment when they let themselves read a book or magazine. The parents of young children often find it is the only time they have together without the kids and this has become precious, even if they are exhausted the next morning.

Make it a top priority to get a full night's sleep. You will regain the "lost" time sleeping in refreshment and productivity. It may take concentration and will to break the pattern, but you can get out of the habit of being sleep-deprived. When you are exhausted and feel too tired to even get yourself to bed, start telling yourself that you will feel much better if you go to sleep now. Allow yourself to make a list of what you still need to do, but then put it aside and go to bed. It's worth it.

Remind yourself of your purpose in life, and figure out what your sleep deprivation is costing you. Envision yourself feeling good and rested. You might want to find out how and why you are staying up. Are you on the phone late catching up with friends? Are you leafing through catalogs? Are you watching TV? These are habits that you can break once you become aware of what you are doing. Get support. Tell your partner, family, and friends that this is a priority for you. Prepare yourself: when you first start getting enough sleep, you may feel worse, mostly because you are less numb and more aware of how you feel. But stick with it. You will start feeling better, being more productive, and completing the things that you want to accomplish.

■ ■ ■ EXERCISE ■ ■ ■

Once a day as you are changing your sleep patterns, visualize yourself going to bed a little earlier than you typically do. Imagine yourself in the middle of your late-night activity. Then see yourself deciding that it is time to go to bed one half hour earlier than usual. See yourself deciding to let go of your activity and getting ready for bed. Make a commitment to yourself to go to bed one half hour earlier than usual. When you are actually getting ready for bed, prepare yourself for sleep by thinking calming, restful thoughts. Perhaps repeat to yourself these comforting words: "All is well, all is well, all is very well." As you practice your visualization, and soothe yourself with peaceful thoughts, it will become easier to go to sleep earlier. As with changing any habit, it may take several weeks or more of practice. Changing our body clock is not easy.

■ ■ ■

Eat

Sometimes your brain isn't functioning because you are undernourished. Eat something nutritious. Feed your brain. You may find that skipping meals temporarily saves you time, yet later in the day, you can't think very well. Food is good, healthy, and essential for focus. Try a high-energy drink if you are in a hurry. Go to your health food store and stock up on nuts and protein bars. Even if you are overweight, you need to eat. Also drink lots of water; dehydration can contribute to fatigue and make it hard to focus.

Create the Environment that Works Best For You

Dr. Edward Hallowell, the attention deficit disorder specialist, gives many helpful tips to those of us who suffer from distractibility. He says to make your work environment as "peppy" as possible. "Know that it is okay to do two things at once. . . . Often people with ADD need to be doing several things at once in order to get anything done at all. Know how and where you work best." You may find that you work best with a lot going on around you. If you have ADD or are prone to distractibility, and work at home alone, try getting out of the house to get your work done. Find a restaurant or cafe where you can work uninterrupted, or try working in your local library. Some people work best in front of the TV. As Dr. Hallowell says, "Children and adults with ADD can do their best under rather odd conditions. Let yourself work under whatever conditions are best for you."

Partnering to Keep Our Eyes on the Prize

It's so easy to get distracted by work-style differences. As you have probably grasped, I fall into the group of distractible people. As fate would have it, I married a very task-oriented and organized individual. Our differences around organizing have been challenging (and distracting) for both of us, and we received some help from a framework that was introduced to us by the Learning as Leadership Group in San Rafael, California.

They distinguish between two types of people: D's, who are drawn to a divergent set of activities, and T's, who focus on accomplishing specific tasks. For instance, my husband loves to check things off his to-do list. I don't even like looking at my daily to-do list—so I have learned to write it on brightly colored index cards in interesting colors. Although I place little boxes by the tasks I complete (to experience a sense of accomplishment), I often would rather do anything other than what is on my checklist. My husband, on the other hand, actually loves to check things off his to-do list, and he loves giving me items for my list as well. Another example: he feels great when he has plowed through his e-mail. While I feel okay about getting through my e-mail, task accomplishment doesn't give me the charge that it gives him. And usually I have to bolster myself first so I can get through it.

D's tend to be fuzzy about their goals, and T's tend to be clear. When there is a task to be done, D's tend to focus on the costs of doing it versus the benefits of not doing it, while T's tend to focus on the benefits of doing it as opposed to the costs of not doing it. D's want to feel good before tackling their task, while T's don't feel good until the task is accomplished. If a D misses their target, it's not that bad as long as they had a good time getting there. For a T the outcome is more important than the enjoyment of the journey. D's tend to respond to anxiety with inaction, and T's respond to anxiety with action. D's tend to criticize people who are too action-oriented, while T's criticize people who are too enjoyment-oriented.

So D's and T's are quite different, and, as nature would have it, they often become life partners or close work colleagues. Without awareness of the distinct and valuable qualities that each person brings to the relationship, they can slip into criticizing each other. I would criticize my husband for being "run" by his to-do list and he would judge me for letting things go and not staying on top of my assigned tasks. What we often don't realize is that neither orientation is the "truth" of how to relate to time and tasks. We could see that we *both* tended to avoid doing what are often the most meaningful yet difficult tasks for us in support of our goals. D's tend to avoid difficult tasks through focusing on how they feel, while T's often do everything but the most important (and hardest) thing for them to do. When we viewed our own approach as the one right way, we could end up just getting on each other's case (and nerves) and not achieve what either of us really wants. What we most wanted to do was learn how to support each other in achieving our deeply meaningful goals.

Try to remember that each person's weakness is also their asset—when viewed through an appreciative lens. Try to remember, too, that your partner or colleague may have something to teach you. D's often can teach about enjoying life, and T's have much to teach about accomplishing tasks. Both lessons are important. Moreover, each partner often needs support in doing what is most difficult for him or her to do, and often the other partner holds the key to providing that support.

The Wisdom of Focusing

We have so many choices. When we focus we give ourselves the gift of depth and presence. We can focus on what is important to us, and we can bring our attention to the present moment. Both of these types of focusing will deepen the quality of our lives. Life is a practice of coming back to the richness of the present moment, and coming back again. In the next chapter, we explore more deeply the power of focusing on the present, and the synergies of organizing and spirituality.

11

Make Music Out of the Ordinary:
Spirituality and Organizing

There's a popular theater production that travels the world called *Stomp*. In it, gifted performers create an exhilarating musical using only the "instruments" of daily life. The "orchestra" consists of brooms, trash cans, lids of pots and pans. Even plastic bags and newspapers are used to produce rhythms that transform them into vessels of music. Through ingenuity and attention, these daily objects become sources of art. The stage rocks with the energy and dance—of spirited human beings who are "playing" a few mundane objects. You can do that, too; you can make music out of the tasks and things of daily life. It takes attention, ingenuity, and joy. This is the essence of the spirituality of organizing. We take the seemingly mundane aspects of life and find the joy, the spirit, and the sustenance. In so doing, you may feel as if you are turning your old ideas of organizing and spirituality upside down.

Spirituality means different things to different people. For some people, living a spiritual life means being open and welcoming the day, whatever it may bring. It means being available, heart and soul, for the present moment and for other living beings. For others, it can mean living with passion, being creative, or receiving divine inspiration. Living a spiritual life may mean being generous and compassionate, resonating with the suffering of others, being of service, and being reliable. It can also be about raising one's consciousness, feeling serenity, clearing the mind of the clutter of resentments, jealousies, and other misperceptions. It can mean seeing God's presence in all things, carrying God's word into the world, and doing God's will. In our pluralistic world, this barely begins to describe the rich and diverse aspects of spirituality. Being touched by a piece of music, noticing the sun glisten on the intricate web of a spider, laughing and playing with a child, helping serve supper in a shelter for the homeless, and awakening for a brief moment to a sense that we are all one—these are all spiritual experiences.

But what, you may ask, does spiritual life have to do with my personal mess and chaos? One of the reasons we have created such a mess is that we haven't learned to bring care and awareness to the details of life. We don't see spirit in everything. When we ignore the details, we create chaos.

Whatever spirituality means to you, you may be surprised to discover that organizing can contribute a great deal to your spiritual growth. Everything that we engage in as we live our daily lives can help us grow and be more present. Gary Thorp, author of *Sweeping Changes: Discovering the Joy of Zen in Everyday Tasks*, notes that in Zen practice, "You learn that taking care of all the little details of your life really matters. Having the car serviced is better, both for the car and for you, than neglecting it. Attending to a dripping faucet helps the faucet, the sink, the water source and yourself. When you give your attention and care to another being or object, your life slowly takes on another shape and begins to have more meaning than before."

In the Judeo-Christian tradition, God encounters chaos very early in the biblical story. By the second line of the Bible, God transforms this chaos into an initial order by separating light from darkness. Soon, God is creating the whole world. The Bible teaches us that we are created in the image of God, and perhaps like God, one of the most important things that we can do is create order where there was chaos. We can read these early biblical phrases as teaching us the power of making distinctions and separations, surely one key aspect of creating order.

Teachers from many traditions invite us to consider that our everyday lives are the setting for our spiritual journey. Native American teachings emphasize care for the earth, traveling lightly on this planet, and living in such a way that we leave little trace. The Christian mystic Teresa of

Ávila teaches that "God is not only within the altar, but God is within the pots and pans." Buddhist teachers emphasize being present in the moment, making any activity an opportunity for quieting the racket in the mind and perceiving reality more clearly. Rabbi Nachman of Breslov teaches that when we care for everyday tasks with focused intention, we release sparks of holiness that contribute to the healing of the world. All these teachers have a deep respect for engaging with everyday life with awareness and care.

Spirituality is personal, deep, life-enhancing, and may or may not include religion. For some people, spirituality means a connection with God, while other people have a hard time with God and anything that refers to organized religion. Personally, I have found great value in some of the teachings from traditional religion. But you may not. Much of the wisdom I draw on in this chapter comes from the Western spiritual heritage, yet I also draw heavily from Buddhist and Taoist traditions, which are nontheistic paths. Take from this what works for you on your organizational and spiritual path. Like cleaning out, discard what doesn't work for you, and keep what will help you lead a more vital life.

Develop Your Own Philosophy of Organizing

In order to make the connections between organizing and spirituality real for you, you need to develop your own philosophy, based on your experience, about the importance of organizing for your spiritual growth. Pay attention, for example, to what happens in your work space when you've discarded many years' worth of unused training manuals, books, catalogs, brochures, or old papers. Observe whether you feel more grounded in your space. Notice whether people connect with you more easily when you consistently show up on time. No amount of inspiring words can match your own discovery that how you live affects your connection to spirit, and that your connection to spirit can help you find order in the chaos.

To create your philosophy, study your own beliefs. Check to see if you hold beliefs that are in conflict with one another. For example, if you believe that "Living with just enough possessions helps me tread lightly on the earth" and you also believe that "It's not wise to pass up a bargain" or "I can't travel without buying souvenirs," then you have some work ahead in building a philosophy—a set of beliefs—that will help you live more congruently and with less chaos.

Frances started off being caught in contradictory beliefs. "For years," she recalls, "I have firmly believed in letting go of excess. I had been trying to pare down my wardrobe because I had too many sweaters, too many pairs of shoes, too much of everything. I valued simplicity, but I couldn't let go because I didn't want to be seen in the same outfits too often. I kept telling myself to give some things away, but I couldn't do it. The turning point for me took place when I went on a business trip where I had to carry my own luggage. Never had I packed so lightly, yet I still felt that I had plenty. I had a direct experience of how, when I am carrying less stuff around, I can be much more present with people and myself.

"I came home and gave away half of my wardrobe almost painlessly because I was very clear about my goal. I actually love having less. While there are often times when I wear the same outfit frequently, it doesn't bother me because my life is so much simpler and I don't have to deal with so many choices and caring for all those things. I now feel grateful for each garment and my life feels more whole."

As you let yourself feel the spiritual benefits of organizing, you'll naturally deepen your intention to continue with your organizing journey. Keep building a philosophy of organizing that is true for you. It will be one of your most effective organizing tools.

■ ■ ■ EXERCISE ■ ■ ■

Take a few minutes to write answers to the following questions.

1. What are some of my spiritual beliefs?
2. Do they match and support how I am handling my time and possessions?
3. Are there any ways in which they contradict each other?
4. Do I see any contradictions that I would like to work out?

As you answer these questions for yourself, you may be able to design an experiment that will help you work out some of the contradictions. For example, if you intend to set aside an hour a day for prayer, meditation, or inspirational reading, but you never do, experiment with five or ten minutes a day for a week. Now, review your experience of that. Perhaps your goal of an hour a day was too much, but a shorter time period will bring you valuable benefits.

■ ■ ■

Ways in Which Organizing Can Contribute to Your Spiritual Life

People who have been blessed with deep spiritual experiences often report a heightened sense of awareness. The world seems more vivid: blues are more blue, the sun brighter. The Buddhists teach that there is a way to achieve that experience without a special occurrence. Tibetan Buddhist Chögyam Trungpa Rinpoche teaches that we can experience "true magic [which] is the magic of *reality*, as it is, the earth of earth, the water of water." We can achieve this by paying attention to the present moment. How we organize ourselves can help us be ready to receive this magic.

Letting Go of "Stuff" Can Open the Connection with Your Source

Reducing our excess belongings can be a gateway to a sense of being part of something greater than the self. We have a need to be an integral part of something greater than ourselves, to feel that we belong to a larger universe, yet often we are overwhelmed by the presence of things, rather than the presence of the Divine. We wish, perhaps, that we were overwhelmed by awe, but we can't create sanctuary because of our carelessness with our belongings and our commitments. Our material excess can induce a kind of stupor, as if we had eaten too much. The sense of bloat is tangible. Since we spend so much time just managing our possessions, we have little energy or inclination remaining to appreciate the sense that we are part of a larger universe.

We may turn to material objects to give us what we might receive from a spiritual source. In *The Overspent American*, Juliet B. Schor cites a woman who says, "I bought a diamond ring for myself. It made me feel worthwhile, loved, secure. My husband doesn't believe in giving diamond rings, so I had to accept the fact that I had to buy one for myself if I wanted to get all those good feelings." This might seem extreme, but we try to get good feelings from buying ourselves things quite often. Recently, I went shopping at a local mall, and I noticed that the experience of wandering through the shops, thinking about what to buy, gave me a feeling of excitement and belonging.

We may have to deliberately turn away from our habits of accumulating things and explore how to turn desire for possessions into desire for spiritual connection. You may feel a sense of fear and emptiness at first; one thing about material possessions is that they seem so real. Sometimes, opening to spiritual connection is like opening an unused faucet: at first rusty water pours out, but soon clear, fresh water flows, and you are in touch. Paring down to the essential can help us experience this sense of the sacred. There is good reason why many spiritual teachings discourage accumulation. We can get hooked on the stuff and forget that there is nourishment in the intangible. Less becomes a whole lot more, because our less becomes a doorway to the transcendent.

■ ■ ■ EXERCISE ■ ■ ■

Choose something that you don't use but have been holding on to for a long time. Pick it up or touch it and consciously let it go. Give it away to a friend or a charity or put it in the trash. Allow yourself to feel the fear of letting go. Let yourself think all the thoughts that go along with letting go: What if I need it? What if I miss it later? But don't follow them. What do you feel after the initial fear? Are you aware of another kind of experience?

■ ■ ■

Clearing Up Your Physical Spaces Can Open Up Spiritual Spaces

Who has not felt the impact of entering a space that is full of harmony and balance? A simple room with a few items can emanate spirit, as can a mighty cathedral with soaring spires and complex design. Sacred external space is an invitation to discovering the sacred space in oneself. Creating such a space at home can begin with finding a place for everything, and putting each thing in its place. As you put things away with awareness and love, you can transform the energy of your spaces.

Clearing spaces externally allows us to experience more spaciousness internally. As we uncover our spaciousness, we also feel accessible, can deepen our connections with ourselves and others, and experience more awe. We can begin to settle down because we are not always battling external and internal disarray. As you create this sacred order, you gain a sense of intimacy with the things of your own life that gives you a sense of who you are. When things are familiar and cared for, they can give us an external sense of place, which helps us develop an internal sense of place.

Chögyam Trungpa Rinpoche, one of the foremost teachers of Tibetan Buddhism in the West, describes how important it is to create sacred space:

> You see that you can organize your life in such a way that you magnetize magic, or drala, to manifest brilliance and elegance in your world. [You can do this by] invoking magic in your physical environment. This may be as small and limited as a one-room apartment or as large as a mansion or hotel. How you organize and care for that space is very important. If it is chaotic and messy, then no drala will enter into that environment . . . when you express gentleness and precision in your environment, then real brilliance and power can descend onto that situation.

If we are used to a chaotic space, it may take time to experience the magic of a cleared and open space. In the beginning, I missed my mess. In time, I learned to welcome the sense of spaciousness that my cleared spaces allowed me to feel.

■ ■ ■ EXERCISE ■ ■ ■

Take a small, messy spot in your home or work space and clean it up. Now, notice. Do you feel more energetic? Do you feel more creative? Do you feel calmer? You might feel scared. Spend some time jotting these feelings down on paper or in your journal. Let those feelings sink in.

■ ■ ■

Managing Time Well Creates Openings for Spiritual Awareness

The commonly accepted purpose of time management is to get more done more efficiently. Yet, as I've noted earlier some of us suffer from trying to fit too many activities into a day. As we learn the basics about time—how long things take, the preparation-action-completion cycle, allowing for transition time—we can start to use these skills to discover deeper levels of time. We can start to live more closely with our own natural cycles. We can pay attention to what Professor Joel Bennett, author of *Time and Intimacy*, calls the soul forces of time—acceptance, flow, presence, and synchronicity—so that we can be aware of what is emerging, not just what we are doing or creating. We can use the bits of free time in our busy days to open to deep soul-nourishing awarenesses and ask some intriguing questions: What is emerging now? What "wants" to come through in this time period?

We can also use our time-planning skills to consciously create intervals for spiritual practice. Your practice may include yoga, meditation, prayer, or quiet times to listen for that which is calling to you. You may want to build in a time to walk. Try walking barefoot on the earth first thing in the morning, or just look at the sky.

As you get more organized, you will find spaces in time. Perhaps, at first, you will experience a few openings during the day, when you are neither booked for an activity nor rushing because you are late. Instead of filling up those intervals with action, you can learn to tune in to yourself. You can listen to what is calling to you, the "still small voice within." As it is written in the Bible, "This word is not far from you. It is not in the heavens . . . neither is it beyond the sea It is very close to you, in your mouth and in your heart" (Deuteronomy 30:11–14). Hearing this word is life-enhancing, yet we need to create receptivity to honor it.

Ruth Mason, who took one of my workshops in Israel, describes her experience of learning to arrive on time in an article in the *Jerusalem*

Post. One evening, she had a few open moments before leaving for an evening class. "On Monday night, I have planned and made and eaten dinner with the thought in mind that I need ten minutes free before leaving for the workshop. I look at my watch and see the time is at hand. But I have packed my bag earlier and my shoes are on. All I have to do is get my jacket. I suddenly find myself with ten minutes on my hands and nothing to do.

"It's our anniversary and I suggest to my husband that we have a slow dance. He puts on a Stevie Wonder song and we dance. Like magic, everything seems to change: The atmosphere in the house, the vibes between us, how I feel inside." When you are on time or early, you can feel spaciousness inside. Contrast that to how you feel when you are rushed, running late, or coping with too many scheduled appointments.

As we do the hard work of time management, we come to understand that we cannot do everything that we want to do. That realization, while disappointing at first, can also yield to an insight that we must learn to make wise choices. We see that we are shaping our lives when we "set priorities." When we make our time management choices with awareness, we find that we must get to know ourselves more deeply. Otherwise, we are going to wreck our lives. Many people want to take quiet walks in nature, meditate, pray, or just pause to notice what is going on around them. They tell themselves that they don't do these soul-nourishing activities because they don't have time. But it may not be time that they don't have, it may be the courage to make their soul's needs a priority.

Spalding Gray said, "I've been circling my meditation pillow for twenty years." Yet, circling is not the same as doing; you just can't get the spiritual development you want without making time for your spiritual practice. Managing our time with an eye toward creating sacred intervals can help us create practices that allow us to hear the One who is always speaking to us, or tune into the abundant, rich qualities of life.

■ ■ ■ EXERCISE ■ ■ ■

Take out your planner and schedule a time for an open interval once a day. Start with even as little as five minutes. Don't think that five minutes isn't enough; for many of us, it's a great start. Quiet your mind. Focus on your breath. Perhaps you can get some fresh air or stretch for a minute.

Do what is comfortable for you to just quiet down. Keep this scheduled interval as a part of your daily routine and try increasing the amount of time or the frequency you allot to it.

■ ■ ■

When Your Word Is Good, You Can Deeply Support Each Other

Mutual support can be one of the most rewarding aspects of our spiritual lives. When our word is good, we are more likely to receive support from others because they know that they can count on us as well. We are also more able to support others when we can count on ourselves to do what we say. Together, we can create a climate of mutual trust and connection, which is one way to experience the holy spirit between us.

Knowing that we can count on others gives us courage to take on the difficult things in life with a feeling of support. For example, friends of mine adopted a child from Russia. As they were discussing their experience, they said that they could never have done it without the friends who were there for them, twenty-four seven. Their friends showed up when they said they would, helped with paperwork, emotional support, and meeting them at the airport. This kind of reliability gave them the courage to go through with the challenge of an overseas adoption. Imagine not knowing if you can count on people to be there for you. What have you held back from doing because you didn't know if you would be supported?

When our word is good, we also feel that we count—that we can make the difference in other people's lives that we want. We can contribute more to our families and our neighborhoods, to our schools and workplaces. We can volunteer our time knowing that we will follow through. For example, when she began managing her time better and keeping agreements, Helen discovered that she could take the lead in organizing the annual Christmas party in her neighborhood, something that she had wanted to do for years.

When we are able to count on each other, we deepen our trust and connections. We no longer have to test each other because we know that we will back each other up. We can enjoy the benefits of feeling that we are part of a community. We can better manage life's challenges because we know that people will show up to help, deliver their work on a joint project, or simply remain present with us as we experience what is difficult.

Managing Distractibility Helps Develop Focus and Presence

Clearing off the desk, doing one thing at a time, creating an energizing to-do list, and setting a timer so that you can start a difficult task all help to focus the distractible mind. Our presence is a precious gift, yet so often we are not here. We are preoccupied with what we didn't do or what we have to do. As we create systems for tracking tasks, action items, and priorities, we can be more present with what is at hand. Psychologists are beginning to explore the new problem of what they call "presenteeism." In contrast to absenteeism, workers do show up at the workplace, but there is no one at the helm. Managing distractibility helps us be at our own helm.

Belinda is an advertising executive who has been interested in meditation as a way of spiritual growth. She wrote, "I can't think straight with a mess all over my desk. My mind scatters with the piles of notes and papers, the half-drunk cups of coffee. There are wires from my computer and other equipment in tangles on my desk and little notes to myself that I can barely read. So, when I sit down to work, I am sitting down to what feels like a minefield. I don't know what disaster I will step on next. I can feel the tension in my body."

She realized that the mess was getting in her way and decided to clear off her desk, "I took all the little Post-it Notes and quickly made notes in Outlook. I untangled the computer and the mouse wires. I was amazed at the relief. And then I did something that I have thought about for a long time. I meditated for five minutes right at my desk. I just closed my eyes, and I allowed myself to feel my body breathing. I could feel myself calming down and bringing my attention back to the moment. When I opened my eyes, I was ready to focus and return to my work with serenity."

Belinda experienced the ways that she created an environment that made it challenging for her to focus, let alone be mindful. As you learn to pay attention and be more present, you may find that focusing on finishing work tasks becomes easier and more rewarding. You are more likely to remember what is on your to-do list or find things that you just had in your hands. Managing your distractibility is one step on the path to developing a practice of being more present, and you will find it easier as you become more skillful in understanding how you distract yourself.

■ ■ ■ EXERCISE ■ ■ ■

At the end of your day, think back on the moments when you were fully present and when you were not "there." What were the differences between the two experiences? What would you need to do to become more fully present?

■ ■ ■

Use Spiritual Practices to Help You Get Organized

You might have a thought that you will develop your spiritual life after you have gotten organized. After you have pulled yourself together, you'll start meditating, saying a morning prayer, or observing a Sabbath. You don't have to wait. To the contrary, it is engaging the mundane that will give you the perfect chances to deepen your spiritual life. The good news is that our spiritual practices can help us accomplish the tasks of everyday life that we so often avoid: folding the laundry, filing papers, washing the dishes, paying the bills. We can do both—engage our spiritual practice and get organized at the same time. (Life is full of amazing bonuses.)

Meditation Can Help You Let Go of the Accumulation

Meditation is a way of synchronizing your body and mind. When you sit quietly, your brain waves change. You start to feel your breath and your body again. You settle down. Your brain refreshes itself. This need not be a formal meditation. You can "sit" behind the wheel of your car when you are stuck in traffic, or pause at a coffee shop and close your eyes. Alice Domar, director of the Mind-Body Center for Women's Health at Boston IVF, calls these "mini-relaxations," which are short forms of meditation.

The important thing to practice is observation. Some people call it quieting the mind; in reality, what you do is create the conditions for your mind to quiet down. The way you do this is to watch your mind. Watch your thoughts. You will start to realize that your thoughts are not you. As you practice this, your mind will naturally quiet down.

Meditation helps you with organizing by helping you clear your mind. You can begin to see how you create your own confusion and disorganization, seeing your mind grasping for happiness through acquisition, attachment to things, and overcommitment. In Buddhism, greed is one of the hindrances to peace of mind. Through meditation, it becomes easier to experience directly how piling things up around us eventually creates more pain than pleasure. You can see how your cravings develop in your mind, and you can practice separating from them. Buddhist teacher Larry Rosenberg explains in his book *Breath by Breath:*

> We might, for example, be sitting and notice greed arises in the mind. The fact that it does is out of our control; it arises and departs when it wants. Typically it propels us into action, often some foolish action, because we overestimate the object that we want. We thereby find ourselves suffering.
>
> But the reason our greed is so powerful is that we identify with it. We regard our particular need as part of our self. The energy takes us over, and when we emerge, we find we've done something we regret. With practice, we develop the capacity to examine craving as a phenomenon.

This capacity to examine our cravings and get some distance from them can be very valuable when wishing for new belongings. We can learn to ride the waves of desire for things, and slowly desire, like fire, burns out. It can be quite a remarkably healing practice to choose to sit down and meditate in the middle of a firestorm of longing for a possession. Very often, you will get a new perspective that sheds light on your current shopping dilemmas. You may gain insight into what you want even more than the new purchase.

Meditation can also help you cut back on your accumulated obligations. When you first start reducing the frenzy and overwhelm, life may seem a little flat because you are coming down from your adrenaline high. You may wonder if this is all there is. Chögyam Trungpa Rinpoche says one of the best paths to awakening is disappointment, because disappointment results from the removal of illusion. If we can use our meditation to sit with these feelings of flatness and disappointment, and tolerate being more present, the flatness soon turns into richness. But this is not the richness of grandiosity and running after great things, it is the fullness of reality just as it is.

Moments of Stillness Help with Priorities and Direction

Take a moment to pause for prayer or inner listening; use it as a time to enter into a dialog with the Unseen. Pausing can allow you time to catch your breath and quiet your mind. It is a recognition that, if you listen, you may hear a calling or intuition that points you in the next direction. You can refocus when you pause, gathering your scattered wits about you. We often don't know what to do next. Pausing can help.

Pausing also supports us in appreciating the abundance we already have in our lives. Our lives are so full, a banquet of temptations so rich and lavish, that we often cannot recognize true nourishment when we see it. We are busy, but not satisfied, full but not fulfilled. When we slow down to pay attention to our own experience, we open ourselves to the love and richness that is here all the time.

These are moments that can nourish your connection to your heart. As theologian Henri Nouwen says in *Making All Things New: An Invitation to the Spiritual Life,*

> It is clear that we are usually surrounded by so much inner and outer noise that it is hard to truly hear our God when he is speaking to us. We have often become deaf, unable to know when God calls us and unable to understand in which direction he calls us. Thus, our lives have become absurd. In the word *absurd,* we find the Latin word, *surdus,* which means "deaf."

These moments of stillness can grow as your skill in managing time grows. Sam describes a moment of insight that took place when he was heading to a meeting through Central Park in New York. He said, "Normally, I would be walking very fast, ignoring everything around me. But on this occasion, I allowed time for a slower walk. It was a beautiful day. I saw several ducks paddling quietly in the water. I heard an inner voice saying 'All is well.' For a moment, I experienced a kind of resting in the full abundant goodness of life."

Stillness also gives you a chance to attend to your intuition and intention. What are you sensing in the moment? What do you want in this situation? What is truly important to you here? Take a moment and ask; perhaps you will be surprised. Such a pause can interrupt the reactivity of your old familiar patterns and help you attend to what is new or fresh for you. The Tao Te Ching asks, "What is it that can make muddy water clear?" And then notes: But if allowed to remain still, it will gradually become clear of itself.

A good time to pause is when you are starting an activity—before you start to do the dishes, turn on the car, or when you sit down to work. Get into the car, put the key in the ignition, and just stop moving for a moment. Take several deep breaths. Feel yourself breathing. Scan your body. It won't make you much later than you are already, and you can get your bearings. Endings are also good times for pauses.

You can use your moments of stillness as a way of defining your intention for the next period of time: "I am dedicating my time and energy and spirit to creating order in this kitchen, and through intention and focus, I can evoke the energy to do that." Or "I am dedicating the next two hours to enhancing openness or serenity." Often we are racing through the moment and we haven't consciously asked, "What is this time about?"

■ ■ ■ EXERCISE ■ ■ ■

You need stillness to discover your intention. Even just a few moments of stillness can allow you to discover what it is that you want at a deep level. What is your soul longing for? Use a small, regular check-in with yourself to ask:

- How am I doing?
- Am I on track?
- What do I have energy for?
- What do I need right now to undertake my tasks with awareness and love?
- What is my intuition telling me?

As you make this a daily or hourly practice, your mind will become clearer. You will feel more centered and remember what's important.

■ ■ ■

Prayer Brings Us Help for the Everyday Tasks

From the perspective of the mystics, everything we do can be a prayer, even breathing. When we engage in everyday activities with the words of the Divine in our hearts, we bring a sense of holiness to every moment. You may be someone who has a problem with prayer. You may feel that nothing happens when you pray, or that there is no one to pray to. You don't have to pray to or pray for—you can simply hold an awareness of the Mystery. Prayer consecrates the moment by directing our attention to something greater than ourselves. When we pray, we recognize ourselves as holy beings and our daily work as holy work. As the poet Gunilla Norris writes in *Being Home*, "Prayer and housekeeping—they go together. They have always gone together. When we clean and order our homes, we are somehow cleaning and ordering ourselves."

Some of us use prayer as a way to ask for the strength to accomplish our everyday tasks. Prayer opens up the possibility for a greater force in our lives to provide support. We can't reduce the chaos alone. But we can do it with help.

Prayer can also help us get perspective and clear our minds. The Irish poet John O'Donohue puts it this way in his book *Eternal Echoes*:

> In prayer, we come nearest to making a real clearance in the thicket of thought. Prayer takes thought to a place of stillness. Prayer slows the flow of the mind until we can begin to see with a new tranquility. In this kind of thought, we become conscious of our divine belonging. We begin to sense the serenity of this clearing. We learn that regardless of the fragmentation and turbulence in so many regions of our lives, there is a place in the soul where the voices and prodding of the world never reach.

As prayer helps us discover an inner clearing, it helps us to be readier to clear up space around us.

▪ ▪ ▪ EXERCISE ▪ ▪ ▪

Try stopping in the middle of a difficult moment of sorting or discarding. Quietly ask for help. If you are not accustomed to praying, this may seem quite odd and awkward, but try it and see what happens.

Perhaps it is late at night. You are at the office trying to put together a presentation for the next morning, or at home facing a sink full of dirty dishes. Ask for the strength to continue. Ask for the courage to do what you must do, that you need heart to do. Here is what you might say:

> *God, who is the creator of all things, bring me strength, courage, and hope as I finish my work tonight.*

> *Source of all life, help me cut through my confusion. Help the fog lift and help me feel the blessings in my life. Help me do these dishes with gratitude.*

■ ■ ■

Keep a Sabbath to Create Structure in Your Week

After six days of creating, God stopped and rested. God rested on the Sabbath, and so can we. The Sabbath is a retreat from the everyday world. Rabbi Abraham Joshua Heschel calls the Sabbath "a cathedral in time," a time for renewing the soul.

Sabbath observance helps with getting organized by giving you a weekly deadline for finishing tasks and cleaning the house. This is particularly valuable for people who work at home and can find themselves working at all hours, seven days a week. Observing a Sabbath also helps with organizing because you stop rushing and trying to get everything done. You acknowledge that you will never get everything done and you cannot wait for completion in order to rest. On your Sabbath, you put getting things done aside. For this Sabbath time, enough is enough.

You do this because you know that when you work all the time, you do not get more done. Extended breaks are essential for your well-being and your long-term productivity. "No problem can be solved from the same level of consciousness that created it. We must learn to see the world anew," Albert Einstein once remarked. When we are refreshed, we can bring great insight and energy to solve problems that seemed insoluble just the day before. Designated rest enhances creativity, gives you regular family time, and provides time for one of the most special of human activities, gathering together. Yet, keeping a Sabbath seems impossible for busy people. There is so much to get done, and already there isn't time enough to do it all. For some people, it involves breaking their work addiction and facing the fears that drive it.

You can start keeping a Sabbath for an hour or two, then move on to a whole evening. Then, rest for an evening and a morning. Perhaps later, you'll take a whole day and dedicate it to rest. You'll close the door to the office, put the laundry basket down, let go of the world of deeds, and enter into the world of awe. The Sabbath allows us to move toward the Great Mystery, so that we can stop being so sure of ourselves and allow another kind of energy to enter into our hearts, minds, and souls.

On the Sabbath, you stop trying to get anything done. What happens will happen. Quiet comes, stillness comes, blessing comes. All the efforts to get somewhere, to be someone, to make something happen, good efforts, rightful efforts, they all cease now that you have entered your Sabbath. The Sabbath is a time for gratitude. In his book *Sabbath*, Wayne Muller cites the Christian mystic Meister Eckhart, "who asserted that if the only prayer we ever prayed our whole life was 'Thank you,' that would be enough." Gratefulness cultivates a visceral experience of having enough. As we cease all our doing for Sabbath rest, we know we are enough, we have enough, we can stop, and we are grateful.

■ ■ ■ EXERCISE ■ ■ ■

Set aside a Sabbath time for three weeks in a row. You can pick a few hours in the morning or an evening. If you want to find other Sabbath observers, it is helpful to know that the Christian Sabbath is on Sunday, the Jewish Sabbath starts at sundown on Friday evening and continues until nightfall on Saturday, and the Muslim Sabbath is on Friday. Yet, you don't have to make your Sabbath religious to experience its value.

Now, guard this time with your life. It will give you life if you give it life. Pick some activities that are spiritually renewing for you. Perhaps you like to meditate or walk on the seashore or in the woods. Perhaps this is time to play with the children or grandchildren. Perhaps it is time to read. Perhaps you take out those watercolors that have been drying up in the closet. The important thing is to break your normal routine. You might try taking the phone off the hook or not engaging in commercial activity. Remember, this is not just leisure time. It is time for spiritual renewal.

■ ■ ■

Practice Mindfulness to Make Clearing Up More Satisfying

Making the bed, doing the dishes, picking the toys up off the floor, it all counts. It is part of engaging directly with our world. We can do all our activities with the direct, sensual, nourishing contact that they offer. But mostly we resist and end up creating more unhappiness within us. We try to avoid certain experiences. We are averse to dealing with paperwork, we dislike scrubbing a burned pot, we cannot stand keeping track of business expenses. Mindfulness is a practice of bringing one's attention to the present moment, so that you can pay attention to what is, rather than paying attention to the chatter in the mind. By practicing mindfulness, we attempt to remove the labels that we put on the experience and stay with the actual experience itself. Scrubbing a burned pot becomes transformed from "a stupid waste of time" to an opportunity to clear the mind, and simply be present with the soap, the charred areas, and the scouring pad. Tracking business expenses loses the label of "tedious bureaucratic bull," and becomes an opportunity simply to write down expenses and store receipts.

You can do the dishes in the same way. I had such an intense aversion to doing my dishes that I would rather put my dirty dishes in a big plastic tub and move them around the kitchen than actually do them. Once I began practicing mindfulness, I learned what Thich Nhat Hanh, the Vietnamese Buddhist teacher, writes about in *Peace Is Every Step*.

To my mind, the idea that doing dishes is unpleasant can occur only when you aren't doing them. Once you are standing in front of the sink with your sleeves rolled up and your hands in the warm water, it is really quite pleasant. I enjoy taking my time with each dish, being fully aware of the dish, the water, and each movement of my hands.

Washing the dishes is at the same time a means and an end—that is, not only do we do the dishes in order to have clean dishes, we also do the dishes just to do the dishes, to live fully in each moment.

In fact, some tasks that you may have hated might actually refresh you if you look at them a little differently. You can bring your loving awareness to washing the lettuce leaves, for example. Take a breath and focus on your hands in the water. Focus on the color and veins of the lettuce leaves. Or bring your mindful attention to putting things away at the end of the day. Watch how you return each item to its place. Observe how you create order in the room.

If you are feeling overwhelmed by intellectual work, bringing mindful attention to something sensual or tactile can be refreshing. Marcia works out of her home office. As a writer, she spends a lot of time at her computer, dealing with words. She said, "I used to just hate doing the laundry. I folded it under duress, complaining all the way (who cares about a few wrinkles!!). But, now, I amaze myself, I fold laundry on my breaks. I love the feel of the fabric, I like taking a big messy pile and turning it into an orderly basketful of usable clothes, sheets, and towels. I have learned how to focus, garment by garment, towel by towel, until my mind slowly calms down from the day's ruckus. This is my mindfulness practice. It takes no more time than my old way of raging at the laundry, and, believe it or not, I get joy from it."

■ ■ ■ EXERCISE ■ ■ ■

Being mindful sounds easy, but to experience its benefits you have to actually do it. Here are two exercises that will get you started.

1. Pick an ordinary everyday task. Now, observe what you are doing with a quiet, attentive mind for just three minutes. Pay attention to your sensations. The feeling on your skin, what you see, the shapes and the sounds. Notice your breathing. If you notice yourself thinking, bring your attention back to the task at hand. Do it as if this were the first time you ever did this task. Try filing this way. Bring mindfulness to your task of filing papers. Notice whether you are experiencing repugnance for the handling of papers. Where do you feel that repugnance in your body?

What are you thinking? Keep coming back into the immediate present. Note the shape of the paper and the feeling as you touch it. There is just this insurance policy to file, stay with it. Feel the weight of the paper in your hands. Now, some notes to file. Where did your attention go? Notice if you become short of breath or find it difficult to pay attention. Keep going for a few more minutes. Keep coming back to the present.

2. Try mindfulness to increase your pleasure in daily tasks. Pick a task that you typically perform with distaste. Practice doing it with joy and simple awareness for three minutes a day for three weeks. Hold the intention of doing it with joy. Observe the results. Could this be a method you want to incorporate into your routine to do more of your daily tasks with a better attitude?

■ ■ ■

A Path of Honesty, Attention, Love, and Patience

Each day, you will have opportunities to explore the connections between your spiritual life and your organizing life. Byron Katie, author of *Loving What Is*, a popular book on spiritual development, says, "Don't be spiritual, be honest." Honesty about your own experience is more real than trying to be in touch with the holy. The matters of this world will keep you honest. Ultimately, organizing can help you build a spiritual life that is real. You will find authentic ways of connecting with yourself, with other people, and with the Divine.

As you travel this path, remember the words of British novelist Lawrence Durrell, who tells us, "Somewhere in the heart of experience, there is an order and a coherence which we might surprise if we were attentive enough, loving enough or patient enough." In all this talk about organizing and spirituality, we are really talking about contacting a deep order in our life. We are talking about how to find ourselves in a crush of abundance amid a culture of heightened expectations. We carry within us our own innate sense of satisfaction. "Just to be is a blessing. Just to live is holy," says Rabbi Abraham Joshua Heschel. The path of organizing can be a path to spiritual wealth. "Who is rich?" asks the sage. "The one who is content with his portion."

III

*Getting the Results You Want for
Yourself, Your Family,
and at Work*

12

Get Traction, Take Effective Action

tep six, taking effective action, is when you make some key changes in your life. First, you get a toehold, then you get a foothold, then you make your first step. Now you will bring to bear all of the tools from the preceding chapters and apply them to the sometimes scary, sometimes boring, and always worthwhile work of organizing your space, time, mind, and work. You want to minimize the amount of time you spend fruitlessly chipping away at the mess and maximize genuine change.

Now, I'll go over the entire process and I'll show how it works as you put all the steps together. I'll also give you additional tips and strategies to implement now that you are familiar with the individual steps themselves.

You will learn a lot about yourself as you as you take action. Viktor Frankl, a psychotherapist well known for his book *Man's Search for Meaning,* says, "It is not enough to observe ourselves, we truly learn about ourselves as we take action towards a meaningful goal."

Tap Your Passion and Purpose

The true starting point for this work is developing your purpose and vision, so if you have not formulated them yet, go back to chapters 2 and 3. Don't just think about your purpose and vision. Pull out a piece of paper, write them down, and place them where you will see them. Put them in your planner, your Palm Pilot, the bathroom, or on your dashboard. They are key to sustaining action and *critical* to your success.

Your purpose and vision will help give meaning to your new choices and new habits. With these tools, you can commit to getting the results you want. Commitment to a meaningful goal is the linchpin of change. You will come back to your commitment over and over again. When you vow to yourself that you cannot go on living this way, and you are determined to experience a deeper sense of order and serenity, you tap into inner energies that come forward to help. Commitment is not hope and it is not prayer. As you commit, you tap into your inner determination that you and your life will be different. You will find the inner and outer resources to make the changes that you want.

Allocate Time

Once you have developed your purpose and vision and are committed to them, you will be much more motivated to devote time to organizing. When you are ready to make some significant changes, pull out your calendar and allocate about four hours per week for getting organized over the next month. *Do this now*. This could be a half hour per day, or two two-hour sessions on the weekend. You'll find a rhythm that works for you. Organizing takes time, and you'll need to plan these sessions in order to develop momentum. For busy people, four hours a week will seem like a lot of time and you'll probably have to let go of some activities in order to do this. If you find yourself resisting, think of this as an investment with a good rate of return. You'll get the time back as you become more effective in your life. You will have more energy for what you really want to be doing. But, at first, be ready to cut back on other activities.

As you start on this journey, organizing may take longer than you think. Don't be daunted by this—plan for it. Remember the preparation-action-completion cycle? It operates here, too, so plan ahead to allocate time and energy to finish what you start in any particular organizing session. Also, plan sessions in which you identify new habits that you want to practice and a system that you would like to experiment with. You'll need time for all these activities. Schedule your organizing sessions when you are fresh and energized if you want your efforts to make a lasting difference. Don't organize when you are tired or during your "off" hours—this only makes it harder.

Use these rules of thumb as you set aside time to get organized:

- Allocate much more time than you think you will need.
- Do less than you think you can. Scope it down.
- Start organizing only what you think you can finish in the allotted time.
- Stop before you think you are done. Then, complete all the little details.
- And a little twist on all of the above—follow your energy. If you started out clearing out the junk drawer but suddenly have great energy to clear out the basement, go for it. Just reset your intention and keep moving. We disorganized people are sometimes best at doing just what we didn't set out to do. So what. Keep the big picture in mind and keep going.
- Remember that small steps actually taken are much more impactful than big steps not taken!!!

Think of organizing as being similar to setting up a new piece of unfamiliar equipment. Susan, for example, recently bought a new computer. Her old familiar clunker was about seven years old (dated and rusty by cyber age time) and her new laptop was sparkling, fast, and up-to-date. But she let her new laptop sit in a corner for months before she made the shift. The transition time just seemed too costly. She felt she didn't have the time to purge or transfer old files, organize her new files, and learn some new programs. It would take hours and hours of work to get up to speed on the new one. Besides, she loved her old white elephant.

Once she finally made the change, she wondered why she had ever waited so long, because she has become so much more effective at her work. As she looks back, the investment in the update was worth it. In fact, the transition time was insignificant compared to how much more she can get done now. Similarly, arriving at your new ways of being organized will take some time, perhaps even months or more than a year, but your life will run much more smoothly. Even more important, you'll have more time and attention for what you really care about. Looking ahead at all the hours that you have to invest to make the change can be daunting. Yet, looking back, it all seems so worth it. You'll wonder what took you so long.

It will help a lot if you designate an extended period of time when organizing will be a high priority. Designate next month as "organizing month." Or decide that this spring will be devoted to organizing. Cut back on your other activities and *focus*. A month or a season is not such a long time. Then, make sure that you have allocated time for your new habits to take root. It will take a while. You'll make progress bit by bit. A month is only a beginning. For many people, who are committed to creating significant change, this process may take years. Don't give up; remember, it took me thirty or forty attempts before I could keep my desk clear. Keep in mind, *the rewards are worth it.*

Arrange for Support

This is the step that most people miss and it is an *essential* step. Who is going to help you? Really. Whom can you call? When? Do you have their phone numbers? Can you meet with them? Share a copy of this book with them. That will help them understand what kind of help you need. Reread chapter 5 about support and identify whom you want help from. Don't postpone calling. If the first person you call can't give you the support you want, call someone else. Arrange a trade of support time.

Create a Plan

Since you can't do everything at once, create a plan that lists the organizing goals that you want to accomplish. Make a list of the projects you would like to tackle and then prioritize the list. Allow plenty of time for each project and identify a specific time when you will do each one.

When outlining your goals for your projects, keep in mind that they should be **SMART**:

- Specific,
- Measurable,
- Actionable,
- Realistic, and have a specific,
- Time for completion.

Plan to Organize Kitchen

Purpose and Vision I want a bright, comfortable place to cook and nourish myself. My kitchen is the warm hearth of my home.

1. Clean out refrigerator. (1 hour, today)
2. Recycle *all* glass bottles and plastic containers. (15 minutes, today)
3. Give away pasta maker and ice cream maker. Call cousin Ellen to pick up. (20 minutes, today)
4. Throw away dead plants. (15 minutes, today)
5. Buy hanging container for onions, potatoes. (1 hour, today)
6. Do all dishes. (1 hour, today)
7. Go through mail piles on counter—save bills only. (2 hours, *date*)
8. Find a better place for recycling bin. (15 minutes, *date*)
9. Put all canned vegetables on one shelf, pasta, crackers, cookies on one shelf, throw out all old chips! (1 hour, *date*)
10. Empty freezer—keep items 2 months old or less. (1 hour, *date*)
11. Clear off all groceries from counter/floor and put away. (1 hour, tomorrow)

When you create a plan, included your purpose and vision. You can sequence your small projects, and you have a picture of the whole organizing project. Then you won't feel pressure to do everything at once. Now, if you are like me, and you are extremely right-brain dominant, you might find that creating a list of projects doesn't help you. It just feels oppressive and too linear. You might find it easier to create a "mind-map" (see next page), which is a way of using your associative mind to create a plan. You'll have a picture of what needs to be done, and you can take

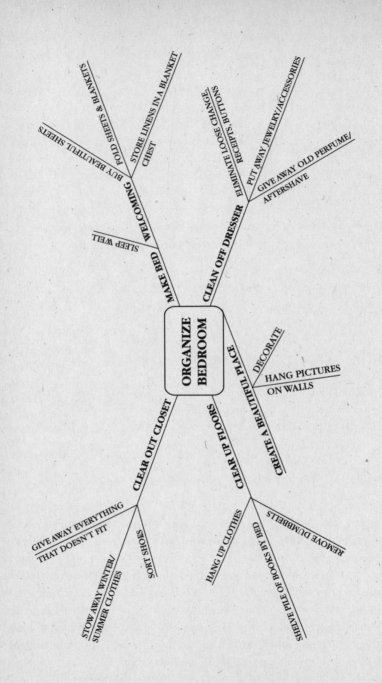

the actions that you have energy for. You don't have to face the creation of a list. You'll let your energy prioritize for you. Do the first obvious thing, and then the next.

Our tendency in organizing is to put only "getting to ready" projects on our lists or mind-maps. Make sure you mentally include time and energy for building new habits and creating new systems. Many personal organizers won't include habits and systems in their organizing sessions with you, so you will have to. Vanessa reported that she had spent the whole day clearing off her desk and office floor, but had forgotten to pay any attention to building systems and new habits. Within a week, her piles were creeping back. It's best to pay attention to systems and habits as you get your areas to ready.

Pick a Starting Point

Once you've established your priorities, pick a very specific area of focus. Don't try to organize your whole office or the whole house, or the whole attic, for that matter. Don't try to get every aspect of your calendar straightened out. *Scope it down.* Remember that your thinking can be confused, so what you think is a small goal might be quite big. Setting big, unrealistic goals will not help you get more done. In fact, it can backfire because you will feel discouraged and may be tempted to give up. Choose one specific area of your life that has been bugging you— whether it's a physical or temporal area.

The challenge in this is not to let your frustration take the lead, since it will say that you simply can't live this way anymore and you have to change everything at once. That kind of thinking will encourage you to try to do too many things in a half-baked manner. Then you won't see much progress and you'll be more frustrated. The truth is, you can't do everything at once. You will have to be patient. Taking time with your plan will yield great results.

As you choose where to start, look for leverage, which means working on the spot where you will get the biggest bang for your organizing buck. Identify the few things that you might change that will have the biggest impact in your life. What items do you spend the most time looking for? What important meetings are you always late for? What vital records can you never find? What bills haven't you paid? What services get shut off? What is the ugliest, most offensive place in your home or office that you can't stand but you have to look at every day? These are good starting points, so you can experience the beneficial impact of your organizing immediately. Some possibilities are:

- The top of your desk—with archaeological layers of papers, mail, lists, and half-drunk cups of coffee.
- One part of your office floor—with years of piles of papers, old magazines, and outdated materials. Identify an area small enough that you can clear it off in one week.
- The front hall closet—with several generations of boots, mittens, coats, and sporting equipment.
- Your car—perhaps it is a traveling storage container.
- One of the kitchen counters—for many people, this is the mail-sorting station, only the mail never gets sorted.
- The bathroom—with assortments of bottles, toys, outdated medicine, and Band-Aids that don't stick anymore.
- Your punctuality for a specific activity—start by identifying just one or two appointments that are important for you to arrive at on time. If you are regularly late for a particular meeting, focus on the key actions that will get you there on time. If you tend to be late for work, start with that.
- Overbooking—focus on one particular type of overbooking. Do you want to completely eliminate double-booking? Or do you want to stop canceling things at the last minute?
- Procrastination—again, choose one area that you want to change. If you chronically postpone calling clients, focus on what you would need in order to do that in a timely way.

When Sandra began thinking about her starting point, she focused on her bedroom. "I wanted to organize the whole bedroom in a day," she recalls. "I wanted to get the stuff off the floor, clear out the closet, hang up the pictures that have been in the closet for a couple years, and clean up the master bath. I figured if I was setting aside a whole day, then I better get a lot done, but I remembered that I often bite off more than I can chew. Then I don't get anything done. I decided to focus on cleaning out my closet. It didn't seem like a big-enough goal for a day, at first, but that is what I really wanted to do. And I did it. It was great. I brought a carload of clothes to the Salvation Army."

Ask what result you want to create from focusing on this specific area. Think about your goals in terms of what would be useful to you. Neatness is not your goal per se. Think in terms of accessibility, attractiveness, or utility. Identify a result that has meaning for you. What Sandra really wanted was to let go of all the clothes that were too small for her. As she thought about it, she decided that she only wanted to keep the clothes she absolutely loved, so that all the contents of her closet would support her aim of being elegant and sophisticated.

Keep reminding yourself that finishing a small organizing task is better than starting something big that you can't complete. Aim for less than you think you can achieve. When you complete your first getting-to-ready project, congratulate yourself and identify the habits and systems that you need to get back to ready. Then, practice your new habits and systems so that you can enjoy the ongoing benefits of your new spaciousness.

Make a Clear Choice

There is an exercise that I do in my workshops that I call "choosing a new habit." In it, you write down how you do things now, including your current habit, your current thinking, your current belief, and your current result. *And* you write down your desired result, the new habit that will get you the new result, and what you would need to be thinking and believing in order to get a different result. Then you make a choice: Which do you really want? I encourage you to try this yourself, using the example that follows as a model.

1. Choose one habit that you want to change and describe your current behavior in simple terms.

   When I eat a bag of popcorn and drink a bottle of water, I leave the empty containers in the car.

2. Write down the thoughts that accompany this habit.

   "I'll come back later and get them."

3. Identify the belief that underlies this behavior; it could be any thoughts you might have that support your current habit and sound true to you.

   Details are unimportant.

4. What is the result that you get from this habit.

   Messy car.

5. Now you describe your desired result and the difference it will make to you.

   A clean interior and much more pleasant transportation.

6. What new habit will help you get that result?

   I bring in everything from the car at the end of the day.

7. What would you have to be thinking in order to carry out this new habit?

   "I enjoy a clean car and it's easy enough to bring in everything right then."

8. What belief (or beliefs) would support this new habit? This new belief might be the opposite of the old belief, but not always.

   Small details make a big difference. I am worthy of dignity.

When you compare steps 1 through 4 with steps 5 through 8, you can see that you can make a choice. At this point, you will see that you will need to make this new choice over and over again until it is no longer a choice. It has become a new habit.

Make One Small Change at a Time: Go Slow to Go Fast

While the "just do it" approach and your own impatience may exhort you to "do it now—all of it," this method encourages you to focus on making small changes, one or two at a time, in order to achieve the results you want. Small changes make the larger process easier to digest. This is a "go slow to go fast" approach. Think about it: if you changed twelve key habits in a year, your life would be very different. It's just hard to say, "I'm going to spend the next month putting my keys back in the same place." It seems too trivial. But these new habits accumulate along with your "ready" areas. If you only sorted, tossed, and filed six inches of archaeological paper piles a week, you could get through twenty-six feet in a year!

At the beginning of this process, if I had told you it could take a year or two or more to get organized, you would probably have protested vigorously. Yet, too many people try very hard and don't get the results they want. They look back and say, "If only I had been patient with the slow pace, because the year went by, and I didn't get anything done." Ask yourself, "How many years have I struggled with this problem?" In comparison, is a year really so long? You will be pleased to discover that these small changes will slowly take root and become a natural part of your life. As you grow accustomed to each new choice and the resulting changes in your behavior, the new habit will start to feel like you. Small changes will build momentum.

Patience is the rich soil from which your faith in your changes will grow. If you can be patient and persist with your small forward steps, you will be amply rewarded. Impatient, nevertheless? Here are some keys to developing patience with the process of organizing.

- Focus on what you *have* accomplished.
- Feel pleasure at every little gain, and consciously congratulate yourself.
- Remind yourself that although you have taken on a big job, you can do it one step at a time.
- Keep telling yourself that as long as you are growing, you are gaining.
- Expect things to take longer than you had hoped initially.
- Trust that you are doing the right thing.

Take your time. Recommit to what you want. Revisit your vision. Be gentle and firm. Be patient and persistent. And you will see results.

Keep Yourself Motivated

If you are a people person, one way to motivate yourself is to set up exciting social events to get to ready for. Invite someone over, give a party, or offer your house for the neighborhood potluck. Make sure to allow enough advanced notice so that you can really prepare for the event; this strategy won't work if instead of throwing things all the way out, you stash them in the closets again. Joyce, who was production manager for a small high-tech firm, used this idea to take her next big step. She decided that for her fiftieth birthday, she would finally throw out all of the books, magazines, software, and documentation that she had been collecting for twenty years. It was a major decision for her to really clear out and let go of all that accumulated material. She left herself several months in which discarding and organizing were her top priority. She then held an office-warming celebration on her birthday, and gave herself a new start.

Reward Yourself

Rewards are essential for getting organized. While the process has its own built-in satisfactions, they generally are not enough to keep you going. Give some thought to extra ways to give yourself treats on this journey, allowing the small moments of triumph their due. No one else may understand that sending in the travel expense report on time is a great victory. No one else may grasp the triumph of arriving on time for three meetings in a row. But you do. (And I do.) These victories may seem minor to others, but let them add up in your own "bank" of success stories. In time, they will lead you to a new way of living.

When you arrive somewhere on time, take a second to celebrate. Give yourself a mini-hurrah, or an "I'm here! On time!" When you finally clear out today's e-mail, reward yourself with a small cheer: "I answered all my e-mail!!" Does that sound silly? It did to me at first, but now these tiny celebrations offset the moments when I say to myself, "You jerk, you're late again" or "This desk is a mess. When are you ever going to grow up?!" When I've made my bed, I gaze for a moment at the smooth sheets and appreciate the sense of closure. I say to myself, "This room looks calm and peaceful." When I bring everything in from the car at the end of the day, I acknowledge the sense of completion. These may seem like small achievements—but they accumulate. Your days are made up of hundreds of tiny actions that determine the quality of your life. Keep acknowledging your small triumphs. Anthony Robbins, a master of personal change, says in *Awaken the Giant Within*, "Don't wait until you've lost eighty pounds. Don't even wait until you've lost a pound. The minute you can push the plate away with food still on it, give yourself a pat on the back."

Using stickers can also help you track your achievements. These self-adhesive little pieces of paper that come in various colors and shapes can be a playful device for recording your accomplishments. You can place them on your wall calendar, in your planner, or anywhere else you find useful. Give yourself a sticker each day that you have practiced your new habit or accomplished a goal. Let the stickers add up and "cash" them in for a bigger reward.

Sally, for example, puts colored stars on her wall calendar whenever she arrives on time or clears off her desk at the end of the day. Eight colored stars in a row got her a special CD, that she refrained from until she achieved her row of stickers. Her incentive for getting through one of her "stalagmite" piles was foot reflexology, something that she would never otherwise do. Jenna compensated herself with a long-distance phone call to her best friend from college; another present she gave to herself was to buy a flowering plant for the dining room table. Rewarding yourself in this way is fun, and it helps generate momentum for the change you're trying to make. The trick is to hold it back until you have collected enough stickers on consecutive days.

Figure out what truly motivates you and feels like a genuine gift. Pick from this list or generate your own. Actually use the reward to motivate yourself. Don't reward yourself too soon, but don't hoard rewards either. Use your prizes to help yourself build new habits and take on some hard tasks.

- A long-distance phone call to a friend
- A massage
- A book or CD
- Dinner out at a special restaurant
- An evening at the theater or a sporting event
- A bouquet of flowers or a potted plant
- A vial of an herbal essence
- An evening out late at a jazz club
- An evening in early with a novel
- A visit to a local museum

Another way in which rewards can be particularly useful is with anxiety-provoking tasks, when you alternate task and reward. Reena described her strategy this way: "When I am faced with a terrifying pile of papers, I set my timer and work hard for fifteen minutes. Then, I allow myself a fifteen-minute reward, a call to a friend or yoga stretching. Under these circumstances, even doing the dishes or the laundry can be enticing. I alternate like this: fifteen minutes on the odious task, fifteen minutes of reward, until I make a good dent. For some tasks, this is the only way I can make progress." You probably have your own ideas of rewards that will help you change your habits. Treat yourself!! It is essential.

What to Do When Your Energy Flags

There will always be moments when being disorganized still feels like trying to breathe underwater or trying to dance with cement blocks on your feet. These are the days when getting organized feels as if you are dragging yourself out of a swamp. You might wonder if you are seriously depressed. On those days, you just do what you can to get going. The suggestions that follow will give you some tools to keep you moving.

Do the Easy Next Thing

Each of us has our particular terrors. Derrick, who feared paperwork, described it this way: "I would sit down and say, 'Now I am going to do it. I am going to pay these bills. I am going to sort out this horrifying pile of papers,' and then nothing would happen. I would freeze, paralyzed. I still feel that fear." It is times like this when doing the easy next thing is essential.

First you need to break the big job into doable tasks, what I call "chunking." Most people who create clutter never learned how to chunk properly, which entails developing the skill of breaking a big job into smaller tasks. Let's say that you are a person who is frightened of dealing with your money and facing the fearsome task of preparing your tax return. Perhaps just thinking "taxes" causes you anxiety. When you chunk, instead of saying, "I have to prepare my taxes" (which is just a huge frightening idea that can cause dry mouth and palpitations of the heart), you say instead, "I need to gather my receipts for the year." Even that may be too big a task, so you could say, "I'll gather my W-2 forms and my 1099 forms." And that will be a good start. Make a list of each tiny step or task and check each one off as you do it.

The next step is psychological in nature. You need to be able to *allow* yourself to do the *easy* thing first. Sometimes, you might feel that the task is only worth doing if it is difficult. Derrick says, "I feel morally obligated to attack the most difficult tasks first. I must prove I can do it. I learned I must eat my spinach before the ice cream. Now I know that when I am facing my backlog, it is critical to chunk it and to do the easy things first. It doesn't mean I'm a wimp, it means I'm strategic." If you keep creating smaller, more manageable tasks, the whole project will be easier and much more doable. Keep telling yourself, "Maybe this is not going to be as hard as I think." Keep looking to do what is easy first. Remember, even tiny steps that you *really* take get you much farther than big steps that you don't.

And Tackle Something Hard with Help and Respect

Inevitably, you will hit a hard spot in your organizing, such as your finances, or throwing out the stash of stuff in the back room. Don't do this alone. Clearing up puts us in touch with our anxiety. Finally throwing out the mess can be terrifying. Know that you are embarking on a task that is very difficult for you. Remind yourself that other people have done such challenging things, but don't minimize your anxiety. Keep breathing; you will get through the difficulty and there is something new and better on the other side.

When Carol called to tell her friend Sally that even though she felt that she was drowning in her taxes she *was* doing them, she was elated. Yes, she was slogging through her swamp, but not alone this time. She called for human contact and for a reminder that she could get through it. Two things were hard for Carol. The first, and obvious, hard thing was doing her taxes, and the next hard thing was asking for help.

You'll feel great when you have moved your mountain. You'll have accomplished something difficult, and next time it will be easier. So, keep doing the easy things and when you are ready, go after the hard things.

Move Your Body

When you are stuck, sometimes it helps to just get moving. When you are confused, distracted, depressed, or just plain sluggish, try jumping jacks, stretching, or standing up straight and taking a deep breath. Breathing into your belly will get you some good doses of oxygen. Raise your arms above your head. Dance. Wiggle. Do anything you can think of to get out of the rut. Moving your body gets your blood circulating, which gets oxygen to your brain to help you think better.

Play Music

Any time you are sorting, filing, discarding, or just moving things around, put on great music. Find a piece of music that is liberating for you. It may be Beethoven's Ninth or Mahler's Fourth. It could be Thunder Drums or rap music. This will sound completely corny, but try the sound track to the movie *Rocky*. Put the music on loud and walk into the office, face the closet, or walk into the kitchen. If you are at work, use a headset or come in over the weekend. Begin to let your energy flow. Let the music help you feel how you are not going to let your mess hold you back; you are in charge of it, it is not in charge of you.

Try Shouting

Raise your voice and yell at your mess. "I'm in charge, not you!" "I am winning." "Get out of here." "This is my house, not yours." "I can do this." "You can't stop me!!" Sometimes, shouting can get your energy moving again better than anything else. Have fun with this. Shouting can unblock you, surprise you, and sometimes it will just seem funny. Warn your family and your neighbors that every once in a while you are going to vent some energy so that you can keep going. Never mind what they think. You are not doing any harm.

Go Outside

If you are blocked, just pick yourself up and get out of the office or the house. Breathe the air, get a change of view, look around, walk down the street, clear your head. Get a new perspective. See if an idea of how to do something easily and productively comes to mind. Take deep breaths. New research shows that as little as ten minutes of walking can shift a bad mood into a good mood. So, get up and move. Take a fast ten-minute walk or run around the block. Your new good mood will help you be much more productive.

Take a Five-Minute Shower

If you are at home or near a gym, take a shower, or at least splash water on your face. Let the water spill over you. Imagine that it is fresh energy. Imagine that this water is washing away all your cares and sluggishness. Try alternating cold and hot water. That can be very energizing. As you dry off, imagine that you are ready to move forward.

You'll start to find your own ways to keep your energy moving. For some people, the very best thing they can do is get someone over or make a phone call. Learn what it is that you need when you are stuck. Spend as little time as possible in that swamp.

Weigh Your Costs and Benefits

When it is hard to change a particular behavior, it can help to take some time and assess what you really want and what is holding you back. For each specific change that you want to make, you can ask yourself six questions that can help you weigh your costs and benefits for maintaining your current behavior.

The first question is about the benefits of your disorganized behavior. This question may stump you at first, because you want to change so much. But become a little curious about your current state: there are probably some good reasons why you do things this way now. Also, there may be some hidden rewards in the current situation. Probe a little. You may discover something interesting or helpful. It is often useful to reveal your current benefits, because then you can consciously weigh them against the costs, and really choose what you prefer.

Here are the six questions:

1. What are the benefits for me in this? (Lateness, pile, mess on the kitchen counter . . .)

2. What are the costs?
3. How would I really like it to be?
4. What beliefs do I hold that might be getting in my way?
5. What is the truth about these beliefs?
6. What are my next steps that will help me move forward?

Andrea was a banking executive who wanted to change her habit of being late, since she couldn't seem to arrive on time, no matter how hard she tried. When she first explored the benefits of being late, she thought that there weren't any. When she became very honest with herself, she could describe them.

"I feel that I have more time to get things done, to finish a project, and to find items needed for the meeting. I have time to talk to others on the way to a meeting. I have a feeling of being more in control. I avoid needless chitchat at the opening of the meeting. Lateness conveys I'm very busy and important."

Yet, when she began to assess the costs of this behavior, she realized: "People view me as unreliable, irresponsible, disorganized, uncaring, disrespectful, lacking judgment, rude, ineffective, arrogant, and someone to be avoided. I provide a terrible example for my employees. I often arrive in the middle of a discussion and I don't know what has already been said about the matter. There are also costs related to my own well-being: I feel anxiety, frustration, and panic. Other people are often frustrated or angry with me. I feel self-loathing, fear, and pain." When she looked at it this way, being chronically late was, in fact, a very expensive behavior.

As Andrea envisioned what she wanted, she said, "I would like to be prompt, reliable, reputable, and in control of my time. I'd like to be more harmonious, serene, and comfortable in my own skin. I'd like to be viewed as organized and respectful of others. And I want to be a good role model for my children. I want it to be easy to be on time, not an energy drain, as it is now."

She was able to identify two fundamental beliefs that might keep her lateness in place. "One is that being late gives me a feeling of having more control, the second is that being late helps me feel busy and important. However, the truth is that being late makes me feel much more out of control, more fearful and incompetent. As far as being important, being late makes me important in a negative way, because often people can't begin without me, but I don't like being important in that way."

As Andrea weighed the costs and benefits of her behavior, it became clearer than it had ever been that she absolutely no longer wanted to run late. It was not worth it to her at all and she identified several next steps.

1. Make sure the only things on my calendar are what I deem necessary and important.
2. Be very attentive to how things get on my calendar.
3. Put transition time between appointments on my schedule.
4. Make a commitment to being on time for everything.
5. Check my calendar the prior afternoon in case I need to make adjustments or get ready.

Andrea amazed herself with the results. The first week after answering these questions, she was on time for every meeting and conference call. She said, "I am so happy, I feel so much freer and more serene. I don't think I realized the price I was paying for my behavior."

Your Take-Action Checklist

You too can achieve these kinds of results. Use the following checklist—keeping it with you when you are working on projects and checking off each action as you take it. (See also appendix 2 for an expanded version with more room to write.)

The area that I am working on is: _____

❑ I have a purpose for organizing this area. _____
    The costs of continuing this way are: _____
    The benefits of changing are: _____

❑ I have a vision for how I would like it to be. My specific goals are:
_____

❑ I have taken stock in this area. A belief that I now want to hold is:
_____

❑ I have good support. It is

Names: _____

Phone numbers: _____

E-mails: _____

❑ I have gotten this area to ready.

❑ I have created a new system. It is: _____

❑ My new habit is: _____

❑ I will draw on the following organizing wisdom practices. (Chapters 7 to 11):

_____

❑ I have set aside time for this. (When?):_____

❑ My reward will be _____ after

_____ (number of) days of my new habit, or for getting to ready.

Take your checklist, all your new tools, and your commitment. These are the elements you will draw on as you embark on the organization journey. You are on that path now and you will reap great results.

13

Going Deeper to Keep Going

Step Seven is when you face the question: How do you keep going? You've taken action. You've made a few a changes in your life, perhaps you've made some progress, but you get stuck or an easy change gets hard. Gremlins start to hide your keys from you or sneak away with file folders or travel receipts that you thought you had found a place for. You were on time for a while, but now you're late again. Stan said, "I thought I got the hang of putting things away, but I had a huge project due at the end of the month and it seemed as if all my gains went out the window." Just when organizing gets a little easier, it gets harder. You thought you were getting somewhere and all of a sudden you have slid back to the old familiar agony.

Our old ways persist despite our best intentions. To continue to grow, you need to learn how to face the deep inner challenges and obstacles that may arise. You may find yourself up against a self that is resistant to change. That's true for all of us. It's helpful to know in advance that change isn't linear, almost everyone who makes changes oscillates on their path to growth. And know that you can use proven tools to dig deeper into the psychological issues that you are facing; you can heal your self-neglect, engage the power of restructuring your beliefs, and face your shadows to continue your path toward freedom.

Familiarize Yourself with the Cycle of Change

Research shows that very few people make a decision to change their lives, and just change. Often there is progress forward, then a lapse. We make more progress, then experience another relapse. Research also shows that forewarned is forearmed. If you know that you may lapse, you start to understand that even "falling off the wagon" is a natural part of the change process. At times, you will feel as if you are moving two steps forward and one step back, or, worse, two steps back and one step forward. That seems to be part of the nonlinear, somewhat mysterious, path of change. The most important thing is to commit and recommit. Recommitting to your purpose and vision is a key part of sustaining change. You have a choice when you lapse. You can give up, which is extremely tempting, or you can pick yourself up, dust yourself off, and just keep going. The route of recommitment will get you much more of what you want in life.

Real Change Comes in Waves

Setbacks are not the end of the story. You put energy into change for a while, and you experience results. Then your energy may flag, and a time of backsliding, perhaps even despair, may follow. Then the part within you that is longing for outer order and inner freedom gets reenergized again and you recommit to action or change. And then you create another change, and then your energy may drop again. That is the nature of change. Sometimes, you take a break from organizing—you may let the clothes pile up on the floor again. It makes sense to catch your breath, do some other things, and then, when you have energy again, you keep organizing. These waves of the energy cycle are natural. The ups and downs are normal, but they contradict our natural expectation that we'll just keep moving ever upward. There will be many moments of success and some moments of despair. Then you recommit to your vision. Don't give up. Keep going. You can do this. After a while hanging up your clothes will be almost effortless for you.

It is vital that you talk to yourself in positive ways even during the lapses. The papers pile up on your desk for a week, or even two weeks. You can say to yourself, "Yes, it looks like I am losing my new habits, but I choose to recommit to my habit of clearing off the desk at the end of the day. Like everyone else, I'm going through a 'lapse' phase in the cycle of change. It doesn't mean that the change is over. To the contrary, I see even more clearly how much I want to be organized so that I can live the life I want. I'm getting back in the saddle." A setback is not possible without some progress first. Remember, in chapter 1, I told you that it took me some forty attempts to clean off my desk and keep it that way. It may have taken more. Yet, each time I did clear off my desk, I was able to recognize that I was making progress that helped me continue to move forward when I slid back into my old habits. There were times when I just wanted to give up on the whole project; it seemed impossible. Now, I am so glad that I stuck with it.

Fear of failure can prevent people from recommitting to the changes that they want to make in their lives. It's hard to face that you have set off on a path and the positive results that you long for seem months, if not years, away. These are the times when you need to remember that you have the strength, the courage, and the support to keep going. Remember not to misread a lapse, instead look at it as an opportunity to gain valuable information about what works and what doesn't.

You can also learn more about your negative thoughts and beliefs (as if you didn't know enough already), since they typically accompany "regressions." Helen said, "I had been working on my new organizing habits for *three* years, and I thought they were completely ingrained. I was so discouraged to see that when I signed up for a creative writing class, something that I had always wanted to do, my old messy habits came roaring back. It took me a while to see that I still held the belief that I couldn't be both creative and organized. When I surfaced and reworked that belief, I settled back down into my new order."

A lapse is a great time to dig deeper into your beliefs about order, success, time, and productivity. Don't use it to beat yourself up, but instead ask how you can turn your pain into an opportunity for growth.

Appreciate the Plateau

George Leonard, in his book *Mastery*, describes what it takes to develop a new skill through sustained practice. As an aikido teacher, he noticed that students who are learning this art often hit what he calls a plateau.

He says that you know you are on a plateau when you practice day in and day out and you just don't get any better. You keep going, and it seems that nothing is happening. Leonard points out that as we learn a new skill, such as a new language or sport, we alternate between plateaus and spurts in growth. The same thing happens as we learn the skills and attitudes of being organized. You are going to feel at times that you keep putting effort into staying organized and it doesn't get any easier. Then, one day, your skill level will jump. You'll feel much more competent.

Many people drop out during the plateau phase of learning. They think that nothing is happening. They don't think they are learning, yet they are going through inner changes that are not apparent on the surface. It is important to value the plateau and the activity for itself, without looking anxiously for signs of great progress. Leonard describes how in learning aikido there are months when the students just practice falling. They fall and get up, fall and get up. They are clumsy, feel awkward, get bored. Many quit. And, yet, those who stay with it discover that one day their body is truly ready for more. So when you hit a plateau, recognize it for what it is, and keep practicing. Organizing your papers, keeping your appointments, saying no, it will all start to get easier.

■ ■ ■ EXERCISE ■ ■ ■

Try this exercise if you get stuck, plateaued, or set back.

Part I: Notice your thoughts. Write down all the negative things you have been thinking about yourself and about your setback. Check inside and see if you missed anything. (Save this list for cognitive restructuring, later in the chapter.)

Part II: Notice your progress. Remember back to when you first began your organizing efforts. Chances are that you haven't lost all your gains. What is still working? Even though you are experiencing a setback in one area, are there other changes that you have been able to sustain? Are you overlooking the progress that you have made because you are so focused on the setback?

Part III: What can you learn? Pretend you are an observer from another planet and view your setback from a detached perspective. What triggered this setback? What is working? What needs more work?

Part IV: Bring to mind your purpose and vision. Remind yourself of the costs of continuing this way and the potential benefits of changing. Take a moment to recommit to getting more organized.

■ ■ ■

Dig Deep into Your Emotional World

We started looking into the emotional roots of our mess and chaos in chapter 4. Now, we can go deeper and look at how organizing can truly point you in a direction of deep change. I've talked about the gold in the chaos; as you do your deeper work, you'll be mining for that gold, because you will learn things about yourself that you could not have learned any other way.

Heal Your Self-neglect

After years of being disorganized, you may have some fundamental needs and wants that haven't been met for a long time. You may not have had people over, had a pleasant, comfortable place to sit, had daily nourishing meals, or even had a regular chance to rest and relax. You may have become accustomed to living in a state of semistarvation with respect to your basic needs.

What is self-neglect? It is about not meeting your basic wants and needs and not allowing yourself to fully enjoy life. It is when you don't pay attention to yourself or when you always put the needs of others ahead of your own. It may be that you never read novels, go to theater, or paint, which you love. Or you may eat several meals a day on the run or try to make do with wrinkled clothes. You might find that aspects of yourself, such as the inner artist, opera lover, or the hospitable one, have disappeared. It is hard to feel cared for when you don't know if your phone will be turned off, when there is no food in the house, or you run your car on empty. The opposite of self-neglect is nurturing yourself: discovering or reconnecting with what you like, what you want, what gives you pleasure or comfort, and what nourishes you.

You need to practice identifying your inner wants and needs. Start with the small, special things that might bring more satisfaction into your life. Do you like taking walks? Do you enjoy long showers? Do you like to read short stories? What are the highlights of your life that you don't get around to doing because you are so busy? Remember, some of these things will be so small as to be easy to overlook, but when you start doing them again, your soul will perk up, life will seem a little more livable. Take a moment to list your needs, wants, and joys. Here's a sample list to help you create your own.

- Good food
- Nice clothes
- Feeling fit
- Deep sleep
- A long swim
- Music
- Theater
- Dance
- Reading literature
- In frequent touch with friends and family
- Fresh flowers
- Sitting and doing nothing

You can get very specific with this list, such as:

- A ripe, luscious mango
- Throwing a pot on my wheel
- A long walk around the reservoir
- Baking bread
- Cutting herbs from my garden
- A cup of coffee with the Sunday paper
- Sitting in a cafe and just watching people go by

Identifying your own list may take some time if you've been neglecting your true desires. Start with a few items and add things over time.

People learn a great deal about themselves from creating this list. When Helen did, she said, "Some of these things may be completely obvious, such as good sleep, but I just hadn't made sleeping a priority, even though my life is so much better when I sleep well. I don't like the feeling of wrinkly sheets, but still I don't make my bed. I leave clothes and books on the bed, and just push them aside a little, so I am often too uncomfortable to sleep. Now, I want to make good sleep a priority. This means that I have to, I mean, I *want* to clear my belongings off my bed and start making it every day."

David had a different reaction when he made his list. "I love theater. It would make a huge difference in my life if I just went to see a play every couple of months. But I don't go because I always feel so busy. I have a full life, but I just don't let myself do this. It's a matter of seeing how much I love it, and miss it, but I had forgotten this part of my life."

Chris observed, "I do stretching exercises every morning, and when I pay attention, I truly enjoy it. But I had turned it into another 'to do.' I had forgotten that I love it. I found that if I put on music with a good beat, stretching feels like a luxury, not a chore."

When Jill did this exercise, she noticed how she neglects herself by not eating well. "I love good food but I eat on the run a lot, because I am often late for meetings and I just pick up junk food or tuna salad loaded with mayonnaise. I know it isn't that hard to carry healthy delicious food with me, but I just don't take the time."

Being aware of how you neglect yourself will help you to start doing something about it. Remember that you need to start small, so pick one item from your list that you would like to introduce, or reintroduce, into your life.

- What would you like to do to take care of yourself well?
- When and how would you like to do it?
- How will you create time and space for this aspect of your life that you have been missing?
- Who will support you?

As you reintroduce this one activity into your life, reflect on what this experience is like. Ask yourself:

- What does it feel like to start doing this activity that you love?
- What are you learning from bringing this back into your life?
- Is it enjoyable or anxiety-producing?
- Do you start and stop?
- Can you make it a regular part of your life?

Keep finding ways to bring your chosen experience into your life. It might take several attempts, but when you finally do it, relish the experience. Remind yourself that there is more to come. In her book *Take Time for Your Life*, Cheryl Richardson uses the term "extreme self-care." This is a useful way to think about caring for ourselves, for, at first, paying attention to our needs in a loving way may feel extreme, but it is essential to see that organizing is a form of self-care.

Talk to Yourself in New Ways

One day, a client, Teresa, called me on her cell phone in tears. She had made such progress in creating more balance in her life, but now she was backsliding. Her day had gone out of control. She had to take her cat to the vet; both children needed rides to different places; she arrived at the pharmacy without her prescription; and the phone company turned off the phone because of nonpayment. She said through her tears, "Most of this is because of me. *I* forgot the prescription. *I* over-scheduled the kids' chauffeuring. *I* forgot to pay the phone bill. I've tried to change, but I'm just a hopeless case. I'll never change. My life is always going to be this crazy, and I can't stand it."

This was a chance for Teresa to practice a new way of listening to her thinking and then shifting it. It hurts when we slip back into old patterns. Any of us might say to ourself, "This is never going to work. I'd rather kill myself than face this mess I have to deal with. This pain is too much. I've tried as hard as I can. Other people can do this, but I can't." These are the moments when you might start to see a choice: "Do I go down my old familiar rat hole or do I choose something more healthy and life-affirming this time?" These hellish moments are of value if you can go through them in even a slightly different way. The very first thing to do, after crying in frustration, if that is where you've started, is to take a breath and remember that you can go through this differently.

A tool drawn from psychology called "cognitive restructuring" can be immensely useful here. Cognitive restructuring is based on the idea that how you think affects how you feel. If you can examine how you think and improve the quality of your thinking, you can shift how you feel, and thus how you act.

When you slide backward and berate yourself, give up, or otherwise fall apart, your inner comments express "learned helplessness," a phrase coined by Martin Seligman, author of *Learned Optimism*. Seligman says that just as we talk ourselves out of desired changes, we can learn to talk ourselves *into* them, to be optimistic about change. The essence of learned optimism is understanding and shifting how we explain our experiences of failure or adversity. The three key dimensions of what he calls "explanatory style" are when people experience their difficult situation as being:

1. Temporary and changeable versus permanent and fixed. Note the difference in tone and impact between "Things can be different" or "I am willing to try again. It will work out better next time," instead of "I've always been this way and I always will be."

2. About a specific area of their lives as opposed to something global and general. Instead of saying, "Nothing ever works out for me," try "I have a lot of trouble arriving at meetings on time."

3. Influenced by an external source as opposed to blaming themselves for an internal defect. Try saying, "I have learned some bad habits, and I can unlearn them." Or "I haven't had good role models for change" instead of "There is something wrong with my brain." This one is subtle. It is not about *blaming* external causes for one's problems (because that can render you helpless as well), it is about noting external influences on one's adverse situation instead of criticizing a supposedly defective self.

We need to learn to work skillfully with our thinking patterns and beliefs because they are so powerful. They shape our perceptions and become self-fulfilling prophecies. If you believe that you are a slob, you will tend to notice the slobby aspects of yourself and miss the disciplined aspects. For instance, Michael, an unemployed single father, told me that he was a hopeless case. He had to find work but couldn't get anything done. According to him, he couldn't follow through on anything and had no discipline. This was part of our first conversation:

Michael: I'm a total slob in every area of my life. I have no good habits.
I can't seem to follow through on anything. I've always been this way.
MP: Did you make this call to me today?
Michael: Yes. But that is only because I am desperate, and I had to.

MP: Do you brush your teeth?

Michael: Yes. But everybody does that.

MP: Do you get dressed in the morning?

Michael: Of course.

MP: Do you get your kids to school on time?

Michael: Yes, but that's about them, and they have to get to school on time.

After a while, we discovered jointly that he had some beneficial habits and some disorganized practices. You can see that his explanatory style led him to be pessimistic about getting organized. He was so sure that he was a complete slob that he had simply screened out the times when he demonstrated discipline.

We took his initial belief and reframed it into the following statement: "In some areas of my life, I am organized and disciplined. In other areas, I have learned some poor habits, and I can learn new, more effective ways of doing things." He found this to be more energizing than telling himself, "I'm a total slob."

The ABCDE Approach

Martin Seligman suggests the ABCDE method as a way to intervene in a familiar, counterproductive pattern that is taking you off course. The A, B, C part of the cycle summarizes our typical reactions and their consequences when we face an adverse situation. We often react to situations that we have created in such a way that locks us farther into a cycle of disorganization instead of pulling us out of it. A day full of these negative reactions can wear us out and prevent us from taking positive steps toward what we really want. The D, E, F part of the cycle interrupts the familiar pattern and directs us toward our goal. Note that I have added an additional step, F, to Dr. Seligman's original ABCDE approach.

Let's look at a case that completes the A–F cycle, and explore how you can disrupt a counterproductive pattern in a constructive way.

A. *Adverse situation or event*

I look at this pile of papers in the corner of my office. I have no idea what is in it.

B. Beliefs and thoughts

I don't even want to look at this pile. I don't know where anything goes. I hate looking at these piles and dealing with them. Going through them is a useless activity. Getting organized is just a complete waste of time. I'll be disorganized forever, and I don't care.

C. Consequences: Feelings, actions, and reactions

Feeling: I feel discouraged and hopeless. I have no energy for this.
Action: Ignore the pile and do something else.
Reaction: You see! I won't be able to get organized, ever.

Your challenge, should you wish to accept it, is to disrupt the A, B, C sequence with a new set of thoughts that will lead you to a new set of feelings and actions. By engaging D, E, and F, you launch a healthier cycle.

D. Disputation or disruption

Whoa!! Stop!!! Stinking thinking!!!! Red light, red light!!!

1. Ask, "What do I really want here? Do I want the familiar and painful results that I currently produce or do I want something new and different in my life? Do I want to go after my purpose and vision?"

2. Affirm your purpose and vision. This is not necessarily an easy choice, because there is something very comfortable about living with the old pains and frustrations. You might try saying to yourself, "I can see this office as a beautiful, calm sanctuary for good work. That is what I want."

3. Reflect on your thoughts in B and consider, "What am I thinking? Are these accurate, healthy, helpful thoughts?" Ask the following questions:

- Are they based on obvious facts?
- Do I see any distortions in my thinking? (Distortions include: jumping to conclusions, exaggeration, black-and-white thinking, ignoring the facts.)
- Are they helpful?
- Are these thoughts going to get me what I want?
- Can I think of alternative thoughts that are more healthy, realistic, and helpful?

Then, restructure your negative thoughts one by one. For example:

I don't even want to look at this pile. Actually, I do want to look at this pile. It is hard for me, but looking at it and seeing the reality of it is part of my journey. I don't like it, but I can handle it.

I don't know where anything goes. I probably do know where some of these papers belong. I imagine that I will throw most of these papers out. I'll keep only the ones I need, and I'll create simple files for some of them or get help with what is confusing to me.

I hate looking at these piles and dealing with them. It's true that I don't like looking at these piles. That is why I want to take some time now, develop some patience and tenacity, and get rid of them.

Going through them is a useless activity. Going through these piles is unpleasant, but I am committed to getting rid of them and creating a great work setting for myself. I can practice mindfulness and patience right now, and that is a very useful practice for me.

I'll be disorganized forever, and I don't care. I do care how disorganized I am. I've made a commitment to myself. I understand that I am upset, but I absolutely intend to work through this, whatever it takes. As Nietzsche said, "What doesn't kill me, makes me strong."

E. Energization and new effort

After you have disrupted and disputed your negative thinking, acknowledge that you are consciously choosing a new course. Notice that this takes courage and commitment and you do have these qualities. You may have more energy and feel hopeful. You can reengage with your organizing, perhaps say to yourself, "I think I'll take fifteen minutes right now to work on the top of this pile and make some progress."

F. Follow up

Build on your momentum. Follow up your good restructuring work with a renewed commitment to yourself. Rededication and recommitment to your organizing path are key parts of following up your work. Try declaring to yourself, "I recommit to getting through this. I feel good about disrupting this pattern, and I'll take a minute every day to revisit my vision and rededicate myself to bringing mindfulness to sorting through these piles."

Now, try the ABCDEF method yourself. You can practice this method at any time. It can be quite powerful in shifting your energy and actions. Reread this section many times. It took me a lot of practice before I could make good use of this method. For more details and support, read chapter 12, "The Optimistic Life," in *Learned Optimism* by Martin Seligman. His work is straightforward and easy to read. Another great resource is a book by Dr. David Burns, *Feeling Good*. Even if you are skeptical, give it a shot; it has worked for many people and it may for you.

Look into Your Shadows

If you have tried everything to get organized and made little progress, it may be that your mess and chaos represent something very important to you, too important to give up. In earlier chapters, we have touched on the idea that there are many benefits of being disorganized. Some of them are obvious: for example, when we are disorganized, we don't have to take on certain responsibilities or we communicate to others that we are not reliable and they shouldn't count on us.

Yet, sometimes there is a hidden message within the mess, chaos, and overwhelm that we can explore by drawing on the very powerful notion of the shadow from human psychology. The shadow, a notion originally described by Carl Jung, refers to the disowned aspects of our selves. These are the parts we don't want to know or look at, and yet they can take over our lives. Through deepening insight into our own story, we can shine a light of understanding on some of these hidden aspects of our being. We start to see that there is an unknown self that is holding on to the mess with all its might, and from its point of view for good reason. Perhaps we hold a belief from childhood that without our mess we would be vulnerable, unsafe, or too successful. We might have the sense that we bury ourselves in chaos so that we don't outshine a treasured parent or sibling in a way that could constitute betrayal. Many of our stuck patterns come from unconscious decisions that we made when we were very young. Those decisions were important then, but may no longer serve us.

It's not easy, though, to recognize that our stumbling blocks come from deep within. Most often, it appears that external forces beyond our control have gotten us into our various fixes. Yet, with courage, help, and insight, we can face that *we* are the gremlin hiding the folder with the crucial data, making us late, forgetting to file the invoices. We can do the inner work that is required to keep moving through the mess and chaos. As cartoonist Walt Kelly's character Pogo said, "We have met the enemy and it is us."

One way you know that shadow is involved is that there is an issue that has been plaguing you for a long time and you don't want to think about it or deal with it, wishing that you could just get rid of it. When you do think about it you experience a lot of resistance or pain. You are blind to how big a price you are paying for living this way. Finally, as you face it, you feel overwhelmed by a sense of powerlessness.

Working with your shadow helps you reintegrate the disowned parts of yourself so that you can regain your whole sense of self. As you do shadow work, you begin to relate differently to those piles of papers all over the office floor, the clutter in the living room, or the clothes on the bedroom floor. You look for their hidden message so you can find meaning in the archaeological layers of food in the refrigerator, the stuffed closets, the car that looks like a wreck. There may be a shadow side to how you keep breaking promises—you don't mean to but you do. If each of these areas of your life could speak, they would give voice to stories that could actually help liberate you from your pain and worry.

One way that you can spot your shadow is to pay attention to the qualities in others that are particularly irritating to you. Perhaps a very friendly, lovely coworker is always late to meetings, but no one holds her accountable. She "gets away" with it. This really bothers you; it seems truly unfair. And, yes, she is late, a lot, but for someone else, it's not a big deal, but you are really bugged. This is a good sign of a shadow. Take a look at your own lateness; you might not even be aware of it. Or ask yourself, "What am *I* 'getting away' with?" Another question that you might ask about the same situation is: "Are there ways that *I* use my friendliness to keep people from holding me accountable?" Or is there a part of you that would like to get away with something? Owning the shadow can give you self-knowledge and power that will free you to be more of who you are.

Harold was so indecisive that he suspected a shadow was at work. He simply could not go after what he really wanted. He said, "There is so much that I am interested in, so much that I want to do, that I get paralyzed, I don't know what to do first. I often end up doing nothing and feeling that I have accomplished so little." When he started to go after his goals, frustrating things would happen. He would lose things, he forgot to pay bills, he didn't return important telephone calls. He came to see that his disorganization held him back from doing what he really wanted to do. This feeling of being restrained from pursuing what he wanted to do in life was very familiar to him, but he didn't know where it was coming from.

He had a dream one night in which he was a gymnast with lead feet. In the morning, he remembered a conversation that he had had with his father when he was twelve years old. He was a superb athlete and had wanted to be a gymnast. His father told him to go out for basketball to build his team skills, saying, "You are not on this planet to do what you want in life, you have to do what's needed." As he remembered this conversation he became short of breath, and then was overcome by rage. He let himself feel the power of his rage, and how it could help him cut through his paralysis. His piles, his losing things, his indecision, were all his ways of keeping himself from doing what he wanted to do, which in his father's view would be selfish.

When you get stuck in your organizing, pay attention to your dreams. Dreams can point you in the direction of the unseen, strongly felt shadow influences. Write them down right when you wake up; they will often provide clues about your stuckness. Explore your dreams with another person who can help you see what you can't see in your dreams. Cultivate an attitude of not-knowing and invite your shadows to reveal themselves.

Matt began searching for insight because he simply could not stop being late despite all his resolutions to the contrary. This tardiness had become a serious performance issue at work. He was in a danger zone. Even though he was extremely good at what he did, his clients and colleagues were losing patience with him. Finally, he decided to delve more deeply into what being "late" meant to him. As an experiment, he took a few moments each day to reflect on how he felt as he ran late, instead of just pushing himself to be on time as he usually did. He asked the question, "What is my lateness doing for me, that I can't seem to do any other way? What is hard for me to see about this?" Interestingly, Matt discovered that he felt a small sense of triumph every time he was late. This discovery surprised him, since he had thought that he was trying his best to be on time.

When he thought more about this sense of triumph, he remembered his father rushing him and his brothers when they were little boys. Whenever they were on their way to school, church, or family gatherings, he heard, "Hurry up, boys, hurry up, boys." He remembered times when he would deliberately slow down, just to show his father that he could not be pushed. By paying attention to these memories, he discovered that he had made a decision that he would never, *ever* let anyone push him to be on time. He would always go at his own pace. His shadow goal in life, more important than anything, was to show his father that he was independent, he was in charge of when he arrived. It looked to him that he would rather lose his job than arrive on time.

With this awareness, he was able to reevaluate the decision he had made so long ago. He said, "Wait a second, I'm an adult now. I'm not a little boy. My father has passed away. I think I can make a different decision. It was right to be mad at my father as a child because he pushed so hard. But, now, there are ways that I can honor my own pace, other than running late." This insight, along with his feeling of triumph, was enough to break his unconscious pattern and allowed him to arrive on time. When he caught himself making choices that would cause him to be late, he would tell himself, "I can honor myself by arriving on time."

When our disorganization triggers deep emotion, chances are we are dealing with a shadow. We could suppress these emerging feelings but we can experience great healing if we let them emerge and learn from them. Greta, a professional photographer, was overwhelmed by film, photographs, and contact sheets. Her home office was a disaster. She described entering her very messy home office as a nightmare which left her feeling like screaming or crying. There were papers and photographs, piled everywhere. There was no room to sit since she had piles of contact sheets on her desk chair. It would take her precious time, sometimes hours, to find what she was looking for. She hired a professional organizer and started to glimpse her office floor for the first time in years. But after about three weeks, she gave up on the organizing project and the paper rapidly flooded back. She would go into a rage and feel so frustrated with herself, yet she was helpless to change the situation. Every time that she tried to clean up, it only seemed to get worse.

Greta learned to slow down and pay attention to her feelings. Instead of gritting her teeth and trying harder to fix the situation, she noticed a pain that felt like a stabbing feeling in her chest. With caring help, she allowed herself to feel this pain and to weep. As she wept with pain, she recognized what her office was showing her. She was unwittingly reproducing the feelings of anger and helplessness that she had experienced as a child in her alcoholic family. With that insight, she could see that for her, cleaning up her office would be a way of letting go of her family, and she had not been quite ready to do that. Like many children of alcoholics she wanted to change, and yet, chaos and helplessness made her feel at home. She started to explore other ways to stay close to her family. She observed that, "I am acting this drama out in my home office in an unconscious way. I don't have to create such insanity in my office in order to be loyal to be my family." It is a paradoxical aspect of human behavior that we sometimes hold on to the very things that keep us small and limit us, precisely because they are familiar.

Another way to do shadow work is to feel the different energies at play in your disorganization and give them names in order to work with them more easily. When I worked with Helen to clear out her closet, she would say, "I want to throw this out." Then she would say, "No, no I don't, I can't throw it out." Each item she touched evoked a similar contradictory dialogue. I suggested that she follow the voices and flesh them out. We discovered that Helen had an inner Good Girl who always wanted to do things just right, stay close to everyone, be nice. We also discovered that she had an inner Wild Woman who helped Helen take things less seriously, didn't mind what other people thought, and could let things go. Helen observed as she threw things out: "I need my inner Wild Woman to be in charge of throwing things out. Through her I have more of a sense of humor. I can throw out obligations like this odious gift I received seven years ago and didn't even write a thank you note for. My Wild Woman would say, 'Throw the thing out, and it's too late to write the thank you note.' This mess is a mausoleum to things I haven't done. But so what, the Wild Woman would just laugh and throw things away. By contrast, my Good Girl just feels guilty. She rushes in and says, 'You're not going to throw that out, are you? You never wrote the thank you note.'" Helen slowly learned to shift this inner struggle between the Good Girl and the Wild Woman, so that she could clear out a small area one step at a time. Like Helen, we are complex creatures, and we have a number of inner parts; if we let them come out we might be surprised at the energy that is newly available to us. We're afraid of becoming Lysol Libby—over-controlling and perfectionistic—but we are also afraid of becoming Lust-ful Libby. We don't let either of them out, we just have a mess.

The mess also keeps some of our good qualities in shadow, our se-renity, our success, our love. Some of us can only see our messiness: "I can't cope, I can't do it, I'm just too frazzled and too overwhelmed." We can't see what other people see, such as our leadership ability, kindness, creativity, how much fun we are, because we are so immersed in feeling terrible about themselves.

Because of the nature of shadow work and the power of your blind spots, you may need to work with a therapist or shadow worker to inte-grate your shadows. In the meantime, you can be appreciative of your disorganization, because it is pointing you toward the deep work that will make your life an adventure in learning about the self and the soul.

See Appendix 3 for more information on Shadow Work.

Begin the Cycle Again

As you go through a first cycle of getting organized, you might find that you are experiencing a little less stress. Perhaps you have deepened your sense of calm and spaciousness. Here and there, you might experi-ence more power and more presence. At this point, you might discover more about what you really want—going beyond your initial purpose for getting organized. The cycle is beginning again. You may want to go back to the beginning of this book to reclarify your purpose and con-tinue the journey of organizing.

There are different rounds of getting organized. The first round is to organize a few areas and change a few habits. This frees you to see that there are other places where disorganization is holding you back. You address those, and then, perhaps, you can clear up one whole area of your life, which allows you to experience a previously unknown level of serenity.

As you stick with this process, as organizing becomes a habit, you may be surprised to find how your life is changing.

Novelist James Baldwin once wrote, "Any real change implies the break-up of the world as one has known it, the loss of all that has given one identity, the end of safety." And the irony for us is that the familiar, hectic, out-of-control patterns represented a kind of safety for us. The end of that "safety" begins to yield to a deeper safety of another kind.

Organizing can result in very deep changes that seem distantly connected to disorganization. Charles reduced his blood pressure substantially and was able to significantly improve his health. Mary found that she took charge of what was important to her, and shifted from feeling like an overwhelmed victim to someone who could make good decisions for herself and her family. Helen created a lovely home for herself and shifted jobs, so that she could live a more meaningful life in all areas.

At some point, you will find that you have integrated enough organization into your life. There will be diminishing returns from organizing, so you've probably done enough. You'll notice that life is just easier and that you are enjoying yourself more. You've arrived at a level that we can call "good enough" organizing, enough to free you up to be more of who you are and to live a better life. And that is the point of all of this good work. We now turn to looking at how to bring organizing skill to your shared home life and work life.

14

Your Home Could Be Your Castle

In this chapter, we explore how to organize the home that you share with others. You'll deepen your understanding of how to share the common space, which could be your retreat, your sanctuary, a place where you renew your soul. When we live alone, we have only ourselves to argue with about keeping house. When we live with others, organizing often becomes a minefield. One person's cozy, homey retreat is another person's eyesore. I remember one day early in my marriage, soon after we returned from our honeymoon. After spending a few hours straightening up, I looked around and thought our apartment looked terrific. I expected my new husband to say something appreciative when he came home, but he said nothing. "Honey, don't you notice anything special about the apartment?" I inquired. He looked around and said, "No, should I?" So I said, "Well, I straightened up and put everything away." He said, "You did? It still looks messy to me." When I looked around again, I saw all the little piles of newspapers, books, and magazines stacked neatly in the corners and on the coffee table. There were no piles on the rug or the couch, so I thought the place looked great. For him, the place looked great with no piles. No piles at all. Hmm, I had to consider that one.

Let's look at what it takes to create a happily shared home life. Comfortably sharing space, food, and things; creating a place to relax and be oneself; and learning to count on one another are all aspects of building a satisfying home life. As Cheryl Mendelson, author of *Home Comforts*, says, "This sense of being at home is important to everyone's well-being. If you do not get enough of it, your happiness, resilience, energy, humor and courage will decrease." Our home can also be a place of holiness, a small temple, where we elevate our spirits and cultivate harmony. Hestia, the Greek goddess of hearth and fire, provided help to those who tended the sacred arts of homemaking.

Often, though, our homes are covert or overt battlegrounds, the place of numerous small offenses that can escalate and deeply wound. What we call the small things are often what drive our partners the craziest. Let's look at how to find creative ways to organize together, respect one another, and transform conflict into learning. In this arena, we are also looking for "good enough" organizing. Organizing that will allow us to live well, but perhaps without the level of precision and compulsion that gives homemaking a bad name.

One of the challenges of organizing our home is that we just see things differently. The unmade bed may mean freedom to one person, but the crumpled sheets and tossed blankets are an aggravation for the other. One person doesn't even see the piles of paper on the kitchen counter, but their partner finds them a painful eyesore that diminishes the beauty and destroys the sense of space. One person doesn't care if they run a few minutes late (or even half an hour late) for a gathering, while being on time is an essential matter of respect and care for the other. And so it goes. Sometimes, it seems that a mean gremlin purposefully matches people whose organizing preferences are opposites, to make us live in a state of constant irritation.

Through things and time, tasks and agreements we shape our lives. If we treat these important topics as trivial, we risk deepening our sense of fragmentation and making family life, and thus our individual lives, harder. We need to respect household organizing because often it is the setting of power struggles, value conflicts, and confrontations about commitment. How we organize our homes can trigger deep hidden feelings about how we love and are loved. It is the rare family that can skillfully navigate the treacherous waters of household organizing without fighting, wounding, and pain.

Organizing can be particularly frustrating because household members keep having the same fights over and over again. They try solving their organizing problems, for example, by allocating the household tasks. But one person doesn't keep his agreement to take out the garbage, and the other person doesn't keep hers to make the bed. Or people try to make new commitments and fail to keep them. Bill promises to arrive on time, yet is still a half hour late, leading Sarita to be angry, even though she knows punctuality is not his strength. What's going on?

Fights about organizing often persist because people think they are arguing about one thing, when really they are fighting about the bigger questions: Whose work is valued? How do we value one another? How do we develop a shared vision of our home? How do we handle earning discrepancies? Do we trust the division of labor to be fair over the long run? How do we break through gender discrimination and stereotyping? Who is controlling whom? Also, we are fighting because of our deepest self-perceptions: "I'm a creative free spirit and you are trying to hem me in by asking me to put things away." Organizing is just loaded with emotional freight. Yet, as you learn to recognize and deal with the bigger questions, chances are the mechanics of household organizing are more likely to fall into place, albeit slowly.

We are also entering the dreaded terrain of housekeeping. Housekeeping has a bad name in many circles. Housekeeping is viewed as worthless, repetitive drudgery that has held women back. My mother didn't know how to keep house, nor did she want to. My friends and I never talk about housekeeping; it's a taboo topic. Yet, here is something to consider: Cheryl Mendelson, who is a successful lawyer, loves to keep house—not in the Victorian sense of everything being just so, but in the sense of creating a warm, loving, hospitable place for living. She says, "Modern housekeeping, despite its bad press, is among the most thoroughly pleasant, significant, and least alienated forms of work that many of us will encounter even if we are blessed with work outside the home that we like. Once it was so physically onerous and arduous that it not infrequently contributed to a woman's total physical breakdown. Today, laundry, cleaning, and other household chores are by and large physically light or moderate work that doctors often recommend to people for their health, as evidence shows the housework is good for weight control and healthy hearts." It is possible to view housework positively. As we will see, cultivating a positive attitude toward it will figure strongly in organizing our home.

What Are You Really Fighting About?

Does this fight between Stacy and Craig sound familiar? "I was picking up his dirty socks for the thousandth time, and I said to Craig, 'Do you think I am your mother?' He said, 'They're just socks,' and I said, 'Who is supposed to pick them up?' and he said, 'It's not that important to me. What does it matter? We love each other.' And something just broke loose in me. I love my husband and I know he loves me, but I let him have it. Everything about how he is a prince who expects me to pick up after him, what kind of example he is setting for our children, and the fact that he doesn't even put his plates in the dishwasher. Next, I was telling him how much his mother spoils him, and then things I am very, very sorry that I said. So, now he does put his socks in the hamper, but for the wrong reasons. We haven't come to some good guidelines for how to keep this house a pleasant place."

It looks at first as if Stacy and Craig are fighting over who is going to pick up the socks, but there's more to it than that. Answering the question of who does what task is only the beginning of a journey into shared values about power and responsibility. Who is responsible for taking care of the space we live in? Whose home is this, really? Who is going to do the housework? Does housework matter? Is it valued? Who is to clean up after whom? When you cook a meal for me or do my laundry, are you (1) being responsible, (2) showing your love, or (3) being taken advantage of? Who earns the money, and what does that entitle them to when it comes to doing housework? These are tough questions. But facing those questions with an attitude of curiosity and inquiry can be much more productive than yet another fight about who is going to pick the dirty clothes off the floor. This curiosity and inquiry can be an exploration of one's own beliefs and assumptions as well as the other's.

It makes sense to bring up the small things early, before bad feelings fester. Yet, no matter how well we apply our communication skills, small things often have much deeper emotional significance than we are aware of. Home is the place where we first learned what it means to be taken care of. How we care for our home is also how we care for us. How you do your share of the household tasks can communicate at a deep level how much you care for your partner. Yet, this way of communicating caring is often done in code and is misread by the other person. The conversations become quite confusing. The subtext might sound like this: "If you loved me, you would pick up my dirty socks and put them in the hamper for me, without complaining, just like my mom did." And that is secretly answered by a different subtext: "If you loved me, you would take care of your laundry completely and I would never have to think about any bit of it. You would put it in the hamper, wash it, dry it, fold it, and hang it up all by yourself, since you are a grown person."

Dr. John Gottman, well-known researcher and author of *Why Marriages Succeed or Fail,* says:

> Housework may seem like a trivial concern compared to sexuality, but women see it as a major issue affecting their sex life, as well as the overall quality of their marriage. I've interviewed newlywed men who told me with pride, "I'm not going to wash the dishes, no way. That's a woman's job." Two years later, the same guys asked me, "Why don't my wife and I have sex anymore?" They just don't understand how demeaning their attitude about housework is toward their wives. Treating your wife as a servant will almost inevitably affect the more intimate, fragile parts of a relationship
>
> If you are a husband who is now saying, "Not me, I do my fair share," you need to take a really good look at how much you actually do around the house. Men are just not reliable reporters of how much housework and child care they do—almost every man overestimates the time he puts in. Even in dual-career families, women nearly always wind up doing most of the housework.

Conflicting Views of Space and Home

When they got married, Joy moved into Rich's house. Eight years later, they still have not worked out how to create a home that they both love, because each has a very different view of how a space makes them feel at home. Rich wants to keep "his" house much the same way it was before Joy moved in. Joy wants to move all of their things out so they can start over and create a living space that she feels comfortable in. Right now, neither of them is happy with the situation. Some of the time, Joy just wants to move out, ostensibly because of Rich's clutter. But there is more to it than that.

Joy

"I love space and openness and light. I want to walk into a room and sense the openness. Clutter bothers me. There are so many small things around. I think he has things out to show that he is successful. I like his taste, and I can see that these things are beautiful, but to me they take up living space, and they take up mental space. I walk into the rooms in our house, and there's no room for me. There is so much stuff clamoring for attention. He likes this closed-in feeling. I told him once that he uses his mother's decorating style. Our house looks just like his mother's house. He didn't mind my saying that because it doesn't bother him. I'm just not comfortable here. The bedroom is the only room that I like. I saw a house recently that I loved: lots of light, lots of space, very simple. Cream-colored walls and a great sense of calm. I could have moved right in and loved it."

Rich

"I like having my stuff around. It makes me feel at home. Everything has a memory for me, and some of these items are truly beautiful. And it's true, I keep years' worth of magazines, but I use those magazines. I know where everything is, everything is organized, and I need that information. I can put my hands on that information whenever I want to. The thing is, I told Joy, 'You do the bedroom any way that you want to.' She bought everything that she wanted, and she loves it. I also said that we could renovate the kitchen, and she can be the project manager. She can be in charge. But I do want to be able to have a final say because I live here too."

It is unlikely that Rich and Joy will work out the differences until they share what home means to each of them, as well as what they mean to each other. Clare Cooper Marcus writes in *House as a Mirror of Self*, "Creating a home together may be one of the most taxing negotiations any couple has to make. Each person brings to the situation a history of environmental experiences, dating back to his or her first awareness of home in infancy and childhood. Each has—largely unconsciously—created spatial and aesthetic preferences that will influence feelings about a range of issues about home, including location, size, form, style, decoration, furnishings, privacy, territory and use.[5] Therefore, it is not surprising that having to live with someone else's belongings scattered around can lead us to feel not at home in our own house.

Although the conflicts seem to be about how much clutter is on the surfaces or how to decorate a room, embedded in them are questions about the meaning of home, the feeling of home, and how the space they live in supports the inhabitants in living their lives well. The space can also reflect deeper questions for a couple, such as: "How at home do we feel with each other? Can we rest with and alongside one another? Can we hold one another?"

Time and Trust

The car is packed. Carlos is ready to drive off on their vacation. An hour ago, Cynthia had said she would be ready to leave in a few minutes. Yet, she is still packing a few more things, just in case. She remembered a last-minute phone call, paid a bill, and is trying to remember where she put the new tube of sunscreen that she bought. "How much longer?" he asks. "Five minutes, five minutes, I'm almost ready," she says, believing it. Yet, half an hour later she is finally locking the door, ready to go. Now he is too mad to talk. As they drive off, he is fuming, she is defensive. Not a pleasant way to begin a vacation. But this is a common experience for them. It happens on the way to social events and meetings as well. He is ready to go. She is often late. He sees her as irresponsible. She uses his sense of time to put some structure into her life but feels judged and irritated nonetheless. She has the impression that he feels superior to her, just because he manages his time a little better than she does.

The tension between Carlos and Cynthia may seem to be over their different ways of handling time and agreements, but it may also be about whether or not he can really trust her. It may be about whether or not she values his time. It may be about the fact that they have drifted apart from one another. He is eager to go on vacation with her, but perhaps she is not so excited about spending all that time with him. She can't tell him directly, so she signals her lack of interest in indirect ways. Alternatively, perhaps he sets unrealistic time lines and uses her casualness in this area as an excuse to control and dominate, so that he doesn't have to look at his own areas of weakness. Or perhaps the subtext of the conversation reads like this: Cynthia thinks, since you love me, couldn't you just factor in that I am usually late? While Carlos thinks, since you love me, you should start getting ready an hour earlier than you think you need to so I don't have to get so upset by our being late to everything.

Part of our work in organizing the family is to surface the subtext in the tensions and deal with the hidden messages in order to ferret out the real ones. If we can begin to read the encoded narratives, we are much more able to have the real fights. As we engage the real issues, we strengthen our relationship and deepen our understanding of one another. These conversations take courage and patience, but they can yield great benefit. You can actually learn how to create a more rewarding way of living together.

Create a Learning Conversation

In a learning conversation, family members explore each other's underlying needs and the kinds of lives they want to live together. They make an effort to respect each other's views and temporarily suspend their harsh judgments about one another. In order to do this, family members or roommates must create a time for these conversations at what we could call council meetings. They build a safe space or "container," developing the capacity to listen and speak deeply together. You can imagine this setting as a sturdy vessel that holds its bubbling hot contents without cracking, allowing them to transform into something of profound value. A strong container helps us bring stability and resilience to life's difficult situations, instead of our rushing in to fix them prematurely or running away from them.

When Sam and Philip tried to have their first council meeting, it was too hard. They were both angry about the state of the house for different reasons. Philip said, "We had let annoyances build up to the point where just looking at each other was irritating. We decided to start by writing each other a letter describing the specific behavior that was bothering us, a solution that we thought might help, and an appreciation of positive efforts that we perceived. That worked as a first step, as we were learning how to do more constructive problem-solving."

Meaningful conversation takes time, skill, and clear intention. Weeks, even months, can go by without a family's carving out time to sit and simply explore what is going on with its members. If there are tensions between various people, it becomes even easier to postpone "family council" time. Yet, gathering regularly to listen to each other, however challenging at first, may diffuse tensions before they build to a crisis. The meetings can help the family or couple identify issues that people are grappling with, or simply offer a time for parents and children to be together and listen to each others' thoughts and concerns. It can be an opportunity to listen for something fresh, for a way to reach beneath the everyday clamor to the surprising wisdom that we each carry inside.

Here are some guidelines for creating a "learning conversation." Start by establishing ground rules, such as:

- Establish an uninterrupted time and place to explore and resolve tensions.
- Slow down and reconnect with your heart.
- Listen deeply and pay attention to both verbal and nonverbal communication.
- Respect other family members' feelings and seek to understand the thinking and experience that leads them to feel the way they do.
- Acknowledge the other person's feelings and reality as true for him or her.
- "Lean into" discomfort. If we can learn to stay with, rather than avoid, discomfort, we often discover a spark of enlivening energy that points to what we can learn from the situation.
- Meet the challenges you and others are facing with commitment, courage, and curiosity. Find a way to become interested in what the others are saying. Let go of your opinions for the time being.
- Trust that difficulties, when handled with care and optimism, can lead to genuine growth.

You can use a learning conversation to explore your underlying beliefs about organizing your lives together. With careful observation, you will begin to see that your conscious and unconscious beliefs have an impact on your perceptions, which in turn influence your actions, and then your sense of reality.

Rich said, "When I finally started listening to Joy, I realized that she's really suffering!! The way I litter the house with my belongings causes her pain. She's mentioned this to me before, but I never took it seriously because it just seemed too trivial. I couldn't believe that clutter could bother anyone that much. But it's hard for her, she has a very different sensibility. I get it, and I do want to limit the waves of clutter that I bring about."

You might use this understanding to explore differences in what people think about performing household tasks or keeping agreements. For instance, you could uncover a difference between how you experience your partner's or child's behavior and what he or she actually intends. This can help you accept that certain actions are *not* intended to hurt you or make you mad, no matter how mad you might feel. You might ask several questions to put yourself in the other's shoes:

- What inner or outer pressures is my partner or child facing?
- What might he or she be intending to accomplish through this action or inaction?
- How might my behavior appear to him or her?
- How can we share our respective intentions and learn about the impact that we have on one another?

As you consider these questions, you might find yourself growing calmer. When you feel ready, you can raise your frustration with your spouse or child in such a way that the other party is more likely to listen with interest and respond with compassion. For example, Brad would leave his breakfast dishes in the sink on the way out the door, assuming that he would do them later. He also never made the bed. Michelle assumed from his actions that he believed that she was supposed to do the breakfast dishes and make the bed. She'd be fuming about how he expected her to take care of the housework while she was dying to get into her home-based studio and do her creative work. At first, she didn't say anything to him, telling herself it was no big deal. But she realized that she was getting increasingly angry with him.

Michelle decided to bring the issue to their learning conversation, even though it seemed so trivial. First she considered the questions listed above, which enabled her to bring up the issue in a calm way. She was surprised to discover that Brad never intended her to do his dishes or make the bed. He didn't make the bed since he had learned that "airing" the bed was important, and he figured he would make it when he got home. He also thought he could do his breakfast dishes at the end of the day. As they talked through the issue, he learned that since her studio was at home, the dirty dishes were an imposition on her space. With this new understanding, both were able to change. Now Brad usually does the dishes before he leaves out of respect for Michelle's work space, and Michelle is occasionally willing to do his dishes since she knows she has a choice. They take turns making the bed.

A learning conversation is a good time to revisit your vision for your family or remind each other of what you are grateful for. It can also be a time to offer special appreciations to each other or new ideas for shaping a comfortable home life. These practices help prevent painful conflicts in the future.

The Essence of Family Organizing

Try to find ways of organizing that are a win-win for everyone in the family. Give each other the benefit of the doubt when you are sharing tasks or trying to find a place for things. If you can, find a way to build new habits and systems together over time. Randy and Rick were both highly disorganized. When Randy decided she was ready to get more organized, it wasn't easy. She explained, "At first, Rick experienced any attempt I made to plan ahead or get organized by making places for things as controlling. Finally, he started to see that if we put things back in the same place, we could find them again. He experienced the logic of 'a place for everything' because it made his life better. He mostly replaces items when he is finished with them, but that was a tough fight."

Organizing Shared Spaces and Managing Possessions

One challenge of family life is to shape our spaces so that we each feel a sense of home, even when we have different tastes, styles, and different levels of tolerance for mess. This challenge includes wisely managing our desires for the many luscious-looking toys (for all ages) and the fantastic variety of products that the American marketplace is so adept at producing. Then, when we have the many things that we have purchased, deciding together how can we store them and use them so that they are valued. And, finally, families must face how to agree to give things away when they are outgrown or no longer fill the purpose they once did.

Sometimes, organizing is catching. Suzanne, who is a massage therapist, sees clients in her home. She decided to prune her books in the family room, without making a big deal about it. Then her husband noticed and joined in. Then her daughter got involved and organized all of her makeup in the bathroom. "I now spend a little more time straightening up and a lot less time being mad about how the place looks," Suzanne said. "Then, an interesting thing happened, I cleaned up the whole family room and it looked beautiful. My daughter came back from a school trip and she said, 'Mom, the family room looks great, but I notice that you didn't touch my room; does that mean it's my responsibility?' "

Managing shared spaces and shared possessions reflects a great deal about your family life. Often, though, people haven't given much thought to how to do this together. Here are some guidelines that can help your household with managing space and things.

1. Recognize that people get their sense of home in very different ways. For some people, the visual field is very important. What they *see* communicates their sense of home. Lots of objects around may bother them. Other people are more kinesthetic. They'll get a sense of home from the *feeling* of being in the space and the texture of the items around them. Talk about what your shared aesthetic is and where you differ. Build on your shared values and make sure that each person has spaces that reflect what really matters to them.

2. Plan your big purchases together, and make sure that you have all identified places for your new things.

3. Regularly give away unused and outgrown belongings together. Create a ritual of giving things away to a cause that matters to you.

4. Discuss and create written guidelines for how you would all like your common spaces to look in terms of amount of stuff versus spaciousness, aesthetic style, standard of cleanliness, and so on.

5. Get off to a good start in the morning by preparing the night before. Make lunch, put out clothing, leave briefcases, cell phones, and knapsacks by the door. Put cereal boxes and bowls on the table. Leave as little as possible to the morning rush.

6. Have a fifteen- to thirty-minute cleanup/get ready time before going to bed. Depending on the ages of children in the household, this could be as early as 7:30 and as late as 10:30. Take turns choosing the cleanup music, then everyone pitches in to put everything away, wipe off counters, and get set up for school and work in the morning.

Not only will these guidelines help you to create a more harmonious home, they can also lead to stronger family bonds, as well as opportunities to put your values into practice. Twice a year, Robin and Ali and their three kids go through the household, purging toys, books, and clothes, collecting and bringing them to the local homeless shelter. They all do their purging at the same time, so it has become a family activity. They know their possessions are going to people in need, reinforcing the family's belief in giving back to the community.

Sharing Household Tasks

Who will do which household tasks? This is often an area of constant negotiation. The question is challenging whether there are two full-time workers and children too young to pick up after themselves; only one working adult and teenage children; or two able-bodied adults in the house who have different values about homemaking. Lynne Weygint, coauthor of *The Joyful Family*, is a professional organizer who helps families get organized. She often works with families in which all members are overbooked and no one has any time to do the household tasks. The challenge that she sees is that often both parents work, and neither parent has developed the skills to run a household efficiently. In addition, the children have a full plate of after-school activities as well as homework. No one has the time or energy to take care of the basic tasks.

In these cases, just getting the laundry done can be daunting. She has seen households where the family might be fifteen loads of laundry behind. At times, the laundry challenge can come from the lack of a laundry system, or it can come from too many clothes. How many pairs of jeans does each child need? How many khakis? Two or three, but some children have seventeen pairs of jeans and throw them into the laundry at the end of each day. Her recommendation to overwhelmed families is to list the areas where individuals are feeling the most stress, and design systems that will substantially reduce or eliminate the stressors.

This family might want to decide on a reasonable amount of clothes for each individual, so that they are beginning a laundry system with an appropriate amount of clothing. A laundry system that has been successful with several of Ms. Weygint's clients is for the family to purchase three large laundry baskets, each one about the size of a large load of laundry. Label the first one "whites," the second basket "darks," and the third "mediums." Each family member (above the age of five) sorts his or her own laundry each day into the three baskets. The baskets should be centrally located, ideally in the area where the laundry will be washed. On the day that a basket is full, it gets washed, dried, and folded by the individual whose task it is to do the laundry. Family members rotate laundry duty either daily or weekly, depending on a prearranged schedule. In a family of three to five individuals, there will be between six and eleven loads of laundry a week, including bed linens and towels.

Here are some other tips for sharing household tasks:

1. Create a family attitude that recognizes that household tasks are an important way of supporting a comfortable family life. As best-selling author Sarah Ban Breathnach says, "Getting our houses in order, and endowing our children [and ourselves] with a respect for and an appreciation of order, is one of the most precious gifts we can give them and ourselves."

2. Recognize that people often slide into agreements about who does what household tasks. They often resent what they "slid" into and may neglect to take quality time to reevaluate the success of agreements that they have made. Allocate family time to seriously evaluate the success of your systems in accomplishing your family goals using "learning conversations."

3. It helps for each person (older than age five or so) to take responsibility for cleaning up after themselves. Everyone should make their own bed, empty their own trash, and put their own dishes in the dishwasher.

4. Create a plan for sharing tasks that builds on people's natural affinities for the work that must be done. For example, let the one who likes to cook, cook. The one who is good at household repairs should do those repairs. Then, divide up the main tasks: collecting and putting out the garbage, doing the dishes, shopping, laundry, and so forth. Sarah Ban Breathnach also suggests the following principles for self-responsibility that everyone should be expected to follow:

- If you take it out, put it back.
- If you open it, close it.
- If you throw it down, pick it up.
- If you take it off, hang it up.
- If you use it, clean it up.

5. Treat doing household work as a collective, worthwhile set of tasks, supporting the creation of a shared homey space. Make housework more pleasant by choosing musical accompaniment for clearing the table or create "laundry time" when everyone sorts and folds their laundry together in front of a favorite TV show.

6. Appreciate each other's contributions. When your partner makes the bed or your child sets the table, don't forget to say "Thank you." It helps when everyone is looking for small ways to appreciate each other.

Melinda had to formally resign as "maid of the house" in order for her family to start contributing to their share of housework. She explained to them that now that the children were teenagers, she would no longer be doing their laundry, nor would she do all of the cooking and cleaning up after meals. She acknowledged that she had perpetuated her role as "maid" and that it would take some time to reallocate responsibilities. She had given her husband a "heads up" that this was coming and they held a family meeting to decide together what to do next. They adapted a "win-win" system that she had found in Stephen Covey's book *The*

Seven Habits of Highly Effective Families in which the children's clothing allowance was dependent on their pitching in with the laundry. When they did their laundry, they got their clothing allowance. No laundry, no new slacks or dresses.

Helping Children Do Their Share of Household Tasks

Keeping the house clean and organized can be a challenge in homes with children, but it is not impossible. If children learn responsibility for helping out around the house, and are taught basic organizing principles from an early age, they can avoid some of the problems we find ourselves experiencing as disorganized adults. Gary, a highly successful lawyer, says that his three boys tended to be disorganized like him. Part of his incentive for becoming more organized was seeing how his children were modeling themselves after him. It was important to him that his kids learn to pitch in, and he realized that they didn't mind doing work around the house as long as the tasks were split equitably. "They don't like it when we ask them to do more than their brothers have to do. Everybody clears and rinses their own dishes and puts them in the dishwasher. Fred takes out the garbage, Harris sets the table, and Donald brings down the laundry. They all make their own beds. If they think it's fair, they have no problem doing it. I try to help them build good habits now and I tell them that my life would have been a lot easier if I had been more organized."

Here are some guidelines for getting children involved in the collective effort of maintaining a well-organized home:

1. Model your own standards. Children learn more from what you do than from what you say.

2. Adjust your attitude. If you hate housework, chances are you will teach your children to hate it as well. If you secretly think that cleaning up is women's work, your children may pick this up. Gloria told her ten-year-old son that he needed to be more conscientious about picking up after himself. She was shocked when he informed her that he didn't have to clean up after himself because his (far-into-the-future) wife would pick up after him. She figured out that her 1950s upbringing and attitudes must have been leaking through.

3. Once you assign a task, let your child decide how to get it done (within reason). Teach them how to make their own beds and let them do it, even if it isn't perfect. An easy bed-making system is a comforter with a duvet cover. They can pull the comforter over the bed, and, poof, the bed is made.

4. Be matter-of-fact about housework. Cleaning up is not a punishment. It is an integral part of taking care of ourselves well. Give everyone household tasks as soon as they are old enough. Even a three-year-old can pitch in. Don't disdain household tasks or make them appear as undesirable work. Rather than call them chores, call them tasks, jobs, housework, or other more neutral terms.

5. Have patience and refrain from cleaning up for your children; let them take some time to pick up after themselves. Leave "cleanup and put-away" time at the end of activities. It may be easier now to clear up after them, but you can help them build useful lifetime habits if you can be more patient.

6. Make sure that there are plenty of places for children to put things away at a lower level that they can use without your help. Clear out closet and drawer space for them. Put shelves and hooks at their level.

7. Teach your children to put one toy back before taking another one out to play with. It gets distracting and confusing for children to be in a place with toys all over the floor. And as they put them back, they learn to treasure their playthings.

Wendy Mogel, parenting specialist and author of *The Blessing of a Skinned Knee*, says that what makes it hard for parents to assign household tasks to children is their own ambivalence about the value of the tasks. And it's often just quicker and easier for parents to do the jobs themselves. "If we aren't sure chores are necessary to our children's growth, why go to all the trouble of assigning them? The fewer chores we require of our children, the more free time and peace we will have." Once parents determine that there is value in assigning, however, they often stumble on which tasks should be assigned when. Three-year-olds can carry their plates to the table and help put their toys away at the end of the day. Four-year-olds can water plants and put their dirty clothes in a hamper. Children of all ages can straighten their beds. As children get older, they can take care of their own room and help set the table. Participating in caring for themselves and their home gives children a sense of mastery and the feeling that they are making an invaluable contribution to the household.

Some parents feel very strongly that their children should be spared household tasks. Anita held that belief when her children were little, wanting them to be children as long as possible without any household responsibilities. As the years went by, she was faced with the fact that her preteens had neither the inclination nor the habit to help around the house. She says, "I wish I had given them tasks when they were younger. Now they have the feeling that I am meant to clean up after them, and I can only get them to pitch in when they feel like it, which isn't that often." Melinda, who resigned as "maid of the house," says, "I wish I had taught my son how to pitch in earlier; I have an entitled prince of a son."

Giving children the responsibility of contributing to household tasks helps them develop the self-reliance they will need later. Wendy Mogel points out, "The lessons we instill by insisting that our children do mundane tasks may very well be the ones that stay with them longest, helping them to become self-reliant adults, responsible community members and loving parents."

Making and Keeping Agreements

Families often struggle with respect to time and punctuality. They need to figure out together how to make and keep agreements so that they can build trust and confidence in one another. Each morning, nine-year-old Johnny knew that he had to finish his long shower only when his parents started yelling at him, "Get out of the shower." Even though they regularly reminded him of water scarcity and the importance of limiting his showers, he seemed impervious to their exhortations. Finally, they put him in charge of timing the shower by giving him a timer and a three-minute guideline. At that point, he was happy to take responsibility for getting in and out of the shower in a timely way. His reward was built in: more time to play with their puppy each morning.

You may want to use some of these guidelines to help you make and keep family plans and agreements.

1. When planning ahead, get input from all family members on their preferences.

2. Make your agreements explicit. Sometimes, one person thinks that a commitment has been made and the other person is unaware of it.

3. When one person thinks an agreement has been made and the other person didn't follow through, review what happened so that you can learn where the breakdown occurred. Was it in the original request? Were there different perceptions of the importance of the agreement? Was there an unclear time line? For example, I agreed to call the electrician, but I didn't say when. My husband expected me to call immediately, while I assumed that calling within a week would be time enough. Remember that agreements will have differing levels of importance for each person.

4. Recognize that people have very different senses of time. The person who is always running late is probably not doing it on purpose. They often don't know how to be on time and may need compassionate support to learn time management skills.

5. When you have events that you need to arrive at in a timely way, try back-casting together so that you have a shared detailed perception of what is required in order to be there on time.

6. Plan a buffer. If you need to leave at 8:15 to be at the airport well before flight time, plan to leave at 8:00. That will give you some time for all the unforeseen things that can take place before traveling.

7. It is helpful to create ways for children to learn to be responsible for their own time, such as giving them a timer.

Planning, like agreements, is another area in which family members often differ. One wants to plan ahead and get all the details squared away, the other doesn't want to plan. Marty, a physician, says, "On the weekends, I like spontaneity. My life at the hospital is so structured that I can't imagine planning my weekends at all. If it's a nice day, I'll go out on the boat; if it's not, I've got some projects to work on in the basement." April, his wife, says, "I need to know what we are doing on the weekends. If he goes out on the boat, then I want to have a tennis game set up with a friend. He wants me around, but he won't make plans with me. If I do go ahead and set up a game, then he's upset that I am not around to do projects with him." One way out of their bind is to make one plan per weekend. It won't structure Marty's whole weekend, and it will give April something that she can count on for family time. The challenge is that family members often dig their feet in a position: "I am spontaneous, I hate planning." Or "I have to know what I am doing the whole time." And they miss the obvious compromises that are right in front of their eyes.

Part of the work of making and keeping agreements is learning how to repair trust when one family member has broken yet another agreement—whether to pay the phone bill, to arrive at a restaurant at a certain time, or to pick up the groceries. Don't just blithely ignore that you broke an agreement, even if it is a small one. I could never understand why it bugged my husband so much when I forgot to make the phone calls that I had promised to make. He often needed to remind me to call a repairman several times before I would do it. It took me a while to learn that if I agreed to make the call, then I should make the call without reminders; otherwise, I shouldn't make the agreement.

When you break an agreement, apologize. Apologies can be powerful. One caveat about apologies, though: If you keep repeating the mistake, after a while, your apology won't hold much water. If you have a pattern of breaking certain kinds of agreements, explore why you keep making and not following through these particular commitments. Then figure out new systems that you need so that you don't do it again or take on different tasks that you will complete.

Organizing for Happiness

A well-run home can be a much happier home. Getting your house organized can yield surprising benefits, making your family stronger, better able to enjoy each other, and more at ease both with each other and in their sacred space they call home.

15

Organizing Your Organization

If you work with other people, in a small company or large, you are probably affected by disorganization at work. We've already addressed ways for you to deal with your own individual organizing issues, which you can apply to your work. Now it is time to examine the larger issue of how teams and companies as a whole often allow disorganization to creep in and disrupt both productivity and worker morale. "Organizations" are often anything but what the word implies!

Whether you are in top management or on the front lines, share these ideas with your colleagues and see if others would be willing to join with you to implement some of these suggestions, many of which you can put to use right away.

Organizations Out of Control

What does a disorganized workplace look and feel like? Let's listen to what people in such organizations have to say.

"We are overwhelmed and exhausted. We push hard to get through one project, and then there's another one that we have to do," says a manager of a large social service organization.

"We race to get products out the door, but often we find major errors, since we have been pushing so hard and everyone is tired. Then there is the major push to rectify the error, plus the yelling and blaming and trying to figure who did the bad deed," says the operations manager of a manufacturing plant.

"We e-mail everyone to keep them informed; then nobody has time to read their e-mails. A typical day leaves me with two hundred e-mail messages in my in-box," says a marketing director of a major pharmaceutical company.

"I can't trust anyone here to do what they said they were going to do. I like them, and we are all friendly, but I can't count on anyone. If you want to get anything done around here, you have to do it yourself," says a foundation director.

"This place is a mess. People leave dirty coffee cups in the kitchen, there are dead plants in the window, and someone left a bunch of boxes in the closet. We can't agree on how to keep this place looking nice," says the associate director of a grassroots organization.

"I don't have one moment during the day to stop and reflect on what we are doing or why we are doing it," says a management consultant.

"People end up in each other's offices with closed doors, telling each other how they can't work with someone else," says the nursing director of a retirement home.

One of the major challenges of getting organized at work is that people tend to experience workplace chaos as individuals, even though disorganization is generated collectively. A group gets disorganized when people can't agree on what they want to do together, so everyone ends up doing their own thing. The team or work group loses track of what is important: it starts running late, losing valuable information; and members begin to break agreements, not only with each other but also with clients, patients, funders, or others outside the group.

Disorganization takes place when it's not clear who is accountable for managing important tasks. It is a collective experience of being unable to work well together; a collective experience of things falling through the cracks, of missed opportunities, of losing track of priorities, of not knowing who is supposed to do what.

Even in teams of a few people, disorganization can grow exponentially as members inadvertently behave in ways that cause each other to be disorganized. Kim's late arrival to a meeting means that David and

Karen arrive late to their following meeting. Robert's inability to find something important leads to Richard's and Lisa's inability to meet an important deadline. We are interconnected in workplaces and our habits affect each other.

Disorganization increases when fellow employees don't address their frustrations directly with each other. Let's say someone performs poorly on a task or breaks a promise to a colleague. Will anyone tell him directly and kindly that he isn't doing well? Unfortunately, colleagues will rarely let others know that a breakdown has occurred. Often other people know far more about how we are doing than we do, but they won't tell us, because they don't want to be unkind. Then we are often in the dark about how we are doing and we can't improve. Our methods for learning from experiences together are often very limited. Much too often, people are blamed by others for doing a poor job, yet no one will give them the information they need to change. Does this sound familiar? Does this make a mess at work? You bet.

People tend to spend a lot of time complaining about each other's disorganization without effectively addressing the issues at hand. Although those complaints temporarily relieve the pain of missed deadlines and broken agreements, they actually make things worse by reducing trust. In these organizations, people know about the complaining behind each others' backs, and most people participate in the gossip, even though they know that others may be talking behind their backs as well. Without direct feedback, however, they can't improve their behavior. The challenge is to have conversations that help relieve the problems over the long run, rather than simply complaining in the halls, which only relieves the pain temporarily.

These are all symptoms of disorganization at work. These workplaces are difficult to work in and very hard to change. Just as disorganization can become a stumbling block for an individual, it can become a stumbling block for an organization, making difficult work situations even more stressful and frustrating. Just as disorganization can block your personal energy, leaving you drained and frantic, it can block an organization's energy, leaving people dispirited, cynical, and burned out. The pain is experienced one by one, but the cure is in working better together as a group.

Great Things Are Possible at Work

Well-organized workplaces are much more than environments where people return phone calls on time, accomplish their projects, water the plants, stay on top of their work, and clean out the coffee cups regularly. Healthy, well-run organizations foster a greater connection with others, a sense of camaraderie, and an experience of working together for a common purpose. We can bring our best selves to the workplace, gain energy from our work and colleagues, as well as find ways of working together that connect us soul-to-soul and heart-to-heart.

In this sense, being well organized does not mean running like clockwork; rather, it means creating a workplace that helps people:

- **Focus** on what is important both to themselves and to the organization.
- **Take action** to achieve their vision and seize new opportunities as they arise.
- **Complete tasks** in a timely way.
- **Keep track** of important information and be able to lay their hands on it when they want to.
- **Conduct productive, stimulating meetings** that help to clarify and monitor vision, goals, roles, decisions, difficulties, and action steps.
- **Make and keep agreements** that enable each other to get work done effectively.
- **Hold each other accountable** for agreements in a way that the group learns from both successes and failures.
- Do all of the above with a large degree of **presence of mind**. People are able to pay attention to what they decide is important while demonstrating respect and care for one another.

How is it possible to get beyond the frustrations of disorganization and establish a healthy, well-organized, meaningful workplace? You can help create that change by instituting these five powerful work processes:

1. Share vision and coordinate goals so that everyone knows where they are going and if they are on track.

2. Clarify roles so that people know who is doing what and why.
3. Move from blame to accountability in ways that promote learning. Everyone stops looking for the culprit and examines how their systems may make it hard to do work well.
4. Conduct effective meetings to help people get their work done together better.
5. Store and retrieve information in ways that genuinely support the people's work together.

Let's look at each of these issues in turn—why they are important, and what specific tools you can use to achieve them at your workplace.

Share Purpose and Vision, Coordinate Goals

An organization is powerful when people share a purpose, talk about their vision, clarify their team or departmental goals, and take effective action. When people establish their goals together, based on conversations about their purpose and vision, they understand how their goals and activities reinforce each other in order to achieve their shared vision. As organizations have moved from a command and control style of management toward a more collaborative style, shared vision, purpose, and coordinated goals have become the new glue that helps hold people together, giving them direction and a sense of cohesion.

Shared vision and purpose emerge from conversations in which people talk about what is meaningful for them. Visioning has a bad name these days, since it has been misused as a way to build company spirit, and then abandoned when business cycles slow down. Nevertheless, engaging in conversations where people talk about achieving what is meaningful to them can inspire people to persist when faced with tough issues. In the same way that determining your purpose and vision for personal organizing can help you drive toward a new way of living, establishing shared purpose and vision at work can give people heart when the going gets rough.

You might consider setting aside time for clarifying the purpose and vision of your work group, department, or organization. See if you can arrange for your company to set aside a period of time, whether a few hours or a full three-day retreat, to step back and look at the big picture.

You may wish to hire a skilled outside facilitator to run the session. If your company is large, it may not be practical to have every employee present, but everyone should have an opportunity for input on the issues to be raised.

When you are together, begin by having each person consider what is important to them about the work that they do, and ask why they think it matters. Then, ask participants to consider their own vision for the organization, their ideal picture of what they would like the place to be. Ask, "What do you want us to be like five years from now? Whom will we be serving? What will our customers (patients, students, clients, etc.) be saying about us? What will it be like to work here? What are our values? What quantitative results will we have accomplished?"

Next, create a shared vision by looking for the shared values and goals among members of the organization. Continue the conversation until you find the images that can help release the underlying coherence in your group or organization.

Visioning at work is not enough by itself to create positive change. It is important for teams and organizations to ground their vision in a shared picture of current reality and establish a clear plan to bridge the gap between where they are and where they want to be. It is essential, therefore, to take some time to develop a common understanding of where the organization is now. Then, you can identify agreed-upon goals that will enable you to bridge the gap between your vision and your current reality.

After you've gone back to work, one way to keep visioning alive is to make it a regular conversation in which you remind yourselves of what you are creating together. Sometimes, it seems much easier to complain than to envision, but find yourself a few people who are game for talking about a positive future. In *How the Way We Talk Can Change the Way We Work,* psychologists Robert Kegan and Lisa Lahey show how to discover the vision embedded in workplace complaints.

Get support for starting meetings with a short discussion of what you are trying to create together. When good things happen that are in line with your vision, point them out at staff meetings, acknowledge the people who participated in making those things happen. Allow your vision to become clearer as new opportunities emerge, and appreciate the shared passion and commitment it evokes over time. You can continuously ground your vision with a clear picture of where you are and establish new goals to bridge the gap. Obviously, this is easier said than done, but there is plenty of support for this way of thinking. Check appendix 3 for resources that can help you create more of the workplace that you want.

Clarify Roles

When you have clarified your vision and goals, you then determine who is going to do what to achieve them. Roles become an organizing problem when we fail to make them clear, duplicate work unwittingly, or undermine the accountabilities that we have established. You might find two or more people doing the same job, or key tasks falling between the cracks because everyone thought someone else was taking care of them.

The management consultant Tom Peters tells a story that illustrates traditional thinking about roles: "Following a last-minute change in plans, I telephoned a hotel early one morning for a reservation. I was disconnected, then put on hold. Finally, I reached a living person at the front desk. He flatly declared that he couldn't help me. When I asked why (calmly), he responded (calmly), 'I'm not a reservationist.' Staying within his job description was more important to this person than any goals the hotel had for customer satisfaction." But this is how it often is: a limited definition of roles can keep people from serving the organizational vision.

An alternative way of thinking about roles is to define individual roles in relationship to accomplishing the group's project goals. Once you have established your purpose, vision, and collective goals, you determine each person's role in relationship to those broader goals. Who's leading the project? Who will be the primary team members supporting the accomplishment of the project? Whom will the team members consult when they have questions? Does everyone in the department have a say in the project or will input be limited to a few people? Workplaces can become very disorganized when no one is sure who is the lead person on a project, when team members are unclear about what they are accountable for, or when lines of communication are poorly defined or undeveloped.

One way you can define roles for a project is to implement the system popularized by organizational consultant and professor Richard Beckhard, and later refined by the consulting group Innovation Associates. According to Beckhard, you consider five roles in relationship to a project:

1. The first role that a person can take is to be the one accountable for making the project happen. The buck stops with the accountable person. He or she is in charge because of his or her perceived commitment and ability to lead the project. That person has the "A" for accountability.

2. The next role is taken by the people who actively support getting the project done. They lend their vital energy, brainpower, and organizational resources. They have an "S" for support.

3. The third role Beckhard calls "consultant." Here you don't have a primary role in accomplishing the project goals, but you still have a lot of knowledge and expertise to offer. You consult to the project. You offer your knowledge, but you don't necessarily expect to have a lot of influence on the way the project unfolds. You have a "C" for consultant.

4. Alternatively, you might want to be kept informed about how the project is going. You want to know what is going on, but you don't expect to have any input. You have an "I" for informed.

5. Finally, you may have sign-off responsibilities—an okay indicating approval or veto power—for the task or project. It is important to assign this role only for legal, financial, or political reasons. Often people demand an okay because they do not have confidence in the person with the "A." If you aren't willing to trust the person with the "A," challenge the decision to make that person accountable from the outset. In fact, it's best to clarify and agree on all roles as a group, so that people can freely delegate and receive authority from each other to get their part done.

Once you have clarified roles in relationship to a project, you have a clearer sense of how people relate to that project. Next, you clarify who is responsible for what tasks as a result of taking on those roles. These role clarification conversations seem time-consuming at first, but clarity at the outset can save hours and weeks (if not months) later.

Lack of role clarity contributes to a lot of confusion at work. Particularly in organizations that value high levels of participation, these roles must be identified early and reclarified if necessary. Clarifying roles is actually an key ongoing task in creating a "learning organization." Read *The Fifth Discipline* by Peter Senge for more information on learning organizations.

Move from Blame to Accountability

Even if goals and roles are clear, breakdowns and misunderstandings can take place. When something goes wrong in an organization, the first question posed is often: "Whose fault is it?" When there are data missing in accounting, it's the bookkeeper's fault. If we lose a key customer, it's the sales group's problem. "They promised more than we could deliver!" say the people in distribution or manufacturing. When errors such as these surface, blaming seems to be a natural reflex in many organizations. Even those individuals who wish to learn from mistakes fall into naming culprits. Once we figure out who's at fault, we then try to find out what is wrong with the supposed offenders. Only when we discover what is wrong with them do we feel we have grasped the problem. Clearly *they* are the problem, and changing or getting rid of *them* (or simply being angry at them) is the solution.

There's a big problem with this common scenario: Where there is blame, there is no learning. Blame rarely enhances our understanding of our situation and often hampers effective problem-solving. Open minds close, inquiry tends to cease, and the desire to understand the whole system diminishes. When people work in an atmosphere of blame, they are more likely to cover up their errors and hide their real concerns. And when energy goes into finger-pointing, scapegoating, and denying responsibility, productivity suffers because the organization lacks information about the *real* state of affairs. It's impossible to make good decisions with poor information.

All too often, rather than focusing on solving the problem, we tell someone else that we have a problem with the person who has broken an agreement or failed to live up to expectations. Typically, Robin tells Lee about a problem with Tony. Tony never hears about the problem and can't rectify the situation. But, later, when Lee has a problem with Robin, Robin doesn't hear about it either, but Tony does. This becomes a vicious cycle of blame, gossip, and innuendo. No one gets held accountable for their "criminal" activity, and no one gains the skills they need to repair frayed relationships.

So how do we avoid the tendency to blame, and create organizational environments that focus on learning instead? Breaking the cycle of gossip and helpless complaint is one way. A work group can decide to turn their problems, breakdowns, and complaints about one another into learning *with* one another. It takes hard work, commitment, and the patience to live with some blundering, but the results can be deeply gratifying. People can learn from their mistakes when they are willing and able to discuss their common difficulties with more of an emphasis on what is happening and why, rather than on who did the awful thing and what is wrong with them. It takes patience and understanding to look for the root causes of a problem rather than jumping to the obvious conclusion that someone is just a jerk. One of the best books to appear about raising challenging issues is *Difficult Conversations* by Douglas Stone, Sheila Heen, and Bruce Patton. In their book, they offer a powerful process that can help work through the hard topics that we so often avoid.

One way to break the hurtful cycle of gossip is to invite in a neutral third party who can be constructive in helping to resolve a conflict rather than to fan the flames. This could be a work colleague from another department, an outside facilitator, or someone from your own work group. Here is a five-step process that you can use to actually clear up conflicts directly.

1. In your work group, decide together that you want to break the gossip cycle and that you will try out a new way of dealing with mistakes, broken agreements, and misunderstandings. Discuss the costs of gossip and the rumor mill and the benefits of being direct and learning from mistakes rather than punishing people for them.

2. When a mistake or communication breakdown occurs, bring your complaints about someone else to a third person who is objective and can give you coaching on how to raise your concerns. This person should be someone who understands the value of neutrality and the power of resolving conflicts rather than inflaming them. Your coach can use these questions to help you both learn more about the situation.

- Tell me about the situation—what actually happened?
- What results do you want? (From the overall situation? From the conversation that you are preparing for?)
- What's one way of explaining the other person's actions?
- What's another, more generous way of explaining the other person's actions?

- How might the other person describe the situation?
- What was your role in creating the situation?
- What requests or complaints do you need to bring to the other person?
- How will you state them in order to get the results you want?
- What do you think you could learn from this situation?

3. After getting clear on the preceding questions, raise your concerns directly with the other person. Begin by reaffirming your commitment to maintaining a good working relationship and find a way to express your fundamental respect for the person. Then, identify the data that are the source of your concern. Then spell out the assumptions you made as you observed the data and any feelings you have about the situation. Finally, articulate your requests for change. During the conversation, remind the other person that reviewing the concern is part of learning to work together better.

4. Let the coach know what happened.

5. Outside of this framework, refrain from making negative comments about people. For people who frequently hear complaints about a third party and want to create a learning setting, it can be helpful to say something like: "I'd like to help, but only if you want to create a constructive situation. Otherwise, I prefer not to listen to your complaints. I have discovered that listening to complaints about a third party is seldom constructive and often destructive."

Developing accountability skills is challenging; it takes courage and the willingness to learn new ways of thinking and acting. So, why is moving from blame to accountability worthwhile? Because blame is like sugar—it produces a brief boost and then a letdown. It doesn't serve your organization's long-term needs and it increases misunderstandings. On the other hand, developing accountability skills and habits on every level of your organization can be an important element in maintaining your team's ability to work well together.

Create Effective Meetings

People spend much of their work time in meetings, but many, if not most, are seen as an ineffective waste of time. Where do meetings go wrong? Here are some of the many reasons.

- Unclear purpose. ("Why are we meeting?" people might say as they come in. "What is this about?")
- Clear purpose, but no agenda. ("What are we covering today in this meeting and how long do we estimate each agenda item to take?")
- The wrong people. ("How come John isn't here? How come Mary *is* here?")
- Late start. (People typically come in ten to twenty minutes late. Nobody says anything.)
- Poor facilitation. ("We are way off track now.")
- Unskillful speaking. ("He's so long-winded. Why doesn't she speak up?")
- People push their opinions without listening to each other. ("I'm right, he's wrong, how come he doesn't get it?")
- Unclear decision-making processes. ("Is this the boss's decision or one that we are making by consensus?")
- Unwillingness to bring up conflict. ("I don't want to hurt anyone's feelings. I don't want to open Pandora's box.")
- Raggedy finish. (People start leaving early. It's not clear what has been decided.)

It takes skill to change the meeting norms of a group. One way to do that is to recognize that effective meetings require that all participants develop the necessary skills. You cannot just depend on a good manager or facilitator to create a good meeting. Everyone can pitch in to make your meetings work well. There are several basic elements of running good meetings, whether on the phone, video, or face-to-face. The following points should be considered in sequence:

1. Before you meet, consider alternatives to meeting face-to-face; sometimes you don't have to meet in person at all.
2. Clarify the purpose of the meeting. Link it to the vision and values of the organization.
3. Invite only the people who really need to be at the meeting.
4. Identify a facilitator. (You can all take turns as facilitator.)
5. Choose people for other roles for the meeting, including a time-keeper and recorder.
6. Determine the agenda in advance, if possible, so that people can come prepared.

7. Design a realistic agenda with time frames.
8. Clarify the decision-making process.
9. Apply skillful speaking and listening skills in order to understand the matter at hand and come to good agreements.
10. At the end of the meeting, clarify and agree to all decisions.
11. Establish a follow-up process.

Learning to speak and listen well are perhaps the most neglected and important skills for successful meetings. The problem is that most of us think that we are good at this already. Yet, when you observe people in meetings, however, you rarely see good listening. Mostly, people are figuring out how to express their viewpoint in a persuasive way. Trying to understand the other people in the room is often far from their minds.

In truly productive meetings, there is a genuine desire to understand each person and develop a shared understanding of the situation. Speaking up in meetings is then not just a matter of stating your opinion, but stating it in such a way that others can respond meaningfully to your thoughts. This entails a willingness to state an opinion as an opinion, not as the ultimate truth. Try saying things like: "I see it this way" or "This is my view." Rather than "*This* is the way things are."

Effective advocacy is also balanced by a willingness and ability to inquire into other people's points of view. Often, asking people why they think what they think is experienced as a challenge or a threat. You can learn to inquire in a respectful and constructive way by:

- Being genuinely willing to learn from others' experiences.
- Respectfully asking them to share their data and assumptions that underlie their opinions.
- Building bridges with your own data and assumptions to develop a more complete picture of what is happening and what might be done to improve the situation.

When people speak and listen well, the group can use its meetings to enhance collective wisdom and support constructive action.

Store and Retrieve Information

In some organizations, information management consists of personal conversations. In others, it consists of people running around screaming,

"Where's that report?" or "Why isn't it in your file cabinet?" Whether people in your organization take it seriously or not, information management is a critical aspect of creating effective workplaces. Good information is a source of knowledge. Too much information or the wrong information overwhelms and confuses people, diminishing their ability to work well together. Here are two basic questions you need to consider about information management: How do you create, store, retrieve, and share information and knowledge in such a way as to enhance your current ability to work together? And how do you design your information system so that you can develop your capacity to do more and better work together in the future? People need to build a system that can track what they know—including financial data, reports, new ideas, meeting minutes, learnings from a feedback session, or photographs (museum, photography studio)—and anticipate what they might need to know based on the vision they want to achieve.

Your information system should be easy to access and easy to use. It is far better to keep your system ridiculously simple and usable by everyone in your company than complicated and state-of-the art if only the technologically minded people will use it. When people don't use their information system, they may duplicate each other's efforts because they are unaware that someone else has done the work already.

Lack of documentation is enormously expensive because it leads to duplication and repetition. In one international development firm, most people were not motivated to document their experiences because they thought that it was a waste of time. The employees were under a lot of pressure to get work done, and documentation only added to the pressure in their view. When they searched the company's database for information that they needed for their work, however, they often came up empty-handed, since few people had documented their case experience. This firm needed to help people value their input so that it could benefit from output. Simplifying database management can help make your systems be user-friendly and usable.

If you rely on Microsoft Office for your information needs, you can easily create an information network through file name protocols. That is, choose a consistent method that everyone can use to name their files, and a system for sharing input files with colleagues. Even a simple system like this provides an edge by greatly enhancing each other's work and knowledge. Many organizations have much more information management power at their fingertips than they are aware of because they have not tapped the potential of their software systems. By getting good training and people-friendly consulting help, you can often greatly increase the value of your information system.

Things You Can Do on Your Own to Decrease Organizational Chaos

Much of what I have described so far are actions that you can take as part of a group. There are also a number of actions that an individual can take that can start to reduce the organizational chaos and overwhelm.

- Limit the amount of e-mails you send out. Don't push "reply to all" when you send an e-mail unless you are sending a general announcement.
- Keep time agreements. Warn people in advance if you can't be on time.
- Have the courage to be realistic: Don't say yes when you just can't do something. Don't make impossible commitments to clients, bosses, funders, employees, colleagues, or people who work for you.
- Follow up on what you say you will do. Don't make people track you down.
- Leave transition time between meetings.
- Use back-casting for your planning and don't leave things to the last minute.
- Stop when you are tired. Go home, do something different on the weekend, or when burned out, go on vacation.

You've seen these suggestions before in other chapters but now you are aware of how your own behaviors may detract from the performance of others. Noticing that these habits can not only improve your own performance but also that of your team and your organization may give you the extra incentive to stay on track.

Another important thing that you can do to reduce chaos at work is learn to manage your anxiety about work-related challenges. Management consultants Ronald Ashkenas and Robert Schaffer identify ways in which managers will avoid job-related anxiety by doing what they already know, even if it is unproductive. Their classic article in the *Harvard Business Review*, "Managers Can Avoid Wasting Time," argues that managing and modifying daily work patterns, improving performance under pressure, and getting subordinates to be more productive causes so much anxiety that many managers retreat into performing more routine tasks that they already know how to do. Ashkenas and Schaffer say that managers—and this is probably true for most of us—escape into busyness, doing familiar tasks or fighting fires. This retreat into "doing" means that many managerial tasks such as truly improving work performance are neglected: "It takes a number of people working together in an unconscious conspiracy to perpetuate too many time-wasting meetings, too much paper and useless information. . . . Once these activities become part of a culture, they can be self-perpetuating." They suggest that we need to be much more aware of our unconscious ways of wasting time.

Workdays That Increase Group Productivity

At times, it make sense to allocate special days for the sole purpose of increasing productivity. One such approach is Amnesty Day, a method used at Pegasus Communications and described by their managing editor Janice Molloy as follows: "Amnesty Day is a time for everyone on the staff to 'clear the decks' of all the detritus that has accumulated over the past several months in order to move ahead with renewed vitality, energy, and lightness.

"We schedule Amnesty Day well in advance so people can clear their calendars of any conflicting obligations. People can then work on anything that serves as an impediment to work productivity. One person may spend the entire day cleaning her office, while someone else may catch up on paperwork in the morning and make long-overdue phone calls to potential vendors in the afternoon. Amnesty Day works best if each individual chooses his or her own priorities and activities.

"To avoid diluting the process and cutting into the available time, we activate the 'do not disturb' buttons on our phones and let the answering machine pick up any messages. Nor do we send or respond to e-mail—unless doing so fulfills one of our personal goals for the day. To ensure that everyone has a chance to come up for air and share their experiences with others, we all meet for pizza at noon. The staff gathers again at the end of the day to discuss what the process has been like for each of us and to suggest improvements for the next Amnesty Day."

At Pegasus, they also use amnesty time at the beginning or end of new projects as well as before any sort of organizational transition. "We have found that people feel more energized and clear-headed after spending a day tidying up," Molloy comments. "And each of us has noticed lasting, if incremental, progress on our personal organizational challenges."

Another way to radically improve the level of organization at your workplace is to set up regular department-wide retreats. A retreat is time that you and your work group take to focus on how to improve working together. It is very helpful to find a nonwork setting for this time: organizations often choose a place in nature and support people to gain new perspectives on old problems.

Think of retreats as a tune-up on the basics. They are times to revisit your purpose and vision, check in on roles, learn meeting management skills, and, perhaps most important, learn from your collective experience. What is going well? What is challenging? Can you talk about some of the breakdowns and misunderstandings?

Retreats give people a chance to be with each other outside of their typical work patterns. Often people see a different side of one another. Relationships can be enhanced. It is a time to relax a little and share a meal. Even going to lunch together as a group can be a little "retreat"— by honoring the personal relationships at the heart of the workplace. Regular retreats also give your team or department a chance to experiment with new ways of communicating and making agreements that can significantly change the atmosphere at work.

Slow Down to Go Fast

Sometimes, you have to slow down to go fast. There is a point at which adding one more thing to your plate, one more project for your team, or saying yes to one more client will actually tip you into a decline in productivity, creativity, and results. Here's the challenge. You won't know exactly when that point is, and you may not find out for a while that you are over your limit. But, slowly (or sometimes very quickly), productivity and quality will decline, as will goodwill, fun, energy, and creativity. You'll be tired most of the time, and the people around you will be dragging. The problem is that pushing hard works in the short run, but if it becomes a long-term pattern, it can cause damage. When you are sprinting, you can run very fast. If you try to keep that same pace up for a marathon, you will end up hurting yourself. And, once you take on too much, it becomes difficult to reduce your workload in a mindful way.

Periodic pauses to renew energy, have challenging conversations, and reconsider mission and vision at work are essential for people to perform well, to do and feel their best. Yet, during times of overload, the very idea of stopping to refresh the body of the organization is hard to imagine. "We don't have the time," everyone will say. Yet, much like an individual who works better when taking periodic breaks and getting reenergized, teams and departments benefit from the same experience. After a while, people will sneak in their breaks anyway, but those breaks will consist of standing in the hall and complaining about deadlines, or about other people who are bugging them for some reason. You'll see staff members complaining about their managers or the employees, overworked doctors complaining about the overworked nurses, overworked teachers complaining about the overworked principal. Everyone becomes irritable. People waste a lot of time complaining. Often, what they really want and need is renewal.

Much of this dysfunction goes back to one very pervasive, very persuasive idea: The harder we work, the more we will get done. This is true up to a point, after which working harder produces a sharp dropoff in results. Slowing down to clear things up might feel as if we are diverting our energies from the real work of the organization. Yet, taking on more projects, setting more deadlines, working longer hours, and ignoring maintenance tasks does not necessarily increase productivity. Sometimes, pausing to catch your breath and creating a context—revisiting vision, purpose, goals, roles, and learning—can be the most productive work you can do.

In Norway, the government launched a campaign for a national break to pause and rethink purpose and goals. Their campaign is called "Time for Change" and was launched on June 7, 2000, the anniversary of the national liberation from Sweden, which took place on June 7, 1905. They want to use the launching of "Time for Change" as a new liberation, this time from the increasing time squeeze that people experience. They see in Norway what we are seeing here: increased consumption and stress, leading to a threat against health and the environment. The government sent an invitation to the entire nation to participate in a "time-out." Norwegians all over the country joined in to consider how to have a good life with less environmental impact. Brandeis University picked up on this idea and sponsored an "Hour of Presence," a time for the university community to take an hour off from the pressures of work and just be with each other or do something different. Both the Brandeis and the Norwegian experiments were very successful.

Pausing together to consider the serious issues that face us at work and as a nation can build community and give us the connections that many people are longing for. You can experiment with different ways of establishing these pauses and new conversations. The need for new ways of thinking about how we work together healthfully and live together well on our planet is great. Slowing down for a moment may help us change direction slightly and move faster toward manifesting our highest aspirations.

Epilogue

There is a famous Sufi story about Mullah Nasrudin, who is a combination of fool and wise man. Several people come upon Nasrudin and are surprised to see him outside of his house on his hands and knees searching the ground under a lamppost. "What are you doing?" they asked. "I'm looking for my keys," he answered. So they got down on their hands and knees and starting looking as well. After a little time went by and they had no success, one thought to ask him, "Where did you lose your keys?" "Inside my house," Nasrudin answered. "Then why are you looking out on the street?" they asked. "Because there is more light out here," he replied.

At first we tend to think that Nasrudin is just being ridiculous. How silly, we would never do something so absurd. But, upon reflection, perhaps we are much like him. We look for lost items where there is plenty of light, where we can see. However, it's hard to find your keys when you are looking in the wrong place. One way of thinking about this story is that, when we lose a precious item, we tend to look in the obvious places outside of ourselves. Perhaps, we first need to investigate the darker areas inside ourselves in order to find what we are looking for. If the keys are on the inside, we can look outside all we want and never find them. Another completely different way of thinking about this story is that Nasrudin wasn't really looking for his keys at all. Rather, he just wanted to get help with his search, so he looked outside, in the light, where people could see *him*. As his neighbors joined him in searching the street, he got exactly what he wanted: companionship.

The path of organizing is about finding the keys inside ourselves and the companionship to make the search easier. If there is one thing you gain from reading this book, I hope it is that you can find help and fellowship in clearing up. You may have to reveal to others that you are "on the path" of organizing. Risky, perhaps, but worth it. Some of us have the feeling that we are always looking for something, usually alone. Now, perhaps, we can look together. The journey does not have to be so lonely. What we are looking for may be our keys, wallet, checkbook, a bill to pay, or a letter from a friend. Perhaps the item may also represent something deeper that we seek: wisdom, soul, or spiritual knowledge. We can join together in this quest and learn from each other.

In his book *Going on Being*, Dr. Mark Epstein relates the tale of "a Muslim man who was put into prison for a crime he did not commit. A friend came to visit and smuggled him a present, a prayer rug. The jailed man was disappointed, he did not want a prayer rug, he wanted a hacksaw or a knife or something. But after some time he decided to make use of the rug, studying the beautiful and intricate patterns in the rug as he did his daily prayers. One day he started to see an interesting pattern in the rug, a diagram of the internal mechanism of the lock to his cell. He picked the lock and was free." There are two aspects to this story. One is that someone may offer us a key that does not look like one at first. The second is that the path to freedom may be right in front of us: in our values, assumptions, and experiences. We have only to look carefully, and we will see the way out.

Getting organized is a path to freedom. Part of the freedom to be found in "good enough" organizing is that we transform our energy from nervous tension and anxiety to a rich source of vitality that naturally flows through us. *Chi* is the Chinese word for energy, and when I first created this work, I used it as an acronym for Choices—Habits—Insights. Perhaps it was a little too cute, but I liked it because it summed up some of the key aspects of this approach to change. It also helped my clients remember what to focus on. You make new choices—of behavior, thought, or focus. You build new habits—again of behavior, thought, feeling or focus. Finally your new choices and habits yield insights that can lead you to revisit your choices at an even deeper level. As you develop organizing skills and focus more on what is truly important to you, you experience more of this rich, nourishing energy flowing through your life.

It is important to know what this genuine energy feels like. Chögyam Trungpa Rinpoche once said, "What you call energy is tension." Many of us count on our highly stimulating lives to keep us going. Yet our fundamental vitality is depleted. Healthy energy is at once vital and peaceful, bigger than we are, yet very personal, sustaining, and steady as well as flowing.

Fighting the basics of life does not improve the quality of our energy. When I collected my dirty dishes in the sink and refrained from doing them for as long as possible, it simply diminished my energy. Avoiding my mail didn't help either. Running late amplified my anxiety tremendously. I felt as if I were living a high-wire act; it was dangerous and I could fall at any moment. I felt a lot of anxiety a lot of the time. Interestingly enough, from what I understand, true acrobats don't live with that anxiety about their work. They can catch the next trapeze with split-second timing only because they are fully present, and in a sense, completely relaxed.

As you become more organized, you will find that it is possible to shift from taking action based on anxiety to acting from deep intention. Being disorganized is like our other reactive patterns: it is compelling and provides the illusion of engagement. You can become less entranced by your reactivity and more available to discover and live in accordance with your deeper purpose. You can ask yourself what it means to you to make a difference. What is deeply important to you? It might take some time to discover your answers, but organizing your personal world helps you create a context for that. As someone I work with said, "When I am at peace and caught up on my work, I am extremely motivated to help my clients. And I am much more likely to enjoy my work."

It doesn't mean that, as a disorganized person, you cannot do important things that make a difference. When I was running myself ragged and losing track of my paperwork, I was still able to engage in some projects that were deeply meaningful to me and to others. But, since adopting some organizing disciplines, I've been able to achieve several things I truly wanted that had been eluding me. I published several papers, created my own body of consulting work, built a professional practice, found a husband, and created a vibrant marriage.

I occasionally look back with a sense of amazement. How did I, who resisted doing my dishes at all costs, who would not wash them until I was totally bereft—until I had used every last plate, spoon, and bowl, until I had dirty dishes all over the kitchen—how did I learn to appreciate doing my dishes? How could I, who could never clean my counters, who in fact was mystified by how people kept their counters clean—for mine were always covered with newspaper, loose mail, purchases, groceries or, of course, dirty dishes—how could I find genuine pleasure in the clean kitchen that I now leave behind me each night? Now, instead of avoiding my household tasks, I often think to myself, "If I have to do these dishes (or open the mail) eventually, I might as well do them now, while the pile is manageable."

I have offered you a framework, a set of steps, some good ideas on organizing, but, ultimately, healing is a mystery. This is a rich, nourishing, valuable, and yes, mysterious, path to travel. Part of the mystery is that help and growth will come from some surprising places.

I am still learning. There are still days when my office looks as if a hurricane blew threw. There are times when I have to cancel at the last minute and when I completely lose my focus. But now I know that this is indicative of how I am feeling. Instead of getting the flu or getting drunk when I feel bad, scared, angry, or overwhelmed, I get messy. Then I know that I need to ask myself what I am upset about, or what difficulty I might be avoiding, and how I am going to take care of myself. I still dislike sorting papers and whittling down my in-box, but I know how to get through it. I do my best to be mindful and responsible. I still make my messes, but I don't have to use them to diminish myself, and I am no longer hoping for someone (probably Mom) to come clean up after me. I now consider cleaning up after myself one of the privileges of being alive.

Living with more order and less chaos now seems like a big gift. I love living more lightly on the earth. I'm glad that my old belongings are circulating somewhere, not stuffed into my closets. I have freed myself of needing to have so very many things. When I shop, I now know to ask: "Where will I put it? When will I use it? Do I already have something like it? To whom can I give it?" These are not questions signaling deprivation. These questions have become a part of how I respect myself, our home, and our planet. I have grown to appreciate my limits. I no longer think that true abundance is when every closet is full to overflowing. I believe that it is the ability to breathe and to love, to experience a listening heart, to give things away, to be able to make wise choices, and to make the contribution that I am here to make.

One of my favorite sayings is from the Native American tradition: "Sometimes I go around pitying myself, and all the while I'm being carried by great winds across the sky." Perhaps the biggest gift of becoming more organized is to reconnect with the blessings that we have received. No longer so frantic, we can deeply experience that despite all our suffering, our human existence provides great opportunities for love, connection, healing, and contribution. We can wake up to our extraordinary capabilities.

There is a Hindu story that goes something like this. Brahman, the master of the gods, saw that human beings—who were divine—were abusing their divinity. Brahman turned to the other gods and asked, "What shall we do so that human beings no longer abuse their godlike powers?" They all said, "Let us hide divinity from the humans. Let us hide it beyond the highest mountains." "No," said Brahman, "they will find it there." "What if we put it in the deepest oceans?" they proposed. "No," said Brahman, "surely they will find a way to penetrate the depths of the seas." Finally, one of them said, "Let us hide it in the deepest recesses of their hearts, for surely humans will never look there." The journey of organizing points us toward the opportunity to find the keys in our hearts, and to make the difference that we have always wanted to make.

I wish you strength, courage, and companionship on this journey and may it lead you to many interesting places, including truly home.

Appendix 1

Areas of Disorganization:
Self-Assessment Survey

You may find it useful to use the following self-assessment survey to help you pinpoint your areas of disorganization. I have used my basic definition of being organized as a set of categories for you to examine your own behavior. Remember, do this self-assessment with a strong commitment to compassion and learning. It is simply useless to beat yourself up over this. You'll see some patterns that can help direct your organizing work.

❏ You can *find what you want* when you need it.

I usually can find _____

_____

I put things back when I am done with them. Mostly _____ Rarely _____

I don't put things back when I am done with them because _____

_____

I often can't find _____

_____

I don't know where to put the following things. _____

_____

❏ You can *complete your tasks* in a timely way.

I always finish _____

_____

I have a number of tasks without deadlines. How many? _____

I have started many projects that I have not been able to complete.
How many? ____

I enjoy finishing up my work and putting things away.
Mostly ____ Rarely ____

❏ You can *focus* on what is important to you.
I can focus when _____

_____

_____

I am often confused about what to do next. Yes ____ No ____

I find myself easily distracted when _____

_____

_____

I waste time [check the items that are true for you]
____ Looking for lost or misplaced items.
____ Leafing through catalogs.
____ Being confused about what to do next.
____ Duplicating errands.
____ Returning things I shouldn't have bought in the first place.
____ Talking to people who aren't important to me.
____ Late at night.
____ Reading e-mails.

❏ You can *arrive at your destination when you choose.*
I am always on time for _____

_____

_____

I run late for [check the items that are true for you]
____ Work-related activities.
____ Family-related activities.
____ Community-related activities.

I run late because _____

_____

_____

❏ You can *keep agreements* and you make agreements that you can keep.
I always keep agreements with _____

_____

_____

I don't write down appointments or list tasks that I have to do.

    Yes _____ No _____

I cancel appointments because [check what is true for you]

    _____ I am not ready.

    _____ I am overbooked.

    _____ I am too tired.

    _____ I forgot.

I often have to apologize for [check what is true for you]

    _____ Being late.

    _____ Breaking an agreement.

    _____ Not returning a phone call or an e-mail.

    _____ Forgetting an important date (birthday, anniversary).

❑ You can *take action when you want* and seize new opportunities as they arise.

    I feel prepared for [name the activity] _____

_____

_____

    I postpone

    _____ Meetings.

    _____ Decisions.

    _____ Social occasions.

    _____ Other important activities.

    _____ Household tasks.

    _____ Office tasks.

I often find myself doing something other than what I set out to do.

    What percentage of time? _____

I am often not prepared to seize opportunities when they arise.

    Yes _____ No _____

I plan time for organizing, but I don't really do it.

    Yes _____ No _____

❑ I can keep track of *important information* and lay my hands on it when I need it.

    I always keep track of _____

_____

_____

My disorganization causes me to lose money through

_____ Paying credit card bills late.

_____ Other late fees.

_____ Losing checks or financial records.

_____ Lost receipts so that I cannot return items.

I lose track of

_____ Phone messages.

_____ Appointments.

_____ Birthdays.

_____ Anniversaries.

I don't know where my or my children's important records are (check what is true for you).

_____ Medical.

_____ Financial.

_____ Educational.

_____ Housing (lease, mortgage papers).

_____ Personal (birth certificate, passport).

❏ You can do all of this with a degree of *presence of mind.*

I am able to pay attention to what I decide is important.

What percentage of time? _____

My disorganization keeps me from being present.

What percentage of time? _____

Appendix 2

Your Take-Action Checklist

Use the following checklist—keeping it with you when you are working on projects and checking off each action as you take it.

❑ The area that I am working on is: _____
_____

❑ I have a purpose for organizing this area. _____
_____
_____

The costs of continuing this way are: _____
_____
_____
_____
_____

The benefits of changing are: _____
_____
_____
_____
_____

❑ I have a vision for how I would like it to be. My specific goals are: _____
_____
_____
_____
_____

❑ I have taken stock in this area. A belief that I now want to hold is: _____
_____
_____

❑ I have good support. It is:

Names with phone numbers and e-mails:

1. _____

_____

2. _____

_____

3. _____

_____

4. _____

_____

❑ I will call them when I need what kind of help: _____

_____

_____

❑ I have gotten this area to ready.

❑ I have created a new system. It is: _____

_____

_____

_____

_____

❑ My new habit is: _____

_____

_____

❑ I will draw on the following organizing wisdom practices (chapters 7 to 11):

_____

_____

_____

_____

_____

❑ I have set aside time for this. (When?) _____

❑ My reward will be _____

after _____ (number of) days of my new habit, or for getting to ready.

Appendix 3

Guide to Helpful Book and Web Resources

I've included many books and organizations that have been helpful to me on this journey. Many of the authors have Web sites that you can review before buying or borrowing the book. I have found it essential to continue learning about how people find inspiration on their path to growth. I hope you can use some of the following resources to your great benefit. This is but a small sample of the intelligent resources that you can tap.

Purpose and Vision

Beck, Martha. *Finding Your Own North Star: Claiming the Life You Were Meant to Live*. Three Rivers Press, 2001.

Covey, Stephen R., A. Roger Merrill, and Rebecca R. Merrill. *First Things First*. Simon & Schuster, 1994.

Fritz, Robert. *The Path of Least Resistance*. Fawcett Columbine, 1984.

Levoy, Greg. *Callings: Finding and Following an Authentic Life*. Harmony Books, 1997.

Sher, Barbara. *Wishcraft*. Ballantine Books, 1979.

Taking Stock

Attention Deficit Disorder

Hallowell, M.D., Edward M., and John Ratey, M.D. *Driven to Distraction*. Simon & Schuster, 1994.

National Attention Deficit Disorder Association
(847) 432-ADDA
www.add.org

Myers-Briggs

Kroeger, Otto, and Janet M. Thuesen. *Typetalk*. Dell, 1988.

www.knowyourtype.com

www.personalitypathways.com

Getting Support

ReEvaluation Counseling
www.rc.org

This group teaches people how to do peer counseling or co-counseling for the purposes of finding freedom from emotional distress.

Richardson, Cheryl. *Take Time for Your Life*. Broadway Books, 1998.

Cheryl Richardson offers life-change support groups through her Web site. www.cherylrichardson.com

For getting-organized support groups:
www.flylady.net

To locate a professional organizer:
National Association of Professional Organizers
(770) 325-3440
www.napo.net

Organize Your World
www.organizeyourworld.com

This company provides extensive information about professional organizers and organizing tools.

To find a personal coach:
International Federation of Coaches
(888) 236-9262
www.coachfederation.org

Coach Connection
(800) 887-7214
www.findyourcoach.com

This is a coach matching service.

For help with overspending or being chronically in debt:
Spenders Anonymous
P.O. Box 2405
Minneapolis, MN 55402
www.spenders.org
E-mail: info@spenders.org

Debtors Anonymous
General Service Office
P.O. Box 92088
Needham, MA 02492-0009
(781) 453-2743
www.debtorsanonymous.org
E-mail: new@debtorsanonymous.org

Getting Organized

Allen, David. *Getting Things Done: The Art of Stress-Free Productivity.* Viking Penguin, 2001. David Allen's Web site is full of helpful hints: *www.davidco.com*

Kingston, Karen. *Clear Your Clutter with Feng Shui.* Broadway Books, 1998.

Morgenstern, Julie. *Organizing from the Inside Out.* Henry Holt, 1998.

Young, Pam, and Peggy Jones. *Sidetracked Home Executives.* Warner Books, 1981.

———. *Get Your Act Together.* HarperPerennial, 1993.

Managing Time

Ashkenas, Ronald N., and Robert H. Schaffer. "Managers Can Avoid Wasting Time." *Harvard Business Review* (May–June 1982).

Eisenberg, Ronni, with Kate Kelly. *The Overwhelmed Person's Guide to Time Management.* Penguin, 1997.

McGee-Cooper, Ann, and Duane Trammell. *Time Management for Unmanageable People.* Bantam Books, 1994.

McGee-Cooper, Ann, Duane Trammell, and Barbara Law. *You Don't Have to Go Home from Work Exhausted!* Bantam Books, 1992.

Morgenstern, Julie. *Time Management from the Inside Out.* Henry Holt, 2000.

Rechtschaffen, Stephan. *TimeShifting.* Doubleday, 1996.

Spirituality

There are so many outstanding books on spiritual practice that I have chosen but a very few here. If you are particularly interested in mindfulness and meditation, start by looking for books by Jon Kabat-Zinn, Jack Kornfield, Sharon Salzberg, Pema Chödron, Thich Nhat Hanh, or Larry Rosenberg and see which ones are readable for you.

Dawn, Marva J. *Keeping the Sabbath Wholly.* Eerdmans Publishing Company, 2001.

Heschel, Abraham Joshua. *The Sabbath: Its Meaning for Modern Man.* Farrar, Straus & Giroux, 1951.

Muller, Wayne. *Sabbath.* Bantam Books, 1999.

Norris, Gunilla. *Being Home.* Bell Tower, 1991.

Nouwen, Henri. *Making All Things New: An Invitation to the Spiritual Life.* HarperCollins, 1981.

Trungpa, Chögyam. *Shambhala: Sacred Path of the Warrior.* Shambhala, 1988.

Going Deeper to Keep Going

Self-Nurture

Beattie, Melodie. *Codependent No More: How to Stop Controlling Others and Start Caring for Yourself*. Harper/Hazelden, 1987.

Domar, Alice D., and Henry Dreher. *Self-Nurture: Learning to Care for Yourself as Effectively as You Care for Everyone Else*. Penguin Books, 2000.

Mellody, Pia, with Andrea Wells Miller and J. Keith Miller. *Facing Codependence: What It Is. Where It Comes From, How It Sabotages Our Lives*. Harper and Row, 1989.

Cognitive Restructuring

Bennett-Goleman, Tara. *Emotional Alchemy*. Three Rivers Press, 2001

Burns, David, M.D. *Feeling Good: The New Mood Therapy*. Avon Books, 1992.

Seligman, Martin P., Ph.D. *Learned Optimism*. Knopf, 1990.

Shadow Work

Ford, Debbie. *The Dark Side of the Light Chasers*. Riverhead Books, 1998.

Zweig, Connie, and Jeremiah Abrams, eds. *Meeting the Shadow: The Hidden Power of the Dark Side of Human Nature*. Jeremy Tarcher, 1991.

———, and Steve Wolf *Romancing the Shadow: Illuminating the Dark Side of the Soul*. Random House, 1997.

Shadow Work Seminars
(970) 203-0400
www.shadowwork.com

This group offers workshops and training in shadow work.

Organizing Your Organization

Doyle, Michael, and David Straus. *How to Make Meetings Work*. Jove Books, 1976.

Kegan, Robert, and Lisa Lahey. *How the Way We Talk Can Change the Way We Work*. Jossey-Bass, 2001.

Learning as Leadership
(415) 453-5050
www.learnaslead.com
E-mail: info@learnaslead.com

This is a training and consulting firm that offers outstanding workshops for personal growth and leadership development.

Paul, Marilyn. "Moving from Blame to Accountability." *The Systems Thinker* (February 1997).

The Systems Thinker is published by Pegasus Communications, which is a good source of books and meetings on organizational learning. Their annual conference, Systems Thinking in Action, is the best one that I go to.
(781) 398-9700
www.peagasuscom.com

Schwarz, Roger. *The Skilled Faciliatator: A Comprehensive Resource for Consultants, Facilitators, Managers, Trainers and Coaches.* Jossey-Bass, 2002. www.schwarzassociates.com

Senge, Peter. *The Fifth Discipline.* Doubleday, 1990.

Stone, Douglas, Sheila Heen, and Bruce Patton. *Difficult Conversations.* Penguin Books, 1999.

"The Interior Life of the Leader: Practices for Renewal"

I recommend this CD, a guided practice for leaders who seek to regain perspective, intercept habitual stress reactions, and return to "center" during the business day. It can be ordered from executive coach Ellen Wingard, whose e-mail is eswingard@earthlink.net.

Your Home Could Be Your Castle

Covey, Stephen. *The Seven Habits of Highly Effective Families.* Golden Books, 1997.

Dacey, John, and Lynne Weygint. *The Joyful Family.* Conari Press, 2002.

Marcus, Clare Cooper. *House as a Mirror of Self.* Conari Press, 1995.

Mendelson, Cheryl. *Home Comforts: The Art & Science of Keeping House.* Scribner, 1999.

Mogel, Wendy. *The Blessing of a Skinned Knee: Using Jewish Teachings to Raise Self-Reliant Children.* Penguin, 2001.

Paul, Marilyn, and Peter Stroh. "The Learning Family: Bringing the Five Disciplines Home." *The Systems Thinker* (August 1999).

You can order this from www.pegasuscom.com.

Acknowledgments

Many people helped every step of the way as this work was coming into existence. More people than I can acknowledge here have assisted me on this path of learning from difficult experiences.

I first want to thank the good friends who generously supported my early workshops on the topic: Nancy Norton, Elliott Freedman, Jody Isaacs, Pam Hoffman, JoHanna Katz, Sally Mack, and my dear cousin Elizabeth Rogers were among those who helped me get started.

There were several pivotal people on the path of creating this book. The seeds of this work were planted years ago during my doctoral program at Yale. I thank Professor Dennis Perkins for introducing me to a personal growth model that I have been able to build on since. Cliff Barry and Mary Ellen Blandford have been teachers and friends over the years. They introduced me to the transformational potential of personal growth work and contributed to my understanding of how people can change very deeply. I thank my colleagues at Innovation Associates for sharing with me their aspiration-based approach to working with teams and organizations. I have been greatly influenced by this approach to change.

I remember the moment when Russ Eisenstat looked at my workshop handouts and said, "This could be a book." Synchronicity unfolded after that. I thank Todd Shuster for encouraging the germ of an idea and suggesting several potential literary agents. Kristen Wainwright, head of the Boston Literary Group, in Cambridge, Massachusetts, for helping me create a lucid book proposal; and Jill Kneerim of Kneerim and Williams for so ably representing the book, and being an extremely knowledgeable advisor and delightful friend ever since. Ginny Wiley, LeAnn Grillo, Janice Molloy, and the staff of Pegasus Communications let me try out my ideas on them, gave me honest critique, provided lots of editing help, and also helped me create an attractive book proposal.

Traci Green helped with good cheer in my office, Kristin Solias provided great graphics, and Alan Hoffman, accountant extraordinaire, offered endless patience and never embarrassed me once during my years of learning how to keep track of financial matters. Patricia Volk helped me hand in my travel receipts in a timely way. Robin Bullard Carter helped transform me from a quivering mass of nerves around financial issues to someone who could bravely open bank statements and credit card bills with barely a whimper. Anna Huckabee Tull, who is far more than a personal organizer, helped me move to the next level of getting organized.

I had the blessing to be living in Jerusalem during the year it took to write this book. I am deeply appreciative of the many friends and colleagues who provided the support, inspiration, and community that is so helpful to the first-time writer. Foremost among them Danny Paller, Rachel Freilich, and Hovav, Shalev, Eden, and Livia. Sharon and Hananya Goodman and Yoav Peck blessed this work from the beginning. Hanna Matt and Sonia Twite both offered supportive friendship and read versions of chapters. Danny Matt, Robin Twite, Betsy and Menachem Kallus, and Dina and Chaim Zlotogorski offered much encouragement. Yedidya and Susan Fraiman provided ideas, books, and biblical references. David and Ronit Ziv-Kreger offered support for visioning. David Jaffe, Janette Hillis, and Andrew Shiller provided Jewish references and a passionate exploration of the spiritual path of everyday life. Ruth Mason wrote the first article about me in the *Jerusalem Post*, which set off a flood of inquiries.

Back in the States, I've also experienced great friendship. I thank Karen Erickson, Emily Wheeler, Kathleen Lancaster, Margaret Newhouse, and Mary Eisenberg for getting me unstuck and helping me to keep moving. Amy Metzenbaum has regaled me with great stories of disorganized people during our years of friendship. I could not have come this far without the loving support, deep listening, humor, and love of my dear friends Beth Sandweiss, Mishy Lesser, Susan Berger, Ellen Wingard, Nicola Kurk, and Maxine Freedman. Sara Schley and Joe Laur, Ron and Susan Kertzner, and Jim and Elana Ponet were cheering me on from various parts of the country

Special thanks to Hilary Pennington who let me run ideas by her, read drafts of the proposal and the book, brought me into her workplace, and offered valuable counsel and good friendship. Grady McGonagill, Joel Yanowitz, Chris Ives, and Benyamin Bergmann Lichtenstein read drafts and provided comments. David Thomas provided tough love and courageous feedback. Robin Ely gave me some key insights. Rebecca Shrum and Elizabeth Michaud became avid readers and editors during the final months of preparation and their comments have been invaluable. I thank Lara Nuer and Marc André Olivier of Learning as Leadership for coaching me toward a path of greater personal mastery. Jane von Mehren of Penguin Books has been a sensitive, patient, and enthusiastic editor. Brett Kelly has been endlessly helpful. I appreciate the team at Penguin Books who contributed their design skills and enthusiasm to create this beautiful book. Donna Zerner of Boulder, Colorado, was a superb editor, who helped me discern, over and over again, the essential meaning of what I wanted to say.

Participants in my groups have been fellow travelers every step of the way. Their passion for learning, their good questions, and their personal progress inspired me to write—and keep writing. I'll let you remain nameless; you know who you are and I thank you a lot.

Members of my immediate and extended family were very helpful. My mother-in-law, Eve Stroh, provided never-ending support and interest and was always ready to hear about the next step. Dev Rogers, David Paul, and Kathy Schultz were great, and I offer special thanks to my dad, Dr. Norman Paul, who gave me financial support while I was working on the proposal. Many thanks to Jan Athos who showed up in my life just as I was completing the manuscript. She read it and provided words of support just when I needed them.

I received a great gift from my mother, who is no longer living. She demonstrated the possibilities of true personal transformation and the power of taking responsibility for one's actions. I am ever grateful to her.

My dear husband, David Peter Stroh (A Neat Person) has been an encouraging partner who provided a constant sounding board, helped edit the manuscript, and pitched in whenever I needed help. Both of us have come to recognize and respect our great differences in how we organize ourselves. I learn from him. He learns from me. We learn together. I am grateful to be part of such a rich and flourishing marriage. Thank you for everything.

FOR THE BEST IN PAPERBACKS, LOOK FOR THE Ⓟ

In every corner of the world, on every subject under the sun, Penguin represents quality and variety—the very best in publishing today.

For complete information about books available from Penguin—including Penguin Classics, Penguin Compass, and Puffins—and how to order them, write to us at the appropriate address below. Please note that for copyright reasons the selection of books varies from country to country.

In the United States: Please write to *Penguin Group (USA), P.O. Box 12289 Dept. B, Newark, New Jersey 07101-5289* or call 1-800-788-6262.

In the United Kingdom: Please write to *Dept. EP, Penguin Books Ltd, Bath Road, Harmondsworth, West Drayton, Middlesex UB7 0DA.*

In Canada: Please write to *Penguin Books Canada Ltd, 10 Alcorn Avenue, Suite 300, Toronto, Ontario M4V 3B2.*

In Australia: Please write to *Penguin Books Australia Ltd, P.O. Box 257, Ringwood, Victoria 3134.*

In New Zealand: Please write to *Penguin Books (NZ) Ltd, Private Bag 102902, North Shore Mail Centre, Auckland 10.*

In India: Please write to *Penguin Books India Pvt Ltd, 11 Panchsheel Shopping Centre, Panchsheel Park, New Delhi 110 017.*

In the Netherlands: Please write to *Penguin Books Netherlands bv, Postbus 3507, NL-1001 AH Amsterdam.*

In Germany: Please write to *Penguin Books Deutschland GmbH, Metzlerstrasse 26, 60594 Frankfurt am Main.*

In Spain: Please write to *Penguin Books S. A., Bravo Murillo 19, 1° B, 28015 Madrid.*

In Italy: Please write to *Penguin Italia s.r.l., Via Benedetto Croce 2, 20094 Corsico, Milano.*

In France: Please write to *Penguin France, Le Carré Wilson, 62 rue Benjamin Baillaud, 31500 Toulouse.*

In Japan: Please write to *Penguin Books Japan Ltd, Kaneko Building, 2-3-25 Koraku, Bunkyo-Ku, Tokyo 112.*

In South Africa: Please write to *Penguin Books South Africa (Pty) Ltd, Private Bag X14, Parkview, 2122 Johannesburg.*